The New Humanism

A CRITIQUE OF MODERN AMERICA

1900–1940

The New Humanism

A CRITIQUE OF MODERN AMERICA,
1900–1940

J. David Hoeveler, Jr.

UNIVERSITY PRESS OF VIRGINIA
CHARLOTTESVILLE

THE UNIVERSITY PRESS OF VIRGINIA
Copyright© 1977 by the Rector and Visitors
of the University of Virginia

First published 1977

Library of Congress Cataloging in Publication Data

Hoeveler, J. David, 1943-
  The new humanism.

  Bibliography: p.
  Includes index.
  1. Humanism—20th century.   2. United States—
Intellectual life—20th century.   3. Babbitt,
Irving, 1865-1933.   4. More, Paul Elmer, 1864-1937.
I. Title.
B821.H59   144   76-25168
ISBN 0-8139-0658-X

Printed in the United States of America

This book is for Diane

Preface

This work deals with what I believe is a significant chapter in the intellectual history of the United States. The New Humanists, under the leadership of Irving Babbitt and Paul Elmer More, have received scattered attention from scholars interested in the various aspects of American life and thought upon which the New Humanists turned their critical attention—art and literature, education, society, politics, and religion. But there has been no effort to examine the collective thought of the New Humanists and usually they have received passing consideration in works in which not Humanism but another topic is the main focus.[1] It is not surprising, therefore, that no analysis of the New Humanists has described their thought in terms of the organic whole from which their approach to different facets of American society and culture derived. But a pervasive theme did underlie New Humanist thought. Their concept of the dualism of human nature, extrapolated in part from Greek philosophy and Eastern religions, provided the criterion for their assessments of all aspects of modern culture and guided their efforts to reconstruct modern life.

It has been my primary intention in this work to present a comprehensive intellectual portrait of this group. For this reason I have included most of the important biographical information, joined to a narrative of the Humanist movement over four decades, in the first chapter. The second chapter prepares a foundation for all the succeeding ones by exploring in depth the philosophical dualism that continues as the central perspective in the later subjects. I have not been sparing of criticism in exploring the manifold aspects of Humanist thought, but neither have I sought to comment on every point where people could reasonably disagee, and have disagreed. The New Humanists were not popular in their own time. They are not popular today. But if we concede that most literary and intellectual history has been written by scholars of a liberal (and sometimes distinctly anti–New Humanist) point of view, we may be prepared to admit the need for a fresh look at Irving Babbitt, Paul Elmer More, Stuart Sherman, Norman Foerster, and the rest of their group. I do admit to viewing my subject from a rather sympathetic position, believing especially that although the Humanists were often unable to offer

[1] A long list would be possible here, but see, for examples, William Van O'Connor, *An Age of Criticism, 1900–1950* (Chicago, 1952), Walter Sutton, *Modern American Criticism* (Englewood Cliffs, N.J., 1963), Ronald Lora, *Conservative Minds in America* (Chicago, 1971), Michael R. Harris, *Five Counterrevolutionaries in Higher Education: Irving Babbitt, Albert Jay Nock, Abraham Flexner, Robert Maynard Hutchins, Alexander Meiklejohn* (Corvallis, Ore., 1970).

a realistic cure for the ills they diagnosed, their diagnosis was always a perceptive one. At their best they offered a thoughtful critique, a useful alternative to the prevailing liberalism of their generation of thinkers.

The Humanists' effort to restore the premises of a Western classical tradition in America provided a noteworthy voice of dissent from the relativist consensus of the early twentieth century. The intellectual revolution of the late nineteenth century, despite its unquestionably important and useful insights, too often became a sterile obsession with the unique, the individual, the immediate, and the changing—with the pluralistic diversity of an "open universe." In an institutional setting the impact of this movement away from a concern with the permanent and the universal in human experience was most apparent in American higher education.

I began this work seven years ago at the University of Illinois, Urbana-Champaign. The vociferous calls for "relevance" that then besieged the university were cause for serious reflection on the New Humanists' pleas for tradition and the wisdom of the past. The Humanists pleaded for a different kind of relevance, but the sharp and conflicting perspectives raised anew some ancient questions, not only about the meaning of humanism, but about its place in the modern university, and indeed in the contemporary world. How important, if important at all, are the traditional humanities to a nation that still reflects the social and religious diversity, the mobility, and the faith in technological progress that are central themes in its history? Although I have concentrated my efforts here mainly on intellectual analysis of the New Humanist movement itself, I hope that it will be useful in a continuing discourse on the larger subject.

Finally, I have endeavored to outline the collective thought of the New Humanists, including the important applications that different individuals gave to the dualistic consensus. I have not tried to incorporate all aspects of each individual's thinking. Especially in the case of Paul Elmer More, who has received extensive treatment in other studies, that effort would be impossible here. Irving Babbitt, the dominant mind in the Humanist movement, has been unjustly neglected by American intellectual historians and awaits a fuller study. Stuart Sherman and Norman Foerster are also candidates for scholarly attention.

Chapter 7 of this book appeared in modified form as an article entitled "The New Humanism, Christianity, and the Problem of Modern Man," in the December 1974 issue of the *Journal of the American Academy of Religion.* I am grateful to the editor for permission to reprint it here.

Any scholar's work is always to some extent a collaborative effort, intellectually and physically. At an early stage this work was read with insight by Leonard Bates, J. Alden Nichols, and Robert W. Johannsen at the University of Illinois, and by Winton U. Solberg, to whom I am indebted beyond the rewards of an immensely enriching intellectual relationship. Harold Wechsler, of the University of Chicago, read the manuscript and suggested improvements during our separate appointments in the Institution for Social and Policy Studies at Yale University in 1973-74. For the friendly and competent assistance of the staffs at the libraries and archives of the University of Illinois, Princeton University, Harvard University, and the University of Iowa, I am most grateful. That this manuscript has undergone significant improvements over several years owes much to my wife, Professor Diane Long Hoeveler. She has assisted me generously with her own expertise in English literature and, as the "Rousseauist" in our family, has forced me to think critically about my subject. The dedication of this book to her represents more than I can here express.

Milwaukee
August 1975

Contents

Part I

FOUNDATIONS

CHAPTER ONE

The New Humanists

Fighting a whole generation is not exactly a happy task.
—Irving Babbitt

THE NEW HUMANISM sprang from a profound disaffection with the modern age. Centering its attention on the governing ideas of the contemporary world, it surveyed the triumph of relativism in philosophy and social thought, of materialism in daily living, and of romanticism and naturalism in literature, and was convinced that twentieth-century man had lost his bearings. The New Humanists sought first to expose the misconceptions that had set him adrift. Believing that modern society could not right itself without a return to first principles, to a precise and adequate conception of the nature of man, the New Humanists answered the modern ideologies with their own diagnosis and prescription for the improvement of society.[1] In carrying out this task, the New Humanism produced the first outline of an intellectual conservatism in twentieth-century America. Its proponents were cultural traditionalists, defensive of classical principles of art, deeply skeptical about human nature, and neo-Burkean in their political and social views. They were not popular in their own time, for they were the first to wage a sustained attack against the naturalism and relativism that had gained consent with the emergence of Darwinism and pragmatism at the end of the nineteenth century and the beginning of the twentieth. Not until the end of the 1920s did they win a wide audience for their views. Nonetheless, the Humanists anticipated several important movements that appeared later, for their own case against modern society and its ideologies showed significant parallels with the Southern Agrarians, Protestant Neo-orthodoxy, and the New Conservatism.

At the base of the Humanists' critique was their conception of the human condition. Their case against the present age rested in large measure in the neglect by the modern philosophies of certain essential human truths. Two intellectual movements in particular were responsible for this loss of first principles. First, a romantic tradition that dated from Rousseau had

[1] Hereafter the terms *Humanism* and *Humanists* will be synonymous with the *New Humanism* and the *New Humanists*. But *humanism* and *humanists* will designate the generic terms.

sought to measure personal values by celebrating individual uniqueness at the expense of the common elements of human nature, spawning, the Humanists charged, a monotonous cult of individualism and a heedless submission to emotion. Praising the virtues of the primitive man and falsely promising to liberate civilized society from its chains, the romantic influence had promoted an irresponsible disregard for traditional values. On the other hand, the Humanists suggested, naturalism and pragmatism, registering the impact of science on modern thought, overstated man's ties to his environment and pictured him the mindless victim of his animal impulses. Both ideas, the Humanists felt, de-emphasized the human part of man's nature that exercised will and restraint over the natural impulses. The Darwinian influence, they further charged, placed a premium on adjustment to external conditions as a measure of progress, belying their own assertion that the only meaningful reform was a conscientious spiritual recovery along Humanist lines.

Although the core of New Humanist thought centered on a few basic principles, these found a variety of applications. They served first to formulate a Humanist aesthetic that was critical for their own controversial discussions of contemporary American literature. Here the Humanists discerned all the symptoms of the decadent modern spirit and romantic chaos, evident in the novels of Theodore Dreiser and others and in the radical subjectivism of the new poetry. The Humanists used the same core of ideas to carry out their longest sustained attack, their case against the nature and goals of higher education in the United States. The elective system, vocationalism, the service ideal, and the German tradition all documented for the Humanists the drastic decline of the classical and humanist tradition of the old-time college and pointed to the complicity of the universities in the materialistic culture of the country. When applied to society, the Humanist outline produced an unrestrained assault on the humanitarian movements and the democratic excess that the group saw engulfing America. But although the Humanists deprecated the romantic reformer and the socialist and though they strongly defended the rights of property, they had a marked distaste for the American plutocracy and severely judged its failures as a leadership class. Finally, the question of religion proved the most difficult for the New Humanism and seriously divided its spokesmen. All were sympathetic to religion as a discipline and as a spiritual antidote to naturalism. But whether Humanism could be a substitute for religion, whether it could achieve in the modern world the unifying effects and spiritual accomplishments of an earlier age, was a question that confounded Humanist opinion. Indeed, on none of these areas of modern American life was there a uniformity of ideas among the Humanists. Although the major proponents concurred on certain basic principles, a rigid ideology never emerged. The Humanist core of belief was in fact capable of immense variety in its application.

Irving Babbitt and Paul Elmer More were the earliest and most important figures in the Humanist movement. Long before it had any significant following, Babbitt and More were solidly laying the intellectual foundations of a Humanist criticism that younger followers later carried beyond Harvard and Princeton. Babbitt was born in Dayton, Ohio, in 1865 and in his youth acquired a wide experience of American life. His family's relocations took him to New York City and East Orange, New Jersey, but he also spent summers in Cincinnati and at his uncle's ranch in Wyoming.[2] Babbitt, however, was never close to his immediate family. His mother died when he was eleven, and his father, Dr. Edwin Dwight Babbitt, was never a sympathetic figure. The doctor, a freethinker and vociferous humanitarian, represented all that young Irving came later to despise. He indulged in a variety of cults, from spiritualism to phrenology, and exemplified by these pursuits an intellectual romanticism that the son recognized as one of the serious maladies of the age.[3]

With the financial help of his uncle, Babbitt began an undergraduate career at Harvard University. Here he discovered the two shaping influences of his life—the classical world of Greece and the culture of the Orient. While many of his college friends pursued modern languages and literature, Babbitt delved into the ancient world and gradually built from it the standards of judgment by which he thereafter measured the present. The world of the early Greeks always remained one of Babbitt's strongest loves. Later in life when he was contemplating a European vacation, Babbitt told a friend that he most eagerly anticipated a rereading of Sophocles while walking through the Acropolis.[4] Harvard also introduced him to the

[2] Dora Babbitt, in Frederick Manchester and Odell Shepard, eds., *Irving Babbitt: Man and Teacher* (New York, 1941), pp. ix-x.

[3] An early letter from the doctor to Irving illustrates the opposing temperaments of father and son. The former chided Irving for being so out of date, for disdaining the modern world even to the point of neglecting the daily newspapers. Edwin Babbitt believed the age was alive and wonderful, full of many marvelous things. His son, he felt, was too much the college recluse, living in the past and closing his eyes to the contemporary scene. On another issue, the father romanticized the American role in the 1898 war against Spain, celebrating the democratic and humanitarian mission of the United States to defeat the European nation, model of Old World barbarism and tyranny. Irving had earlier expressed his admiration for the conservative and traditionalist Spanish character (Edwin D. Babbitt to Irving Babbitt, Aug. 30, 1898, Irving Babbitt Correspondence, Harvard University Archives, Cambridge, Mass.).

[4] George Roy Elliott, in Manchester and Shepard, p. 156.

Irving Babbitt. Photograph by Bachrach. (Courtesy Harvard University Archives.)

Paul Elmer More. (Courtesy Princeton University Archives.)

Eastern languages and these increasingly attracted him to Buddhism. Both these influences became critical cornerstones of Babbitt's Humanist outlook.

Although Babbitt celebrated the virtues of discipline and restraint, in personality and conduct he was the picture of untamed energy. He relished the adventurous cowboy life of his uncle's ranch and later hiked through Europe with a college friend, visiting many of the remote and less familiar corners of the continent. Friends and visitors of Babbitt always recalled restless walks with their host in and around Cambridge, while others remembered vigorous games of tennis. Indeed, an irate Babbitt was not even constrained from throwing his racquet.[5]

Babbitt continued at Harvard long enough to receive a master's degree but chose not to pursue the doctorate. Here began his long revolt against the academic establishment. Even in the study of the classics, Babbitt too often found a cold Germanic pedantry squeezing the zest of life from literature. As an undergraduate Babbitt made his feelings known by refusing to attend classes. That in turn brought a warning from the registrar that Babbitt had more "cuts" than anyone in his class. After graduation Babbitt left the cultured confines of the East and launched a teaching career at the College of Montana in Deer Lodge, in 1889, joining a faculty of eight and a student body of one hundred. Babbitt then taught for a year at Williams College and in 1894 secured a position at Harvard, where he remained until his death in 1933.[6]

Babbitt's Harvard career was vital to the New Humanist movement, and he was clearly the major intellectual force in it. In its early years Humanism won little recognition in the academic or literary world, but Babbitt spread the gospel in his classroom to a younger group that carried it abroad. Stuart Sherman and Norman Foerster readily absorbed Babbitt's ideas, and T. S. Eliot was a partial affiliate of the movement. Babbitt also had his antagonists. Van Wyck Brooks and Walter Lippmann took courses with him but never rallied to the cause.[7]

On many of his students the Harvard Humanist made an enduring

[5] For a complete view of all facets of Babbitt's personality, see Manchester and Shepard, which contains reminiscences by thirty-nine friends and acquaintances.

[6] William F. Giese and Anne Douglas, in Manchester and Shepard, pp. 15, 26–27.

[7] Gorham Munson, *The Dilemma of the Liberated* (New York, 1930), p. 55. The young Lippmann was a classroom critic of Babbitt's viewpoints. When Babbitt tried to trace the intellectual origins of socialism from Rousseauistic humanitarianism, Lippmann penned a letter to his teacher suggesting that the real heritage of Rousseau was the vigorous individualism that produced the Manchester School of economics (Oct. 7, 1908, Babbitt Correspondence).

impression. His classroom lectures were daily exercises in Humanism. Babbitt entered the room with the familiar green Harvard book bag, whose contents he hastily unloaded on the desk. Then the discourse began. Stuart Sherman recalled the ensuing phenomenon: "He deluged you with the wisdom of the world; his thoughts were unpacked and poured out so fast you couldn't keep up with them. . . . He was at you day after day like a battering ram, knocking down your illusions." To another student, "to hear him was to understand the modern world."[8] Babbitt's vast repertoire of facts, carefully chosen cases-in-point from the wisdom and folly of the past, so amazed the students that they made bets on the number of authors he would mention in the course of a lecture. The record, apparently, was seventy-five.

But it was never smooth sailing for Babbitt at Harvard. He taught in the Department of Romance Languages and Literature and in the Department of Comparative Literature. His individual courses included Literary Criticism in France, Rousseau and His Influence, and the Romantic Movement in the Nineteenth Century. But his real preference was the classics, and he won little favor in his own department when as an instructor he once referred to French as a cheap and nasty substitute for Latin.[9] The Classics Department, however, closed the door to him, and in his own colleagues he met protracted depreciation. At one time he had to use an offer from the University of Illinois, obtained through Sherman, to win a promotion, and according to More only a response from the growing number of his good students prevented his being dropped altogether. Babbitt, moreover, was at loggerheads with President Charles W. Eliot. The latter's elective system and the course proliferation under it represented much that Babbitt found intolerable in American higher education, and he openly took issue with Eliot at faculty meetings.[10]

Humanism dominated Babbitt's intellectual career from start to finish. His consistency was striking. Paul More said of his friend that he "seems to have sprung up, like Minerva, fully grown and fully armed. . . . There is something almost inhuman in the immobility of his central ideas." Visiting Babbitt at Harvard in 1926, More observed that "Babbitt's fundamental ideas had not changed by a jot, though they were now reinforced

[8] Jacob Zeitlin and Homer Woodbridge, eds., *Life and Letters of Stuart P. Sherman* (New York, 1929), I, 117; Hoffman Nickerson, "Irving Babbitt," *Criterion,* 13 (1934), 194.

[9] Giese, in Manchester and Shepard, p. 4.

[10] Babbitt to Sherman, Nov. 20, 1910, Correspondence of Stuart Pratt Sherman, University of Illinois Archives, Urbana-Champaign; Paul Elmer More, *On Being Human* (Princeton, 1936), p. 34; William F. Maag, Jr., in Manchester and Shepard, p. 83.

by an appalling mass of erudition at the service of an unhesitating, un-
failing, unerring memory."[11] Babbitt was, indeed, a crusader for Humanism. He proposed to meet the moderns on their own ground and make
Humanism defensible empirically without appeal to metaphysics or
dogmatic religion. When George R. Elliott told Babbitt that he agreed that
America needed a new deal in ideas, Babbitt fired back, "Well, why don't
you get out and fight?" Although for years he quietly despaired at
Humanism's failure to make headway, he rejoiced at its flourishing in the
late twenties. Edmund Wilson reported learning that Babbitt hung a large
map of the United States in his office and marked the appearance of
a new convert by sticking a pin at the proper locale.[12]

Babbitt did not avoid controversy and was often the object of attack.
The irascible Burton Rascoe called him "the nearest thing to an Anglo-
Catholic royalist in America . . . a Boston Brahmin . . . living in academic
seclusion from contact with the world of today . . . [and] shadow-boxing
with the ghost of Jean-Jacques Rousseau." Babbitt's ardent moralism
brought from another critic the charge that "he is Calvinism applied to
literature, the arts, philosophy and science."[13]

Paul Elmer More joined Babbitt to form the vanguard of the New
Humanism. More also was a midwesterner, born in Saint Louis in 1864. His
family, however, had deep roots in New England and traced descendants
to the founders of Connecticut. His father, a bookdealer, moved the family
from Dayton, Ohio, in 1859, following their minister to Saint Louis. More's
parents were strict Calvinists. Enoch Anson More led the family in morning
and evening prayers, while his wife, Katherine Hay Elmer, daily read
from the Bible to Paul and his sisters. A stern moral atmosphere dominated
the household, including even dancing among its proscriptions. Although More later broke dramatically from his father's Calvinism, he did
acquire from his father an interest in literature and a love for poetry.[14]

These pursuits More carried through high school, where he was president
of the literary society, and in Washington University in Saint Louis, where
he became immersed in German romanticism. He wrote a good deal of
poetry before going to Harvard to continue his graduate studies. At
Cambridge, More studied Oriental and classical languages, and began his

[11] More, *On Being Human*, pp. 29, 35.

[12] Elliott, "Irving Babbitt as I Knew Him," *American Review,* 8 (1936), 50; Wilson,
The Triple Thinkers (New York, 1938), p. 7.

[13] Rascoe, "Pupils of Polonius," in C. Hartley Grattan, ed., *The Critique of
Humanism* (New York, 1930), pp. 126–27; Harry Salpeter, "Irving Babbitt,
Calvinist," *Outlook and Independent,* 155 (1930), 439.

[14] Arthur Hazard Dakin, *Paul Elmer More* (Princeton, 1960), pp. 3–5.

lifelong friendship with Babbitt, the two constituting the whole advanced class in Sanskrit and the Pali dialect. And there too Babbitt made probably his first convert to Humanism. After breaking from his parents' Calvinism, More had wandered off on a romantic tangent pursuing what he later called a vague emotionalism in literature and poetry writing. But the encounter with Babbitt reversed More's outlook. "He turned the whole current of my life," More later wrote, "saving me from something akin to emotional and intellectual suicide." In 1913 More wrote to Stuart Sherman: "We seem to be . . . wandering intellectually, like travelers in a country with innumerable roads and no maps, and I.B. is a guidepost pointing always to Rome." [15]

More also rejected the doctoral course at Harvard and went to Bryn Mawr to teach Sanskrit and classical literature. Thereafter he joined the staff of the *Independent* and shortly became literary editor of the *Nation*. More's articles during these years, the most important of which he published in the *Shelburne Essays*, reflected the Humanist ideas he brought from Harvard and are the most important elements of the Humanists' literary criticism. In 1919 Princeton induced More to teach Greek and Patristic philosophy with the promise that he would be excused from faculty meetings and the rest of the academic routine.

Although More carried the stamp of Babbitt's intellectual influence, in character and personality the "Hermit of Princeton" differed sharply from the "Warring Buddha of Harvard." [16] More was always shy and withdrawn. As a youth he was frail and anemic and never joined with his schoolmates in games and sports. At Bryn Mawr, we are told, he felt uneasy before the pretty girls in his class; in fact, the prettier they were, the more conscientiously he avoided looking at them. Never deliberately remote, he nonetheless failed to excite his students with the enthusiasm and conviction that Babbitt transmitted. Basically, More aspired to withdrawal from the world in quiet and private contemplation. He shared little of his colleague's zest for activity. In Shelburne, New Hampshire, More found the isolation and peace of a New England retreat and there continually rediscovered an atmosphere conducive both to his creative efforts and to the otherworldly strains of his personality. When at Princeton, More devoted most of the day to reading; he combined this in the warmer months with activity in his garden. One is close to the essence of More in a letter

[15] More to Maurice Baum, ibid., p. 221; More to Sherman, June 19, 1913, Sherman Correspondence.

[16] G. R. Elliott supplied the nicknames. See his *Humanism and Imagination* (Chapel Hill N.C., 1938), p. 56.

he wrote to his sister: "Plato and a garden, what more should human nature desire?"[17]

More did not have his friend's zeal for popularizing Humanism, but he was equally exposed to attacks from without. Edmund Wilson labeled him "an old-fashioned Puritan who has lost the Puritan theology without having lost the Puritan dogmatism." H. L. Mencken longed to entice More from his "ivory tower" and "engage him on the field of battle." Nonetheless, Mencken respected his enemy: "More has a solid stock of learning in his lockers. . . . he is, perhaps, the nearest approach to a genuine scholar that we have in America, God save us all!" And Randolph Bourne, no friend of Humanism, remarked that More "is an American institution, the ablest spokesman for the idealism of our intellectual plutocracy."[18] More indeed was one of the most esteemed American literary critics and students of Greek philosophy and was widely considered for the Nobel Prize in 1932.

The first major outline of the New Humanism was Babbitt's *Literature and the American College* (1908). It indicted the whole course of modern culture and identified as its twin evils the enduring influences of science and romanticism. Subservience to the first, Babbitt felt, was enslaving man to material pursuits. Inheriting from Bacon a cult of practical knowledge and from his successors a faith in progress through science, the present age was neglecting the spiritual content of human well-being and drifting from traditional standards through a welter of experimentation. Romanticism was the other false goddess of the modern age. Babbitt attributed to the influence of Rousseau the cult of personal uniqueness that was producing a "riot of individuality" in the arts and a confusion of standards everywhere. In higher education particularly these influences were pervasive. A wealth of courses that promised to place "power and service" at the disposal of society testified to the age's faith in material improvement; and a romantic trust in the uncharted course of individual development replaced the older common curriculum with a free elective system that Babbitt judged ruinous to higher education.

For the rest of his career Babbitt reinforced the outline set forth in his

[17] Dakin, *Paul Elmer More*, pp. 20, 53, 154–55 (the quotation). In 1914, as the guns of war rattled in Europe, More wrote to Babbitt: "I sit in my little study among the trees in a profound peace, thinking of things very ancient and withdrawn, and cannot realize in my imagination what is actually taking place in the present" (More to Babbitt, Paul Elmer More Papers, Department of Rare Books and Special Collections, Princeton University Library, Princeton, N.J.).

[18] Wilson, "Notes on Babbitt and More," in Grattan, p. 59; Mencken, *Prejudices: Third Series* (New York, 1922), p. 178; Bourne, "Paul Elmer More," *New Republic*, 6 (1916), 245.

first work. *The New Laokoön* (1910) continued to chart the romantic influence in aesthetics, followed two years later by *The Masters of Modern French Criticism*. The latter was the New Humanism's most incisive statement of the philosophy of art. Babbitt, displaying a rich mastery of his subject, made critical evaluations of the most important French critics and aestheticians, mostly nineteenth-century figures. The study provided him a useful vehicle for surveying the influence of romanticism and scientific thinking on aesthetics, and to both Babbitt responded with his own Humanist prescription. This work helped prepare the way for *Rousseau and Romanticism* (1919), the most important work of the New Humanism. Here Babbitt continued the Humanist case against the present by a critical survey of the intellectual past, searching three centuries back for the sources of drift and confusion that marked the contemporary world. Scarcely a major thinker escaped Babbitt's attention. Altogether *Rousseau and Romanticism* was a plea for the recovery of human law, for self-discipline and traditional moral values against romantic individualism.

Meanwhile More was helping to define the New Humanism in his *Shelburne Essays*. Named for his New Hampshire retreat, the eleven volumes appeared between 1904 and 1921 and marked the period of More's Humanist career. In that period More applied a strongly Humanist framework to his critical writings—religious, literary, and philosophical discussions. The *Shelburne Essays* show him to be almost wholly in accord with Babbitt, defending a positive and empirical Humanism. To this extent, one central idea pervaded the essays and provided the critical framework by which More judged the wide range of topics and persons he examined. The dual nature of the human soul was for More the indispensable fact of human nature. The propensity of man's lower self for evil and spiritual inertia required the vigorous opposition of a higher self, a principle of control. It alone could redirect human energies to moral ends. Despite its essential simplicity, dualism had infinite variations in More's conception, and in his essays (on Pascal, Rousseau, William James, Newman, Huxley, and many others) the subject's perception of this human condition was More's final criterion.

Babbitt and More did receive some reinforcement before the First World War. Frank Jewett Mather, Jr., an acquaintance of both Babbitt and More, contributed essays to the *Nation* and later, in the middle of his career at Princeton, dedicated his major work along Humanist lines, *Modern Painting* (1926), to his Harvard friend. Kenyon Cox was another Princeton associate of the Humanists and the author of *The Classical Point of View* (1912) and *Artist and Public* (1914). Prosser Hall Frye and Sherlock Bronson Gass both taught at the University of Nebraska and were friendly to the

Humanist position. But all of these persons were minor figures who, though sympathetic, contributed little to the enrichment of Humanist thought.

Although Babbitt and More in this period were building a framework that changed but slightly over a four-decade span, they made almost no headway in literary or academic circles. Babbitt said in 1913 that he felt as though he were writing for private circulation. More felt similarly. He later recalled these years: "I used to solace myself with the boast that I was at once the least read and most hated author in existence. Other writers I admitted might be more hated, and I hoped that a few were less read; but the combination I claimed for myself as a unique distinction."[19]

But the appearance of Stuart Pratt Sherman as the first of the young Humanists ended the movement's status as an isolated outpost of protest. Sherman, too, was a product of the Midwest, born in Anita, Iowa, in 1881. He early knew the raw and rough conditions of Iowa farm life and his father's difficult struggles to win a decent living. Stuart attended a little wooden schoolhouse a mile from his home, but it was largely from his father, a great enthusiast of literature, that he heard firsthand the exciting passages from Homer, Milton, and Shakespeare. Problems of health required John Sherman to move the family to Los Angeles, but his condition worsened and he died when Stuart was eleven. Although he was close to his mother, Ada Pratt Sherman, it was his uncle who introduced him to the rugged life of the Arizona mining camps. The experience excited Sherman, and his reaction to the rough democratic character of this part of America anticipated the romanticism Sherman always bore toward this tradition.[20]

Sherman early evidenced eclectic interests and pursued science with enthusiasm in his Dorset, Vermont, high school, well before he concentrated on literature. At Williams College it was Latin that won his interest. Sherman was athletic and excelled at football, and he was judged by his classmates the brightest as well as the most versatile of their members. Like More, Sherman wrote a good deal of poetry and even some short stories, and the world of literature hereafter became his sustaining interest.[21] His involvement then took him to Harvard for graduate work. He became the first of Babbitt's students to enlist in the cause, and at Babbitt's home in Cambridge he made his first acquaintance with Paul Elmer More. More

[19] Babbitt to Sherman, Apr. 8, 1913, Sherman Correspondence; Paul Elmer More, *The Demon of the Absolute* (Princeton, 1928), p. 3.

[20] Zeitlin and Woodbridge, I, 2-29.

[21] Ibid., pp. 43-45.

cultivated Sherman as reviewer and essayist for the *Nation* and tried without success to have Sherman on the permanent staff.

After teaching one year at Northwestern University, Sherman accepted a position in the English department of the University of Illinois. Here he gave most attention to his course in Matthew Arnold, but in his other classes, too, Sherman sought to effect a spiritual awakening in his students through literature. He tried to work out with them a conception of the good life and used Arnold as the best illustration of the general ideas that American society most needed.

The First World War was crucial to Sherman's outlook, for his emotional involvement in the Allied and American cause invigorated the spirited nationalism that henceforth prevailed in his criticism. Like many others in the literary world, such as Edith Wharton, Dorothy Canfield, and Willa Cather, Sherman saw the war pitting German vulgarity and militarism on one side against art, democracy, and culture on the other. His 1918 essay "American and Allied Ideals" levied a blistering attack on German culture: it had made the Germans idolators of war and the powerful state. The Americans and Allies, he claimed, were "fighting for the common interests of the whole family of civilized nations."[22] And for Sherman the Humanist, the war was instructive. He recognized in Germany the weighty impact both of the romantic and naturalist movements and their expansive effects. These forces had deprived the individual of standards for self-control, necessitating external control in the form of a repressive government. By contrast, Sherman argued, the American ideal was the opposite. In Germany it was the government which pronounced *verboten*; in America the individual conscience supplied the necessary restraint. Sherman called the American ideal "Puritanism," the indispensable check on democracy, the principle of external freedom.[23]

In 1917 Sherman published his first two books, *Matthew Arnold: How to Know Him* and *On Contemporary Literature*. The former was as much a statement of belief as a study of the English critic, who was one of the favorites of the New Humanists. But the latter book plunged Sherman into the thick of battle. It was Babbitt and More applied to contemporary literature. Sherman castigated the naturalist movement in American letters and announced that the time had come, not to restore man to God, but to retrieve him from the animals. Denouncing the "barbaric naturalism" of Theodore Dreiser, Sherman insisted that the artist must not merely

[22] Sherman, "American and Allied Ideals," U.S. Government *War Information Series*, No. 12 (Feb. 1918), p. 14.

[23] Ibid., p. 9.

record life; he must capture the ethical center at the core of human experience.

On Contemporary Literature put Sherman in the spotlight and Humanism in the midst of the "battle of the books" that raged throughout the 1920s. Much of that controversy involved the American literary past, then under attack by Van Wyck Brooks from the Left and H. L. Mencken from the Right. Sherman came to the defense and used the American tradition in letters to define the New Humanist program for the present. His new critical efforts, collected in *Americans* (1922) and *The Genius of America* (1923), elaborated his case. In the Puritans, in Emerson, and in Hawthorne, Sherman found useful directives for modern man's spiritual fulfillment and self-mastery. These writers, he maintained, showed the path to the higher life through their insight into the distinctly human qualities. Sherman also joined to this dualism the ingredients for his democratic humanism that he found in Whitman and Twain and thereby forged the "religion of democracy" that he now celebrated as the essence of the American spirit. This was to be the source of unity and cohesion, a spiritual renaissance for American society. The task of American letters Sherman now defined as "the cultural unity of America," which it might achieve by illuminating the national character, specifically its "profound moral idealism."

Sherman was the first of its proponents to popularize the New Humanism. Unlike Babbitt and More, he plunged headlong into contemporary literature, taking on Dreiser and his defender Mencken, Sinclair Lewis, Ben Hecht, and many others. Armed with a wry wit and a fiery tongue, Sherman was a ready match for the caustic Mencken and soon became the enfant terrible of the Humanist circle. Babbitt knew his value. "Sherman's a man I shouldn't want for an opponent," he said. And as for Sherman, he seemed to thrive on controversy and relished the counterattacks of his opponents. "It shows," he said, ". . . that we have got under their skins."[24] For better or worse he was giving Humanism a new and wider reading audience, and his correspondence included many letters from noted writers and critics and requests from the general public for speaking engagements.

But just when Humanism was winning attention, signs of disintegration appeared. More interrupted the *Shelburne Essays* and returned to the ancient world, introducing his *Platonism* in 1917. Here he appealed to Plato's dualism as the basis for a Humanist conception of man. But the work also

[24] Manchester, in Manchester and Shepard, p. 129; Sherman to More, Mar. 12, 1918, Sherman Correspondence. More never thought highly of the Menckenite tactics of Sherman, even when used against the enemy himself. "I can't believe this is the way to go at the thing" (More to Babbitt, Feb. 2, 1923, More Papers).

denoted the beginning of More's movement away from an empirical Humanism. That shift was fully apparent in his new series, "The Greek Tradition." Its five volumes—*The Religion of Plato* (1921), *Hellenistic Philosophies* (1923), *The Christ of the New Testament* (1924), *Christ the Word* (1927), and *The Catholic Faith* (1931)—indicated that Plato's idealism was becoming equally attractive to More and furnishing the means for his defense of religion. Whereas More had earlier used Plato to argue that religious ideas and myths were useful supplements to the Humanist life by virtue of their symbolic correspondence with an empirical dualistic philosophy, More now speculated seriously that the entire Logos of the Christian religion was true in itself because it was a uniquely accurate description of the human condition. The intricacies of that argument received their most elaborate statement in *The Sceptical Approach to Religion* (1934), the second volume of the *New Shelburne Essays*. But these changes in More's ideas left Babbitt and Sherman wholly unsympathetic.

Meanwhile, Sherman was moving away from both Babbitt and More. Some have suggested that his later books, *Points of View* (1924), *Critical Woodcuts* (1926), and the posthumous publications *The Main Stream* (1927) and *The Emotional Discovery of America* (1932) show a marked shift from his earlier Humanism and the abandonment of the Puritan crusade. The charge is only partially true. Sherman relaxed his moral idealism somewhat, but his fight for the spiritual enrichment of American life now superseded that concern, and Sherman was simply casting a wider net. Even on the seamy side of life, where Sherwood Anderson and others expressed the aspirations of restless souls in drab midwestern towns, Sherman found signs of a healthy struggle for qualitative living and welcomed much of the new literature.

Sherman's growing inclusiveness coincided with his removal from Illinois to New York City in 1924 to become literary editor of the *Herald Tribune*. In leaving the Midwest, Sherman denied that he was "deserting the ship." "Loyalty to the provinces," he wrote, "doesn't mean that one must never take a trip to the city to see what is going on there. After seventeen years in the corn I am simply making a 'detour' out of it to learn what is going on outside." Sherman, furthermore, was an exhausted man. He confided to a friend that he worked "like a horse," writing prolifically over a nine-year period and all the while performing his academic duties.[25] He was maintaining this pace up to the moment of his untimely death by drowning in the summer of 1926, the probable result of a heart attack.

Meanwhile, however, Babbitt was worrying considerably over the new

[25] Sherman to "Gensen," May 2, 1924, and to "McNitt," May 30, 1926, Sherman Correspondence.

directions in Sherman's criticism. "It seems to me," he wrote to his former student, "that you have been diverted from [the] anti-naturalistic campaign of late by your desire to defend our American [democratic] idealism. . . . I have rather regretted this diversion of your energies." Nonetheless, Babbitt continued to hope that Sherman, More, and he could still "present a united front to the enemy."[26] Sherman's unyielding democracy, however, did weaken that defense. When he told Babbitt, who was visiting him in Urbana, that he would rather be at the state university of Illinois than at Oxford, Babbitt was appalled. He blamed Sherman's admiration for the average American on his midwestern location, an area he identified in his own mind with a crude philistinism that threatened to swallow up what little remained of civilization in America. Sherman, on the other hand, thought that Babbitt and More were "remorselessly negative."[27]

The breach between Sherman and More was even more serious. Sherman's democratic enthusiasms troubled his friend. More encouraged Sherman to see the good in people but the evil as well. "Don't get slushy," he warned; "human nature is of a strange mixture, and the one thing it cannot stand is too much flattery." Like Babbitt, he felt that Sherman should quit Illinois, and he despaired at his rejecting an Amherst appointment. "I don't like this talk of democracy," he wrote him. "The one supreme duty for a man in a democracy—or anywhere else—is to make the best of himself." More believed that that concern ought to weigh more heavily than the "democratic experiment" that Sherman defended. And, finally, More recommended that Sherman sober his enthusiasm by taking up the classics. "You have read so prodigiously in the modern field," he told him, "that you can well afford to take time for the ancient." The Greek authors in particular would help.[28]

These exhortations only intensified Sherman's grievances with More. Sherman felt that More could do considerably better for Humanism if he would join Sherman in his crusade against the philistines. He charged that More's scholarship, though profound, touched hardly at all on America or the contemporary scene. He bluntly told More that he was too much the Princeton professor. "My quarrel with the professors," he explained, "is that

[26] Babbitt to Sherman, Mar. 18, 1922, ibid.

[27] Warner Rice, in Manchester and Shepard, pp. 250–51; Sherman to Frank Jewett Mather, Jr., Jan. 13, 1923, Sherman Correspondence.

[28] More to Sherman, Jan. 25, 1920, Aug. 6, 1915, Sherman Correspondence. More was repulsed by Sherman's nationalistic literary criticism in the latter's *Americans*. He wrote to Babbitt that it "is no less than a compact signed with the Devil" (More to Babbitt, Jan. 2, 1922, More Papers).

they don't fight. They stand on their dignity—or rather they *sit* on it, till it is as flat as an old hat."[29] Sherman therefore did not reserve his sarcasm for his enemies. The following caricature of More's work was intended to rouse his friend to battle: "I conceive the Shelburne essays," Sherman wrote, "to which he adds a wing year after year, as a many-chambered mansion, conspicuously withdrawn from the public highway, built and maintained for the reception of Indian sages, Greek philosophers, great poets, moralists, scholars, statesmen, and other guests from the Elysian Fields." But More still did not enter the fray. He ploughed deeper instead into Greek philosophy. Sherman despaired, writing to Frank Mather, that More "retreats into a blinding white mist of Platonism, where God himself would think twice before pursuing."[30]

But in spite of these divisions, the New Humanism gained considerable strength at the end of the 1920s. Norman Foerster completed its inner circle. Foerster was born in Pittsburgh in 1887, the son of Adolph and Henrietta Foerster, and pursued an early interest in literature through his undergraduate years at Harvard. He was the student editor of the *Harvard Monthly* and, like Sherman a few years before him, a student of Babbitt. Foerster, in fact, became the most consistent and enduring exponent of Babbitt's ideas and the major Humanist voice after the deaths of Babbitt and More in the middle 1930s. His greatest interest for a while was writing, and for this reason he decided to forego the doctoral program and renounced a life of conventional scholarship. He did do some graduate work at Harvard and at the University of Wisconsin before taking a position at the University of North Carolina, where he taught courses in literary criticism and romanticism.

The outline of Foerster's Humanism became apparent with the publication of his *American Criticism* in 1928, and a second work, *Towards Standards*, two years later. Foerster now undertook the same task in American criticism that Sherman had accomplished in American literature. Surveying the major American statements of the philosophy of art and literature, Foerster subjected the past to a Humanist critique. Although unfavorable to Poe's romanticism, Foerster found Lowell, Emerson, and even Whitman useful correctives to the vogue of impressionist and historical criticism in the twentieth century. He also appealed to Greek standards in defending a fusion of the ethical imagination with the aesthetic as the basis for a Humanist measure of literary value.

[29] Sherman, *Americans* (New York, 1922), p. 34; Sherman to More, Mar. 12, 1918, Sherman Correspondence.

[30] Sherman, *Americans,* p. 320; Sherman to Mather, June 13, 1923, Sherman Correspondence.

Norman Foerster. (Courtesy The University of Iowa Archives, Iowa City.)

Stuart Pratt Sherman. (Courtesy University of Illinois Archives, Urbana-Champaign.)

In 1930 Foerster accepted a call from the University of Iowa to fill a newly created position as director of the School of Letters. This high-salaried office followed the University's effort partially to merge the four departments of Romance Languages, Classics, English, and German. Foerster saw here an opportunity to practice his own Humanist ideas on higher education and now followed Sherman in establishing a second Humanist beachhead at a large midwestern state university. Foerster proceeded to innovate in a number of ways, and his fifteen-year career at Iowa became as controversial as the Humanist movement generally.

Higher education, in fact, was now becoming the major focus of Foerster's attention, for he became increasingly convinced that this was the critical cultural failure of modern America. *The American Scholar* (1930), *The American State University* (1937), and *The Future of the Liberal Arts College* (1938) all severely indicted American institutions for their slavish imitation of popular trends. Like the other Humanists, Foerster saw the American college and university as the last bastions of defense against materialism and romantic chaos; he found, however, that they were neglecting the disciplining effects of the humanities, catering to mediocrity, and worshipping at the altar of material progress. Foerster elaborated a persuasive case for humanist education, and *The American State University* particularly ranks with the best literature of the New Humanism.

George Roy Elliott was one of the brightest in the second generation of Humanists. As a young instructor at Bowdoin, he had corresponded with Babbitt and resolved one day to see the man he so esteemed. This he accomplished by stealing quietly into one of Babbitt's classes at Harvard. Thereafter he enjoyed long walks and conversations with Babbitt at the latter's summer home in New Hampshire. Elliott's *The Cycle of Modern Poetry* (1929) acknowledged the author's debt to Babbitt and More, "our two chief critical thinkers since Arnold." He asserted with them that poetry must fuse the moral intellect and the imagination, and in his critical studies of Shelley, Keats, Milton, and others, he explored the aesthetic possibilities of that prescription. *Modern Poetry* is one of the New Humanism's most incisive studies, but in *Humanism and Imagination* (1938) Elliott failed to match the quality of his first work. Here he joined the Humanists' attacks on naturalism but also shifted to a religious stance in calling for a renewal of the Christian influence on the arts.

Two other figures completed the younger ranks of the Humanist school. Gorham B. Munson came to Humanism from a radical past. A Greenwich Village bohemian and dadaist in the early twenties, Munson cultivated Freud, socialism, and the anti-Puritan crusades of Van Wyck Brooks and Waldo Frank. He was also a close friend of, and influence on, the poet

Hart Crane. Munson joined the expatriate crowd in Vienna and Berlin after the war and was editor of the literary journal *Secession*. Although short-lived, the journal was a forum for a remarkable number of young writers, including Malcolm Cowley, Matthew Josephson, Tristan Tzara, E. E. Cummings, William Carlos Williams, Wallace Stevens, and Yvor Winters. But later in the decade Munson broke sharply with his radicalism and drifted toward the Humanists. Finally, Robert Shafer, a Princeton Ph.D. and later a dean at the University of Cincinnati, added considerable force, if not much intellectual quality, to the Humanist movement. He wrote three books defining Humanism and several articles that show him to be a temperamental and often caustic critic. His *Progress and Science* (1922) and *Christianity and Naturalism* (1926) assaulted the modern age's faith in science. In 1935 Shafer published *Paul Elmer More and American Criticism.*

Babbitt, too, was at work in the middle twenties. His *Democracy and Leadership* (1924) warned that America was in danger of producing "one of the most trifling brands of the human species that the world has yet seen." In this critique of democratic theory and practice, Babbitt challenged every premise of the democratic faith and judged harshly the prevalent texture of American society, from its pervasive commercialism to its indiscriminate humanitarianism. And again on each side Babbitt found the twin evils of naturalism and romanticism. *Democracy and Leadership* was Babbitt's last major work. He published in 1932 a series of essays under the title *On Being Creative*, and in 1936, after his death, his wife, Dora, issued his translation of the Buddhist classic *The Dhammapada*. In her introduction she described the book as the "fruit of Irving Babbitt's whole life's devotion to the study of Buddhism." Babbitt in 1927 had written an accompanying essay, "Buddha and the Occident," which shows clearly the influence of the East on his Humanism and which is one of the most explicit statements of the New Humanism. *The Spanish Character*, a collection of essays, was published posthumously in 1940.

Also important to the advancement of Humanism in the 1920s was the widespread hearing it now received in the literary journals.[31] T. S. Eliot was always friendly to much of the New Humanism and as editor of the *Criterion* sponsored important articles on the movement, particularly on its relation to religion. Eliot himself said of Babbitt and More that "these seem

[31] Seward Collins quoted the following passage from Karl Schriftgeisser in the *Boston Evening Transcript:* "Pick up almost any magazine from the *Bookman* up or down, and you will find considerable talk about Humanism. This philosophy of life and letters . . . is gaining more credence all the time" ("Criticism in America: The Revival of the Anti-Humanist Myth," *Bookman,* 71 [1929–30], 404–5).

to me the two *wisest* men that I have known."[32] Eliot, of course, aided greatly in giving Humanism an audience in England. In the United States, John Farrar and Henry Goddard Leach made a similar contribution when, in the early 1920s, they opened the pages of the *Bookman* and the *Forum*, respectively, to proponents of Humanism. Farrar called Sherman "the logical critic for this hour in America" and sponsored his call for a Puritan recovery in American life.[33]

Seward Collins succeeded Farrar as editor in 1928 and made the *Bookman* avowedly pro-Humanist. He vigorously and often bitterly attacked the Humanists' opponents. Collins regarded Babbitt's *Democracy and Leadership* as "the weightiest book even written by an American." He himself was an ardent right-winger who had earlier supported the Southern Agrarians and later Mussolini.[34] The *Bookman* became the *American Review* in 1933, continuing under Collins's direction. But his connection with the New Humanism won it little credit in academic or literary circles. Many identified it with reaction. Thus Alter Brody wrote in the *New Republic*: "Stripped, with Mr. Collins' aid, of its philosophical verbiage, the New Humanism emerges as the intellectual program of the Boston Chapter of the Daughters of the American Revolution, differing from the Ku Klux Klan by being more exclusive."[35]

It is difficult to draw a composite picture of the New Humanists. Although their origins were overwhelmingly middle-class, a diversity of regional, cultural, and religious influences prevailed. Babbitt and More forsook the Midwest and the democratic philistinism they associated with it, but Foerster and Sherman especially saw that area as holding the greatest promise for Humanist growth. What united the group was not any single external element. The Humanists found their identity as lovers of literature and moral critics of life. More, Sherman, and Foerster each came to literature through an early interest in its art and practice, but Babbitt always judged these pursuits as frivolous. Nevertheless, in a certain sense,

[32] Quoted in Dakin, *Paul Elmer More*, p. 386. Though a student of Babbitt at Harvard, Eliot was apparently more intimate with More. A letter from Eliot to More mentions Eliot's impending separation from his wife and confides that, outside those consulted for spiritual help, More is the only person so far apprised of the event (Mar. 26, 1933, More papers).

[33] "The Fiction of the Uncontrollable," *New York Herald*, Apr. 29, 1923.

[34] Collins, "Criticism in America: The Origins of a Myth," *Bookman*, 71 (1929–30), 361; Arthur M. Schlesinger, Jr., *The Age of Roosevelt*, Vol. III, *The Politics of Upheaval* (Boston, 1960), pp. 70–72.

[35] "Humanism and Intolerance," *New Republic*, 61 (1930), 278. More first met Collins in 1927. He wrote to Babbitt: "Collins is an interesting chap but I wonder how stable he is" (Nov. 27, 1927, More Papers).

literature was their real world. They looked to books to find what life did not give, and in books they sought the realization of their highest aspirations for man. Their recourse to literature afforded the Humanists some of their most useful insights on the human condition, but it was also a source of their weakness. The Humanists too often confused literature and life. If the real world did not reflect the highest human promise, then literature, they felt, must. The ancient Greeks won Humanistic allegiance for showing man at his noblest, but when the modern American writers failed to do so, Babbitt and More turned away. Even Sherman, a more eclectic reader, for a long time renounced the modern works that focused attention on the gutter. Literature was always the sounding board for the Humanists' judgment of life, a fact that may explain the general lack of concern, in their writings and in their own lives, for the fine arts. Few of them found the art galleries and concert halls worthy of more than an occasional visit. All of the major Humanists found inspiration in Matthew Arnold, who more than any single person shaped the Humanists' point of view. One can, in fact, read Babbitt's essay on Arnold in *The Spanish Character* and find one of the most succinct, complete summaries of the New Humanism.

However they might divide on specific issues, intellectually and spiritually the Humanists shared a common quest for certainty in a period when relativism had won respectability. Against the decline of philosophical absolutism in the nineteenth century and the rise of romantic individualism and naturalistic pragmatism, the Humanists found the essence of their challenge in defending a view of life that could uphold general universal standards and values without recourse to metaphysics or religious dogma.

The pinnacle of the Humanist movement was 1930. Journals of every kind published essays and letters pro and con. And in May three thousand people attended a Carnegie Hall discussion of Humanism by Babbitt, Henry Seidel Canby, and Carl Van Doren.[36] The New Humanism had gone public. There appeared also that year the unofficial manifesto of the movement, *Humanism and America: Essays on the Outlook of Modern Civilisation*, edited by Foerster. This collection of essays, with its fifteen contributors, revealed how far Humanism had progressed since the years when Babbitt and More were voices of unrequited protest. But it indicated also that the young disciples had not improved on the intellectual quality of Humanism provided by the older leaders of the school. Many of the essays were good, but altogether the volume did not present the case for Humanism as well as its earlier literature. Opponents attacked the book viciously, some

[36] Seward Collins, "Criticism in America: The End of the Anti-Humanist Myth," *Bookman*, 72 (1930–31), 220; *New York Times*, May 9, 1930.

unreasonably. "If this is all the New Humanism could say for itself," Lewis Mumford wrote, "the writers should have practiced their canonical virtue—the will to refrain." [37]

The Critique of Humanism: A Symposium appeared the same year, close on the heels of *Humanism in America*. Under the editorship of C. Hartley Grattan, thirteen critics of the New Humanism presented their rebuttals. *The Critique* clearly indicated the opponents' concern that Humanism was enjoying its widest vogue. But *The Critique* was even more disappointing in opposition than was *Humanism in America* in defense. There were some perceptive essays, but too much of it dealt with personalities and caricature; little of it examined in depth the important questions the New Humanism raised about the direction of contemporary society. Henry Hazlitt, for example, seemed to think the antinaturalism of the Humanists discredited when he suggested that from the dog man might learn to smell better and from the ant to run his society more smoothly! [38]

And this dearth of useful intellectual exchange was one of the major, unfortunate facts about the Humanist movement. The New Humanism was a perceptive and provocative analysis of modern America. Its proponents saw weaknesses in our society that the more widely read Dewey, Mencken, and others failed to perceive. Its conservatism and traditionalism afforded insights on culture and national character that the relativists and liberals ignored. The New Humanism had its weaknesses and faults, but both its strengths and deficiencies were deprived of effective discussion when personality superseded intellectual criticism in the forum of debate. The liberal thinkers themselves might certainly have sharpened their intellectual axes against the Humanists by critically replying to their major ideas. What might have been one of the most interesting engagements of the period simply did not come off.

[37] "The New Tractarians," *New Republic,* 62 (1930), 163. The contributions by Babbitt and More are particularly good, but see also those of Louis T. More (brother of Paul), G. R. Elliott, T. S. Eliot, Mather, Alan Reynolds Thompson, Shafer, Munson, and Stanley P. Chase. Some of the Humanists themselves must have been appalled at the type of publicity the book received. The publishers, Farrar and Rhinehart, ran a full-page advertisement in the *Saturday Review of Literature,* introducing the book with these screaming headlines: "Is this the philosophy for YOU to live by in the 20th Century? Is the famous 'inner check' of the Humanists the answer to the chaos of our times? Only *you* can decide—Read HUMANISM AND AMERICA" (6 [1930], 875).

[38] "Humanism and Value," in Grattan, pp. 97–98. Malcolm Cowley, Alan Tate, and Louis Mumford wrote provocative critiques. Other contributors included Edmund Wilson, Burton Rascoe, Kenneth Burke, R. P. Blackmur, and Yvor Winters. The anti-Humanist movement continued with the publication of George Santayana's *The Genteel Tradition at Bay* (New York, 1931).

Humanist literature continued to appear after 1930, but the noise of the battle was stilled. The depression, to be sure, was a factor. To many, a note of irrelevancy seemed to accompany the Humanists' call for spiritual conquests amidst economic plight. And most of those who took an interest in Humanism had spoken their piece. Little more remained to be said.

Why did the New Humanism suddenly attain such notoriety and interest at the end of the 1920s and the beginning of the next decade? In part, the movement must be seen as a reaction to a decade and more of liberal pro-test, a vociferous criticism that had been gnawing away at the Puritan moral and classical aesthetic tradition and welcoming a new literature of rebellion. Innovation in the arts and in literature had been riding strong on the wave of aesthetic tolerance and individualism, resulting, in the opinion of many, in a severe loss of critical standards and a meaningless escape from traditional values. From another viewpoint, the decade of the twenties suggested an unprecedented reign of materialism and hedonism in American life. Intellectuals of both a liberal and traditional persuasion castigated a bourgeois society that elected businessmen or their mouthpieces to high political office and measured its social success by the GNP. Certainly the 1929 crash and the ensuing depression constituted a loss of faith to some and a lesson in point to others. Humanism could draw allegiance from critics who now looked for the recovery of traditional spiritual values and the exercise of self-restraint as an alternative measure of the good life. But the Humanists themselves were less concerned with the social and economic roots of disorder than they were with the intellectual and cultural. More significantly, then, the rise of the New Humanism takes place against the most profound revolution in American thought, and this transformation must be considered the starting point for discussion of the subject.

CHAPTER TWO

Human Nature

There are two laws discrete
Not reconciled—
Law for man, and law for thing;
The last builds town and fleet,
But it runs wild,
And doth the man unking.

—Ralph Waldo Emerson

SCIENCE WAS TRANSFORMING American thought in the late nineteenth century and producing a radically new way of looking at man and the universe. The increasingly materialistic and naturalistic tenor of American thought also corresponded closely to the overall character of American life in a period that witnessed the rapid advances of industrialization and urbanization. Significantly, the first group of Humanists grew to intellectual maturity in a period of marked spiritual decline, and although they rebelled with other intellectuals from a workaday civilization and business culture, they themselves could find no solace even in the intellectual community to which as literary men and academicians they belonged. One major focus of the New Humanism, in fact, centered on the prevailing direction of ideas in this country and in the Western world at large.

American thinking during the middle of the nineteenth century inherited a predominantly Christian world view. Although patterns of thought had shifted considerably from Puritanism to rationalism and romanticism over the past two centuries, a strong religious perspective had still preserved a teleological conception of the universe as a moral and spiritual order under the aegis and direction of a controlling diety. The earlier transcendentalists defended the higher, divine self of man that linked him to a universal, benevolent spirit, or Oversoul. Pointing to the reality of "higher laws," the transcendentalists posited a spiritual order of moral absolutes whose postulates were the immediate, intuitive recognitions of natural man. But although the Concord group of thinkers was significant in American ideas, it was largely local in setting and impact. Of wider significance in America were the varieties of Scottish Realism that enjoyed a nearly universal vogue in the American academic community.

The moral philosophy tradition in America was as old as the American campus itself, and in the nineteenth century it was elaborated by such academic leaders as Francis Wayland of Brown, Noah Porter of Yale, Francis Bowen of Harvard, James McCosh of Princeton, and John Bascom of Williams and Wisconsin. The moral philosophers borrowed heavily, though not exclusively, from the Scottish intuitionist school of Thomas Reid and Dugald Stewart. These "common sense" philosophers constructed a system based on dualism, intuitive moral principles, and Christian teleology, to counteract the influence of the British empiricists. The dualistic philosophy defended the strictly spiritual dimension of human nature and lent support to the Christian notion of the separate creation of man by distinguishing him from the rest of animal life through his moral and rational faculties. It also, of course, left defensible the possibilities of the afterlife by arguing vigorously for the radical division of mind, or soul, and body. Furthermore, in their defense of the moral truths intuitively perceived, the moral philosophers underscored the existence of ethical laws independent of the circumstances of time and place. The appeal to absolutism over relativism followed Reid's assertion that "the first principles of morals are self-evident intuitions" which nonetheless needed careful Christian nurture. These conceptions of human nature were linked closely to the free will of man as a responsible moral being. The actuality of divine compensation in the afterlife for the moral injustice of this world lent additional support for a teleological world view that envisaged a governing diety as the shaping and controlling force of human destiny.

The Darwinian revolution in American thought severely challenged all of these prevailing views of God, man, and the world. The immediate controversy, of course, was the turmoil over evolution and traditional Christian thinking about the special creation of man in the image of God. But the implications of Darwinism, as American thinkers began to perceive and elaborate them, were more subtle and far-reaching. The most radical suggestion to come out of the Darwinian model was a naturalistic conception of human nature. Evolution as the British scientist presented it was not, of course, the first to promote this viewpoint, but it greatly enhanced it. The "spiritual" side of man, as heretofore conceived, was now likely to be labeled the "mental," and mind was judged to be only an evolutionary product that reached its most advanced stage in homo sapiens. Human intelligence was but an adaptive device for the survival of the organism. Particularly disturbing to the Humanist, however, was evolution's suggestion that change is the ultimate reality. The consequent fixation on the present and immediate, the "flux," was leading, the Humanists felt, to a disregard for the permanent, the traditional, and the universal, the unchanging aspects of human existence that made man more than the mere product of time and circumstance. Their refutation of this trend dominated the Humanists' efforts. Finally, Darwinism offered the upsetting possibility that purposelessness is the prevailing universal order, that divine plan and rational order leading to preconceived and controlled ends are unwarranted speculations. Indeed, one of the most significant changes in American thought in the late nineteenth century was the demise of a universe teleologically conceived.[1]

In the rise of pragmatism, the implications of Darwinism registered their heaviest impact. The writings of Chauncey Wright, Charles S. Peirce, William James, and John Dewey, its four most important philosophers, took the naturalistic viewpoint in different philosophical dimensions. Wright and Peirce first set mental habits in a biological context. Peirce argued that beliefs are only habits of action and attributed a physiological dimension to the thinking processes by relating them to the entire organism's attainment of an equilibrium or adjustment to its environment. The push of the pragmatic school against the older dualism made its heaviest impact by inextricably linking the mental processes to the whole behavioral pattern of the organism. The "radical empiricism" of William James added to the case against dualism by breaking down the subject-object dichotomy and viewing mind as only a particular organization of the continuous data of experience. James, furthermore, in appealing to an "open universe," articulated a philosophy of the flux that the Humanists came to see as one of the major intellectual nemeses of the modern age. Finally, the instrumentalism of John Dewey completed the Darwinian reinterpretation of the world. Dewey himself recognized that Darwinism had thoroughly destroyed the concept of a teleological or absolutistic order, and he now focused the attention of philosophy on the problematic dimensions of the immediate. Mind became the instrument of pragmatic adaptation to indeterminate situations and was thus intricately related to the organism's entire behavior. Dewey himself was outspoken against the dualistic philosophy and the social disasters implicit in its rigid separa-

[1] Borden P. Bowne, professor of philosophy at Brown University, summarized the implications of the Darwinian message in 1878: "Life without meaning; death without meaning . . . . A race tortured to no purpose, and with no hope but annihilation. The dead only blessed; the living standing like beasts at bay, and shrieking half in defiance and half in fright." Quoted by Paul F. Boller, Jr., *American Thought in Transition: The Impact of Evolutionary Naturalism, 1865–1900* (Chicago, 1969), p. 23. Several others, however, in a prominent new school of liberal theology, tried to link evolution to Christianity and preserve a teleological world view.

tion of mind and body. The problem for philosophy and for society, then, was the healthy integration of both dimensions of the human creature.

These sketches are intentionally abbreviated and gloss over many fine points, but they do point collectively to the central challenge to thought identified by the New Humanists. The "revolt against formalism," the sharp rejection of any appeal to absolutes, the suspension of a higher moral order or even a universe of law—these constituted for the Humanists the intellectual heritage of the nineteenth century. Babbitt defined it as the substitution of the notion of the relative for that of the absolute "in all realms of thought." And that heritage, furthermore, had been disastrous, opening the floodgates to the contemporary cultural confusion. From now on, Babbitt said, the central problem for man was how to live in a universe "with the lid off." But for the Humanists it was not a question of recovering a golden intellectual past. The American Humanists were quick to distinguish themselves from their Renaissance predecessors, who had sought to mark off the boundaries of a human nature from those of a supernatural; the Humanists, on the other hand, had to work toward a similar definition by fending off the inroads of science. This effort could not look back to a religious age, but rather required that they "meet the moderns on their own grounds," by defending a critical and empirical dualism. The Humanists saw this as a middle course that would overcome the romantic chaos on the one hand and the naturalistic fallacy on the other.

Irving Babbitt and Gorham Munson found in Aristophanes an apt description of the Humanists' own age: "Whirl is King, having driven out Zeus." For it was, they said, an age without direction and purpose. Society, Munson complained, showed no central idea for its collective self or its individual members; all were adrift, susceptible to a plethora of ideals and programs that only compounded the confusion.[2] And at no time before was man more free to follow his whims and desires, for a century of democratic advances and material improvements had promoted individual choice and provided the means for its fulfillment. Nonetheless, the Humanists charged, modern man was lost. He had proclaimed that he would find happiness through the pursuit of his desires, but he had not learned to desire the kind of happiness that is possible. Never more free, he was never more slave to his passions and his material ambitions.

Humanism sought to provide principles for self-direction. Unless man could find the measure of his life within, he would continue to be prey to pressures from without. Here was one aspect of the modern predicament:

[2] Gorham Munson, *The Dilemma of the Liberated* (New York, 1930), p. 21; Irving Babbitt, *Rousseau and Romanticism* (Boston, 1919), p. 181.

lacking any standards for the good life, modern man was himself remark-
ably standardized. Without internal direction, he could only center his
activity outward, on the machinery of existence as an end in itself. Social
progress, Munson noted, had become a species of popular religion, a
faith in the ability of applied science and technology to bring well-being to
all men. Belief in progress, the leading article of faith since the Enlightenment, promoted a pursuit of speed and power for their own sakes,
Babbitt wrote, with no subordination to superior purpose. Consequently,
society was increasing its material and physical power faster than it
was acquiring the wisdom to assure its proper use.[3]

Behind this obsession with progress the Humanists discerned a fundamental misconception. The course of modern thinking—Darwinism,
pragmatism, behaviorism, naturalism—showed the power of environment
and placed a premium on adjustment to external conditions. But the
assumption that human happiness depended on mastery of physical
objects was valid only to the extent that the natural world dominated
human nature. That assumption the Humanists rejected. It persisted, they
said, only through blind neglect of the distinctively human qualities that
relied for their exercise on release from the control of the natural. Man,
More insisted, could never achieve freedom by submitting his mind to
things. So long as he persisted in regarding himself a part of nature,
so long would he sacrifice his well-being to physical comforts.[4]

Babbitt cited an even more severe malady of the age. "What is dis-
quieting about the time," he said, "is not so much its open and avowed
materialism as what it takes to be its spirituality." He thought the present
age to be both more mechanical and yet more emotional than any previous.
Altogether, the Humanists noted, much of popular culture was only
emotional indulgence, a watery sentimentality of sex and romance that
nonetheless coexisted with the rampant materialism. What was lacking was
a genuine spirituality. The church had given itself over to a simple and
indiscriminate humanitarianism, a "Social Gospel" denoted by a
materialistic rash of service projects and welfare programs. The college too
had forsaken its humanist past for a program of "power and service,"
all the while indulging the romantic notion that student whim was the
surest prescription for quality education.[5]

In their delineation of these social ills, the New Humanists shared with
other intellectual groups a clear dissatisfaction with modern America—the
ascendancy of material values, the failure of good art and literature to

[3] Irving Babbitt, *Democracy and Leadership* (Boston, 1924), p. 23.

[4] Paul Elmer More, *The Demon of the Absolute* (Princeton, 1928), p. ix.

[5] Babbitt, *Democracy and Leadership*, pp. 16–17.

survive in a business civilization, sensationalist media given to mass appeals, the neon temples to the gods of advertising. But Humanism was nonetheless distinct in its analysis of these symptoms.[6] First, Humanism turned wholly to the intellectual and cultural past to explain this wayward course. For the most part its account ignored the impact of technology and the machine and paid little attention to a capitalist social structure that others saw as the source of American acquisitiveness and exploitation. One can reread today Harold Stearns's *Civilization in the United States* (1921), which documented the young intellectuals' indictment of the philistinism in American life. But that celebrated manifesto was often a call for greater freedom—political, social, intellectual—whereas nearly everywhere the Humanists found the forces of liberty pervasive and dangerous and in turn issued their calls for self-restraint. The sources of modern deterioration, then, were not social or technological; they were rooted in the major movements in ideas since the Enlightenment. Humanists would turn to the intellectual past to find the sources of misdirection and confusion.

[6] As these conditions of American life became noticeable earlier in the mid-nineteenth century, a group of "genteel" critics emerged in protest against them. It is important to define their relationship to the later Humanists. Among the earlier group were Thomas Bailey Aldrich, George William Curtis, Charles Eliot Norton, Richard Watson Guilder, Edmund Clarence Stedman, Richard Henry Stoddard, and Bayard Taylor. They were writing from the 1850s to the turn of the century and were in fact similar to figures such as William Crary Brownell, George Woodberry, John Jay Chapman, and Brander Matthews, who continued their style of protest into the twentieth century. John Tomsich suggests that this group in many ways anticipated the New Humanists. There are similarities, to be sure. Both groups looked for a recovery of manners and morals and for the qualitative improvement of American culture, and defended a moral content in art. Each group despaired of organized religion as an aid in spiritual recovery, and each rejected any kind of teleological perspective. The genteel spokesmen and the Humanists both were apolitical, placing little hope in political reform, and for the most part renouncing personal involvement in politics. Nonetheless, important distinctions should warn against any close affiliating of the two schools. The genteel group was strictly an affair of the eastern seaboard, while spokesmen for the Humanist position originated and flourished in other parts of the country. The former group shared little of the Humanist anxiety over romanticism in America and looked for "an art of individual genius" that would liberate literature from a world of philistines. The literary figures in the group, Aldrich, Stoddard, and Boker, were themselves romantic poets. Above all, there is no philosophical identity between the genteelists and the Humanists. The consistent dualism of the latter is not anticipated in any form by the earlier group. Tomsich believes in fact that the genteel endeavor was amorphous and that it lacked a center of values that dominated throughout. See John Tomsich, *A Genteel Endeavor: American Culture and Politics in the Gilded Age* (Stanford, Calif., 1971), pp. 6–8, 24, 38, 58, 70–71, 83, 151, 167–87.

The foundation of the Humanist critique was its conception of human nature. Humanists gave much attention to definition here, for they believed that the roots of contemporary ills, the romantic and naturalistic fallacies, lay in fundamental errors concerning the human condition. Their reconstruction of modern culture commenced with an attack on natural man. They charged that the varieties of romanticism and naturalism that had persisted for two centuries had deprived man of any recourse to internal controls. They both, as More explained, originate in the denial of that element in man that is outside of nature and is denoted by "conscientiously directive purpose."[7] The Humanists explored that element in depth and urged its cultivation as a counterforce to the physical determinism of the naturalist and the emotional flux of the romantic. Without that control natural man remained inevitably the unthinking victim of external and internal forces.

An effort to define and defend a dualistic philosophy of human nature was the standard Humanist reply to the romantic and naturalistic outlooks; this dualistic philosophy served in the Humanists' discussions of all issues as their criterion of truth and value. Human freedom could assert itself only through an element in man that distinguished him from both the animal and physical world and from his own "natural" self. The Humanists therefore appealed to a "law for man" and a "law for thing." "This," said Sherman, "is the rock upon which the humanist builds his house," and he and his colleagues cited many times over the Emersonian quotation that introduces this chapter. Abjuring any metaphysical defense of the two laws, they simply upheld their empirical reality and claimed that this basic fact of human nature was demonstrable to any careful observer. Dualism was the indispensable fact of the human condition. It referred to one part of man's nature that was constantly changing, vulnerable to the relentless play of feelings, perceptions, and external stimuli. But at the same time the Humanists pointed to another element in man's nature, an unchanging element that was set against the flux. Our mere consciousness, More explained, tells us that we are ceaselessly changing, yet withal the same. Here was "the last irrational fact" of human nature, impervious to precise conceptualization. The Humanists therefore sought to describe in a variety of ways what they judged to be an empirically valid general account of the human self. The constant element of human nature was the "higher self" of each individual, the "inner check" on the natural self, the "frein vital," in opposition to the "élan vital" of

---

[7] More, *The Demon of the Absolute,* p. xi. Sherman too laid the romantic movement to rest: "We have trusted our instincts long enough to sound the depths of their treacherousness" (*On Contemporary Literature,* 6th ed., [New York, 1931], p. 10).

Henri Bergson. But above all, the higher self was the center of the religious and spiritual as well as the aesthetic experience of man and the continuing, essential identity of all the race amid the infinite variety of its individual members.[8]

More found useful illustrations of dualism in the Greek philosophers. The active nature of man, according to Aristotle, is governed by desires and impulses that are themselves incapable of self-restraint and are consequently limitless. Moreover, Aristotle's propensity for locating the good between extremes led also to his identifying this expansive element as a source of evil. Good is that which limits, so that the aim of conduct should be the acquisition of a golden mean—a definite restraint set against the impulses. More elaborated further that a function of the reason is the determination of this limit, and to find it one must look beyond the constant flux of experience. Here Aristotle contemplated the existence of an "absolute unity amid all that moves."[9]

More also drew from Plato's elaboration of dualism. There is, More said, a part of our personality that is subject to variety and change and concerns itself with the phenomenal world. It is the path to self-seeking, competition, lust, and violence. "Its end is despair." But the religious or humanist life rests on the consciousness of another tendency in human nature. The higher direction of the soul, More wrote, is toward unity and completeness. Material concerns subside before the awareness of a higher self that remains constant amid the inconstancy of life. "True liberation," More wrote, "comes only . . . with the consciousness that something within us stands apart from the everlasting flux and from our passions which also belong to the flux."[10]

Recognizing this duality of the human soul, the Humanists often described the human condition in terms of the allegorical "war in the cave." Foerster pictured the struggle as one between two wills, each seeking to dominate the other and control the individual. One, the temperamental, pulled in the direction of endless desire and sought to free itself from the imposition of the other, the ethical will, which restrained desire and kept it within limits. The first was the natural, or ordinary, self of impulse, the second the human self, which is the power of control over the natural

[8] Paul Elmer More, *The Drift of Romanticism* (1913; rpt. New York, 1967), p. 249. More added: "If a man denies this dualism of consciousness there is no argument with him, but a fundamental difference of intuition which follows into every view of philosophy and criticism" (p. 249).

[9] Ibid., pp. 226–27.

[10] Paul Elmer More, *Studies of Religious Dualism* (1909; rpt. New York, 1967), pp. 321–22; idem., *Drift of Romanticism*, p. 263.

self. But in any form or description, Babbitt explained, human dualism must be accepted "as a mystery that may be studied in its practical effects, but that, in its ultimate nature, is incapable of formulation." Its obscurity, however, should not preclude belief in its reality and force. We can use electricity, he said, without knowing the theory of it.[11]

This description, of course, raised specific questions for the Humanists. What was the ultimate significance of the "higher self" or the "inner check?" How were these to be exercised? What was their place in the overall conduct of life? The Humanists first insisted that man's dual nature was his uniquely human characteristic and his capacity for spiritual existence. But the fulfillment of that potential demanded a conscious effort against the natural self. The adjustment between the variable and the permanent in human experience, the Humanists believed, was a difficult struggle. Indeed, the necessary disciplining of his lower by his higher self required overcoming the spiritual inertia and moral lethargy basic to the state of the natural man.

This aspect of the New Humanism is better understood in relation to an equally important issue. The possibility of discovering standards, and the exercise of those standards, depended upon how one dealt with the old problem of "the One and the Many." "For standards," Babbitt believed, "imply an element of oneness somewhere, with reference to which it is possible to measure the mere manifoldness and change." Greek philosophy had supplied useful illustrations of the various concepts of the universal, the ideas or forms that persist among the data of experience, but it was a matter of some importance exactly how one dealt with them. For Babbitt especially, who endeavored consistently throughout his career to uphold a "positive and critical" Humanism, there was always a danger that the effort to posit the One amid the Many could terminate in a speculative transcendentalism, or even in religious dogma. Such in fact, he believed, had too often been the fate of this effort in Western thought, and that was one reason, as we shall see, why Babbitt turned to Buddhism to fortify an empirical Humanism. Thus Babbitt was anxious to point out that his own solution to the problem of the One and the Many "is not purely Platonic. Because one can perceive immediately an element of unity in things, it does not follow that one is justified in establishing a world of essences or entities or 'ideas' above the flux. To do this is to fall away from a positive and critical into a more or less speculative attitude; it is to risk setting up a metaphysic of the One."[12]

[11] Norman Foerster, *The American State University* (Chapel Hill, N.C., 1937), p. 221; Babbitt, *Rousseau and Romanticism,* p. 26.

[12] Babbitt, *Rousseau and Romanticism,* pp. xii–xiii.

Babbitt, and indeed all the Humanists, were disinclined to establish their credo in a precise and technical philosophical framework, and this characteristic is troublesome to some readers who will be sensitive to the imprecision of language and concepts employed by the Humanists. On the issue in question here, however, it is clear that Babbitt borrowed much from Aristotle, whom among the Greeks he most favored for his empirical and positivistic spirit. Babbitt's appeal to the One among the Many parallels Aristotle's discussion of universals. These we come to know by observation and experience of facts. Universals become clear not by some intuitive insight but by the repetition of experience that distinguishes the accidental and incidental from the permanent and enduring. Aristotle thus pursued a concrete and not an abstract universal, for intellect (*nous*) cannot know immaterial substances. His *De Anima* made clear his discontent with those Platonists who boasted of a direct internal vision of truth.[13] Babbitt also wished to dispense with Platonic transcendentalism and defended the empirical viability of universal experience.

For the Humanists a correct approach to this question, furthermore, involved the whole conduct of life. There could be no check to the spiritual and moral drift of the modern world without an effort to locate the norms of human experience and apply them against the expansive tendencies of the romantic ego and the mechanized drive of modern civilization. The problem was to locate a "centre of humanity" that must function as an ideal norm and model of emulation for all persons. This "higher humanity" must also determine each individual's check on his emotions and temperament; the universal in this sense must, in other words, function as a disciplining quality. It was a precarious matter, as the Humanists knew. Babbitt, in a manner that further confirmed his suspicions of speculative philosophy, saw in Neoplatonism a confusion of the concrete universal with the cosmic infinite and perceived in the effort to grasp the infinite an egotistical outreach that anticipated the romantics. Babbitt followed Aristotle in warning against this perversion. "That something in human nature which is always reaching out for more—whether the more of sensation or of power or of knowledge—was, [Aristotle held], to be strictly reined in and disciplined to the law of measure."[14] But the utilization of the universal, the effective perception of the universal as a source of discipline and control, of standards for the just measure of behavior, depended not wholly on the definition of the problem, whether the definition was Platonic or Aristotelian. Ultimately it was a question of the use of the imagination.

[13] John Herman Randall, Jr., *Aristotle* (New York, 1960), pp. 42–43, 94–95.
[14] Babbitt, *Rousseau and Romanticism,* p. 253.

Any rising above the natural level of existence required the imposition of a rational, willful restraint; but the Humanists recognized that the reason itself was powerless before the force of the natural instincts. Reason, in the first place, could not provide a clear conception of the higher reality necessary for transcending the natural. Herein lay Babbitt's departure from Aristotelianism. Babbitt maintained that the Enlightenment was injurious to the humanist movement of the seventeenth and eighteenth centuries because it suspected anything incapable of clear proof in the logical or mathematical sense. The Humanists believed that the higher reality cannot be so demonstrated; "it can only be grasped, and then never completely, through a veil of imaginative illusion."[15]

Here Babbitt touched on one of the most important ideas of the New Humanism, one that it would find useful for its entire program. As a power that might lift man from his natural inertia, reason alone was inadequate, the Humanists said, for the sensual or imaginative appeal of the base instincts would always prevail against it. Reason occupied something of an intermediate level in the human constitution, above the natural but below the spiritual planes. And it was a tenuous position at best. For either as abstract thinking or as uninspired good sense, reason, in the long run, did not satisfy. It was either too difficult or too boring. Man is ultimately driven to sink below or rise above the rational plane. Reason invariably needed outside help in aiding the spiritual ascent.[16]

The Humanists appealed to the imagination for that assistance. The vision of the higher life, the unity of things, the permanent in man's character, was illusionary. This meant, not "false," or "deceptive," but *unclear*—a vague sense or apprehension that cannot be rendered in rational or intellectual terms and cannot be precisely described. But though incapable of such formulation, this apprehension could present itself to the mind through imaginative insight. This faculty alone could render the higher reality concrete by supplying it with specific content. In their pronouncements on aesthetics the Humanists followed this idea to important conclusions, but only after defining carefully what constituted right use of imagination and insight.

The Humanists were looking particularly for means to employ these qualities against the spiritual sluggishness that prevailed at the natural level of existence. They recognized at the same time that the imagination was itself neutral, that its appeal might be at the service of lust and violence, or it might be a moving force in a spiritual or religious life. It would serve most effectively, then, in joining the reason as a counterforce to the natural

[15] Ibid., p. 27.

[16] Ibid., pp. 39–40.

instincts. The humanist, Babbitt explained, will look for a region of insight above the reason, which he will perceive as an element of vital control over his natural state. He recalled Voltaire's statement that "illusion is the queen of the human heart." But illusion may take for itself any content, such that its attraction may be to the natural impulses below the reason, or the spiritual, above it. The rational level, in all events, could not persist against the pull from either side. Babbitt explained the consequence: "When the imagination has ceased to pull in accord with the reason in the service of a reality that it set above them both, it is sure to become the accomplice of expansive impulse, and mere reason is not strong enough to prevail over this union of imagination and desire."[17]

The distinctions that Babbitt was drawing here were central to the New Humanism. They had, as we shall see, several applications, in art and literature, education, politics, and religion. But the Humanists' analysis of the imagination served above all to distinguish their view of life from what they defined as the romantic and naturalistic, and because it was linked directly to the question of dualism it was essential to their entire program. Babbitt therefore differentiated between the "superrational intuition" that supplies a frein vital to impulse, and the "subrational intuition" that is associated with the élan vital. He believed furthermore that the exercise of the higher self, on which the Humanist life depended, was impossible without the correct functioning of the imaginative insight. "One will find . . . that the centre of normal human experience that is to serve as a check on impulse . . . can be apprehended only with the aid of the imagination." In this sense the imagination has a disciplining function and serves as a moral center. It is the antithesis of the use of the imagination by the romantic, and we may cite Babbitt's words, in anticipation of a later discussion, on the use of the romantic imagination in art. "With the elimination of the ethical element from the soul of art the result is an imagination that is free to wander wild with the emancipated emotions. The result is likely to be art in which a lively aesthetic perceptiveness is not subordinated to any whole."[18] For Babbitt, therefore, the quest for moral standards, discipline, and control depended on a quality of imaginative insight that could illuminate a realm of universal experience to be set against all the natural expansive tendencies of the individual ego.

The Humanists, confronting what they took to be the confusion of their own age, sought to discover meaningful standards through the proper use of the imagination. That effort was responsible to a large degree for the

[17] Ibid., p. 53.
[18] Ibid., pp. 200–201, 206.

anti-individualistic tenor of the movement. They were determined to direct modern man away from the intoxicating cult of individualism by emphasizing the norm of human behavior. Man needed to be recalled to the permanent in his own nature by rediscovering the permanent in his own race. Against the romantic's assertion that to be oneself is to cultivate one's own temperament, the Humanists certified that true self-realization is compatible only with restrictions on the temperament. If a man is to attain his true humanity, Babbitt wrote, he must "aim at some goal set above his ordinary self which is at the same time his unique and separate self." These limitations made possible the discovery and realization of the higher self, the ethical self, the self that a person shares in common with his fellow man.[19]

The Humanists were looking not merely for what men held·in common; that indeed would include the instincts and emotions basic to their natural state. The highest sense of the permanent in the human race came only from long and wide acquaintance with what Matthew Arnold called "the best that has been thought and said in the world." That was the general prescription for the entire Humanist program. It was intentionally vague in itself, but a central starting point. The search for the best in man's past, Foerster said, also led the humanist to place less value on the idiosyncracies of the individual and the romantic cult of the unique and separate. "The difficult thing," Sherman said, "is to be normal." Differences, as all the Humanists maintained, were less important than the similarities among men.[20] The progress of humanity did not come naturally; only when persons everywhere worked to discover their higher selves in the common best of their past might they assure the continued spiritual welfare of the race.

Babbitt described the romantic and humanist imaginations in another way. In any individual case, he said, it was largely a matter of how one related to the problem of the One and the Many, and for that reaction the imagination was decisive. For we may be imaginative in two ways. The romantic and the naturalist will see life in its infinite diversity, as a panorama of variety reflecting the differences of time and place and the flux of experience. They will be sensitive to individual uniqueness in the individual and in others. Such an imagination unites a variety of persons who describe reality in intellectually different ways. It unites a Rousseau

[19] Ibid., p. 252.

[20] Foerster, *American State University*, p. 226; Stuart P. Sherman, *Critical Woodcuts* (1926; rpt. New York, 1967), p. 119. Babbitt believed that an event of "almost unparalleled triumph" was the ascendancy since the end of the eighteenth century of the sense of the individual over the sense of mankind in Western civilization (*Rousseau and Romanticism*, p. 114).

with an Henri Bergson and a William James. Bergson's remark that life is "a perpetual gushing forth of novelties" was for Babbitt a "dangerous half-truth." The challenge for the humanist is to see life both in its variety and its wholeness. To his perception of the local, the individual, and the transitory, a wise person will join an imaginative perception of the permanent and unchanging, the enduring elements, the norm, of the human condition.[21]

Placing the intellectual outline of the New Humanists within the context of contemporary philosophical currents makes it possible to show to what extent the Humanists moved against the prevailing currents of thought and to suggest also how their own campaign was a response to these. The Humanists were upholding human dualism at a time when it was receiving its heaviest assault by John Dewey. Not only did the latter articulate a naturalistic philosophy of human nature and locate the origin of all mental processes in the interaction of organism and environment, but he laid at the feet of the dualistic tradition in Western thinking most of the ills of the modern world. Like the Humanists, Dewey believed that a correct conception of human nature was imperative for the qualitative improvement of society; if our age reflected only a drab, mechanical, and workaday atmosphere joined to a shallow and hedonistic spirituality, it was, Dewey believed, because our intellectual tradition had never successfully united the organic with the "spiritual," body with mind. Dewey found the source of this perversion in the Greek heritage in Western thinking and severely attacked its impact at the time Babbitt and More were trying to revitalize it. The Greeks, Dewey felt, were responsible for a split in Being itself, "its division into some things which are inherently defective, changing, relational, and other things that are inherently perfect, permanent, self-possessed. Other dualisms such as that between sensuous appetite and rational thought, between the particular and the universal . . . between matter and mind, are but the reflections of this primary metaphysical dualism." So long as reality was so bifurcated, Western thought, including Christianity, which incorporated the Hellenistic philosophies, traditionally relied upon extrasensual means to gain access to truth. "Higher truth," it was said, dwelled in some extramundane abode, outside the temporal and spatial limitations of the empirical world and beyond the reach of the empirical faculties. This Dewey called the "spectator conception of knowledge," and it precluded the possibility that ordinary experience could enlighten ultimate reality. Dewey of course believed that it was misleading to speak of any permanent structure of being. What we may

---

[21] Irving Babbitt, *The Masters of Modern French Criticism* (1912; rpt. New York, 1963), pp. 53–56; idem., *Rousseau and Romanticism*, p. xiii.

legitimately call the permanent and fixed are merely ratios of change in an unstable flow of experience, and they are the conclusions of scientific inquiry.[22]

The Humanists were closer to this analysis than they or Dewey may have realized, although the absence of an effective exchange of ideas makes conclusions only tentative. There is no doubt, however, that the Humanists realized the weight and influence of Dewey's pragmatism, and Babbitt knew that he would have to "meet the moderns on their own ground" by a strictly empirical Humanism that shunned appeals to metaphysics and speculation. Their dualistic account of human nature relied ultimately for its validity on the "immediate data of consciousness," and however mysterious, this duality was a fact of observation and experience. It could be demonstrated to anyone willing to test its premises by a self-conscious exercise of the higher will, and in this sense could withstand the criteria of the application of the scientific method, the standard Deweyan method of verification. In fact, however, the Humanists were closer to William James than to Dewey in this test. In their effort to verify the reality of the higher will by their challenge to the skeptic merely to resolve to exercise it, they recalled James's reply to the person who aked if God exists. For James the answer was no, not so long as you doubt it. Life, Babbitt said, is an act of faith. We do not know in order that we may believe, but believe in order that we may know. "The answer to the enigma of life, so far as there is any, is not for the man who sets up some metaphysical theory, but for the man who . . . acts."[23]

For Irving Babbitt, however, there was nothing in the Western intellectual tradition that was as useful to him in describing an empirical Humanism as were the religions of the East, and Buddhism first and foremost. Dewey and pragmatism failed precisely because they were too "Western" and merely brought to fruition a movement that had its roots in Bacon. The major features of Buddhism, so distinct from Christianity in form as well as content, made a special appeal to Babbitt as a pure kind of religion. (We shall examine these in a later chapter.) Recalling how easily in the Western tradition Platonic universals found their way into supernatural religion, Babbitt favored Buddhism as a religion without a dependence on the supernatural, a program for the conduct of life which was essentially psychological rather than metaphysical in description and which relied ultimately on self-initiative rather than divine sustenance.[24]

[22] John Dewey, *Philosophy and Civilization* (New York, 1931), pp. 302–5; idem., *Experience and Nature* (New York, 1929), pp. 123–24; James Gouinlock, *John Dewey's Philosophy of Value* (New York, 1972), pp. 73, 77.

[23] Babbitt, *Democracy and Leadership,* p. 228.

[24] Huston Smith, *The Religions of Man* (New York, 1958), pp. 104–8.

Buddhism was especially useful in describing a genuine "spiritual positivism," for Buddhism was in essence a psychology of desire. The world outside is seen in a constant state of flux and change; it is joined to a similar element in the human personality that makes itself felt as expansive desire. "What is unstable [in man] longs for what is unstable in the outer world." But a person may escape from the flux by an exercise of a higher will that corresponds to the permanent or ethical element in that person. This was the Buddhist equivalent of the war in the cave, and the person who drifts supinely with the current of desire is denounced for his spiritual or moral indolence. In the literal meanings of the Buddhist terms *yoga*—a reining or "yoking" of the impulses of the natural man—and *Nirvana* —the going out, or extinction, of these desires—Humanism could find further definition of an empirical dualistic philosophy.[25]

Buddha's value for Babbitt was precisely his ability to cut across Western dichotomies, between the partisans of the One and the partisans of the Many, between strict empiricists in the Lockean tradition and intuitionist schools such as the Platonic and Scottish, between Cartesian expounders of the *cogito ergo sum* and the Rousseauistic expounders of *sentio ergo sum*, both of whom claimed to rely on "the immediate data of consciousness." Furthermore, as Babbitt said in his important essay "Buddha and the Occident," Western thought has been characterized by a kind of intellectual imperialism that aims at wholeness through comprehensive metaphysical systems, such as Spinoza's and Hegel's, and by an emotional expansiveness that also grasps for a total inclusiveness of experience. Each evidences a strong affirmative quality, what Babbitt called a "yea-saying" inclination toward all reality. Buddha, on the other hand, "is probably the chief of all the 'no-sayers.' " "The unification that Buddha seeks is to be achieved by the exercise of a certain quality of will that says no to the outgoing desires with a view to the substitution of the more permanent for the less permanent among these desires and finally to the escape from impermanence altogether." The West had been unsuccessful in following these standards in modern times because its culture had been shaped by the reinforcing effects of romanticism and naturalism. The result was "a view of life that combines the extreme of outer activity with the extreme of spiritual indolence."[26] Just how this came about was a critical concern of the New Humanism.

It is nearly impossible to discuss the subject of romanticism without getting into difficult problems of definition. This broad philosophical,

[25] Babbitt, *Rousseau and Romanticism,* p. 150; idem., "Buddha and the Occident," in Irving Babbitt, trans., *The Dhammapada* (New York, 1936), pp. 95–96.

[26] Babbitt, "Buddha and the Occident," pp. 82–84, 110.

religious, and aesthetic movement had infinitely diverse expressions and was not without its contradictory tendencies. Critics of the Humanists have recognized that what Babbitt and More attacked was something of a parody of romanticism. This was undoubtedly the case, explainable in part because the Humanists' obsession with the confusion in modern culture attributed a long shadow of influence to romanticism and distorted their vision of the movement. Babbitt in fact was willing to concede as much; his portraits of individual romantic spokesmen were admittedly incomplete and even neglected possibly sympathetic qualities of some. His selectivity would be justifiable only insofar as there was in romanticism a certain quality of imagination that warranted the common nomenclature. The following portrait therefore is one of "main tendencies" that grew to force in the early nineteenth century but which the Humanists saw writ large in the twentieth.[27]

Romanticism, the Humanists believed, revolutionized thought by re-defining the meaning of nature. The earlier classicist, they said, recognized the natural as the normal—the representative in humanity. Thus the Enlightenment looked to nature as the symbol of rationality, law, balance, harmony, and control. To this extent, strong emotion or enthusiasm was a departure from the natural and was to be distrusted. But the romanticists defined the natural as the spontaneous play of emotion and impulse. Reason, then, because it might be a hindrance to these faculties, was now suspect, and so also were law and control. Restraint, in fact, was abhorrent to the romantic. He was determined to be at one with nature by finding every possible outlet for his feelings.[28]

The romantics, identifying their emotions and impulses with their own peculiar nature, cultivated these as the elements of their precious uniqueness, worthy and valuable in themselves. More charged that Rousseau, having lost the sense of the war in the cave, became convinced of his own innate goodness and imagined himself the pure, uncontaminated product of nature. But at the same time Rousseau was aware of his lapses into anxiety, despair, and shame. This contradiction of ideal and fact, mankind born free and everywhere in chains, needed a new dualism to

---

[27] Babbitt, *Rousseau and Romanticism,* pp. xvii–xviii. Babbitt's selectivity is no more clearly evidenced than in his treatment of Wordsworth. *Rousseau and Romanticism* has many references to the English poet but wholly ignores the Words-worth of *The Prelude,* who wrestled at length with the problem of living in a world of relatives and the mutable flux.

[28] Ibid., pp. 39, 130; Paul Elmer More, *Shelburne Essays: Seventh Series* (1910; rpt. New York, 1967), pp. 11–13.

resolve the dilemma—a dualism of man in a state of nature and man in society.[29]

This effect, the Humanists believed, was fatal. Now the human moral struggle shifted from the cave to the outside—to an external scapegoat. For if natural man was born good and pure, why should he have become corrupt, why should he be so out of sorts with the world, and why the contradiction between his natural feelings and his actual state? Rousseau blamed society and its articles of civilization and in turn exalted the natural freedom of primitive man. Said Babbitt: Rousseau "is ready to shatter all the forms of civilized life in favor of something that never existed, of a state of nature that is only the projection of his own temperament." Babbitt was certainly right in charging that the new dualism had become a cloak for irresponsibility. His very creed, as Babbitt charged, led the romantic moralist to point the accusing finger at someone else. "The faith in one's natural goodness is a constant encouragement to evade moral responsibility." To accept that responsibility requires maximum effort and discipline, and these the Rousseauist and the natural man forsook for the emotional path of least resistance.[30]

Babbitt ridiculed many aspects of romantic ethics. Some he found downright dangerous, others harmlessly absurd. The romantic's refusal to discriminate on the issues of individual moral responsibility resulted in some serious distortions of truth. Romantic literature extolled as its beautiful souls the drunkard, the courtesan, or the genius betrayed and misunderstood by society. Here was natural man victimized by aritificial standards. Since the Rousseauist denied any of the virtues that implied self-control (and Babbitt figured that these were about nine of ten), he was ready to extend a hand to, or shed a tear for, anyone. Morality was then reduced to an expansive sympathy, a passion itself rather than a restraint on passion. If it could be shown, therefore, that the wayward soul was not motivated by deliberate malice, the romantic would find him sympathetic, even heroic. But most humanitarianism, in Babbitt's judgment, was merely excessive emotional indulgence.[31]

Similar to the romanticist's cult of the noble savage was his idealization of the child, another emblem of innocence and purity. This romantic cult went against the whole grain of the Humanist temper. For in childhood the Rousseauist found the period of unreflective happiness, when the troublesome bother of sober thought and reason never interfered to spoil the fresh surprises of the good life. It was the life of "vivid and

[29] More, *Religious Dualism,* pp. 224–25.

[30] Babbitt, *Rousseau and Romanticism,* p. 155.

[31] Ibid., pp. 140–42.

spontaneous sensation," the very antithesis of the Humanists' code of discipline and restraint.[32]

But it was neither an intellectual system nor a set of values that defined romanticism; it was a common quality of imagination. Lacking any principle to restrain his natural expansiveness, the romantic drifted automatically to the extremes. The pastoral and idyllic imagination of Rousseau, the governing content in most romantic varieties, was answered by a traditional and conservative perspective, prominent in Germany, that glorified the Middle Ages. Thus Babbitt's comment: "Every imaginable extreme, the extreme of reaction as well as the extreme of radicalism, goes with romanticism; every genuine mediation between extremes is just as surely unromantic."[33] An extremism that was defiant of norms and hostile to discipline and control was for the Humanists one of the destructive legacies of the romantic movement.

Babbitt and the Humanists knew that the cult of primitivism was not exclusively a romantic trademark, but they seemed not to have recognized how easily those who, like them, upheld neoclassical standards slipped into the same mood. Arthur O. Lovejoy's suggestive essay "The Parallel of Deism and Classicism" describes how the Enlightenment's quest for universal rational standards in religion and morality was not only anti-traditional in outlook, seeking to relieve the present from the burden of inherited prejudice, but became a celebration of the simple truths available to the natural mind and conscience. If the light of nature is universal and each person may have access to it, nothing can be of great value that is beyond the comprehension of the plain man, and even the basic truths of religion must, as Swift said, be "level with everyman's mother wit." There was in the classical standards of the eighteenth century a kind of "rationalistic primitivism" that was itself hostile to high culture and enthusiastic of an uncorrupted and unspoiled way of existence. The neoclassicists of course held in check the later romantic primitivism by upholding as "pure" models the standards of classical Greece and Rome.[34] If the Humanists were sensitive to this tendency of the eighteenth century, it perhaps helps explain why they abstained from the use of the term *natural man* in any sense and insisted on a dualism that differentiated a lower, natural self, from a higher self that controls it.

[32] Irving Babbitt, *The New Laokoön* (Boston, 1910), pp. 80–82; idem., *Rousseau and Romanticism,* pp. 51–53, 147. Babbitt saw a typical expression of romantic morality in Victor Hugo's poem "Legend of the Ages." Here the poet praises an ass who steps aside in the road to avoid crushing a toad. For this act of compassion the brute is proclaimed "holier than Socrates and greater than Plato" (ibid., p. 146).

[33] Babbitt, *Rousseau and Romanticism,* p. 97.

[34] Arthur O. Lovejoy, *Essays in the History of Ideas* (Baltimore, 1948), pp. 84–96.

But the romantic influence alone was not responsible for the confusion of values. A naturalistic tradition that dated from Bacon had also undermined traditional moral standards by attacking the dual nature of man. Whereas the romantic tradition extolled the subjective to the point of eroding all norms for human behavior, the naturalistic erred in the opposite extreme. The Baconian, Babbitt explained, was inclined to substitute an outer for an inner self. In placing a premium on control of external conditions, he relied wholly on empirical evidence that would yield knowledge for utility and power. In shifting attention outward, the naturalists, too, neglected the war in the cave and promoted a utilitarian ethic that overlooked the moral health of the individual and sought to improve society by perfecting its machinery.[35]

The Humanists saw the naturalistic tradition culminating in the pragmatic movement in philosophy. The pragmatists and "other philosophers of the flux" Babbitt called the "chief enemies of the humanist." Although William James himself was a vigorous defender of free will, he erred fatally, the Humanists believed, in describing consciousness, not as an entity distinct from or above experience, but in conjunctive and qualitative relation to it. This belied the Humanists' depiction of an element in human nature not described by sensational phenomena. James's notion of a pluralistic universe further violated Babbitt's ideal of the One amid the Many. More found the common core of all varieties of pragmatism their taking the flux as the whole of consciousness and finding there the only reality. Such a view was conducive to the pragmatists' own ethical relativism and further alienated them from the Humanists' point of view.[36]

The result again was the merging of man and nature. Thus while the romantic idealized man governed from passions within, the naturalist subjected him to forces from without. Both movements went in opposite directions to arrive at the same point. Both movements deprived man of the *frein vital*, exercised by the individual against himself. For under the naturalistic influence as well, there prevailed the tendency to make society the scapegoat for the ills of the individual. Behaviorism and pragmatism, Sherman stated, were products of the same assumptions. Both viewed man as a nervous automaton and sought to explain conduct in terms of the actions and reactions of the organism to the physical world. All meaning thus derived from interrelationships with the external

---

[35] Irving Babbitt, "Humanism: An Essay at Definition," in Norman Foerster, ed., *Humanism and Modern America* (New York, 1930), p. 34; Babbitt, *Literature and the American College* (Boston, 1908), pp. 34–46.

[36] Babbitt, "Humanism: An Essay at Definition," p. 42.

environment. For man thus viewed, "there is no spiritual centre. . . . Everything is valued in terms of visible behavior."[37]

Much of the Humanist scheme depended on the reinforcing tendencies of romanticism and naturalism. Humanists believed that both could flourish only in a culture that had lost the sense of the supernatural and failed to replace it by a discipline that comes from within. Such a culture left only physical and organic nature as an external measure of the individual and as the arena in which he might play out the drama of life. Both Wordsworth in one tradition and Bacon in the other, therefore, made the critical quest a marriage of mind and nature. Bacon's *Great Instauration* proposed to determine "whether that commerce between the mind of man and the nature of things . . . might by any means be restored to its perfect and original condition." Here was the passage to the new "kingdom of man, founded on the sciences."[38] John Dewey in the twentieth century pursued this redemption of the mind in a similar way, and the burden of his reconstruction of philosophy was the purging of the intellect of inherited abstractions, transcendental ideals, and spirit-body dualities. Extended to the social realm, Dewey's marriage of mind and nature alone promised the needed reforms to liberate the modern world from the anachronisms of the past. The romantic marriage, an intensely personal experience, and the instrumentalist, objective, scientific, and public, nonetheless had the common effect with the naturalistic of referring all experience to the flux of nature and inducing what the Humanists believed was a dangerous relativism.

Two prevailing conceptions about the Humanists should be addressed at this point. The Humanists *were* absolutists in a particular sense: they urged the quest for standards and permanent values on a generation that was highly uncomfortable with these terms. But the Humanists, as their religious critics pointed out, were precariously individualistic. The quest for universals was seriously jeopardized when the Humanists abandoned metaphysical and theological frameworks. Nor were the Humanists willing to rely on an apriorism that had fortified the moral certainties of the prevalent academic philosophy in nineteenth-century America. The Humanists' program, for its successful realization, would have to be tried and tested in a multitude of individual cases in the face of an undogmatic and empirical dualistic psychology. Nor can the Humanists be dismissed as "remorselessly negative." Their unwillingness to appeal to any transcendent and supernatural reality thrust them back on the human species as the single guarantor of its destiny. An awareness of the darker, evil side of the

[37] Stuart P. Sherman, *The Genius of America* (New York, 1923), p. 103.

[38] Quoted in M. H. Abrams, *Natural Supernaturalism* (New York, 1971), p. 60.

human personality was no cause, however, for a pessimistic determinism. The Humanists' program appealed to the tested accomplishments of the race and everywhere evidenced its faith that human triumph over nature was not merely a matter of building better bridges. The Humanists were skeptics in a healthy sense and did not permit the invocation of the "negative" values of discipline and self-denial to spoil their faith in the capacity for human growth and achievement.

Ultimately Humanism became a question about the conduct of life. The dualism by which they described the human condition amounted to nothing in the Humanist scheme if its acceptance did not lead to greater personal satisfaction and the qualitative improvement of life and society. In a period that was becoming more complex, and has become more complex since, Humanists tried, in the manner of an Emerson, to remind their generation that there were things that mattered more and things that mattered less. The essential Humanist message today might be the assertion that there is more than Superbowls, television talk shows, and beauty pageants to make life interesting and worthwhile. The Humanists would surely condemn the present American society for the quality of imagination that prevails in it, a subrational imagination that thrills to crime and violence in movies and on television and revels in the technicolor passions of our contemporary cultural freedoms. Amid all the events and activities that vie for attention in the modern world, the Humanists asked Americans to distinguish between those of transient and those of permanent concern. Knowing the difference is the mark of a wise person, and the wise person is the hope of civilization. Two fools, Foerster wrote, will live poorly together; a fool and a wise man better; but two wise men best.[39]

[39] Foerster, *American State University,* p. 227.

CHAPTER THREE

The Creative Life

The chief problem of criticism, the search for standards to oppose to individual caprice, is also the chief problem of contemporary thought in general; so that any solution that does not go back to first principles will be worthless.
—Irving Babbitt

Genius is merely the capacity for being reasonable in a superior degree.
—Eugene Delacroix

WHEN IRVING BABBITT pointed to the need for first principles in matters of art and criticism, he appealed to the standard Humanist remedy in all categories of life and thought. Not the least serious malady of the age was what the Humanists judged to be the long and pervasive revolt against classical values. It had waxed with increasing strength from the early nineteenth century and found expression through two major intellectual movements. In one case a romantic aesthetic proclaimed a unique or special quality for art and established for the artist a separate world sanctified in its remoteness from the common intellectual and moral judgment of the race. On the other hand a naturalistic protest sought to link art with the forces of biology, economics, and society and to explain cultural history by the empirical standards of scientific inquiry. These new directions fostered much diversity in criticism, and the Humanists' own outline took shape against the major spokesmen for each. But more important to the Humanists was the fact that both the romantic and the naturalistic movements shared a common ground in their opposition to any idea of universal norms. Both were seen to be attacking the use of standards by fostering an individualistic or empirical relativism in art and criticism. The Humanists sought to overcome the excesses of both extremes by upholding the validity of higher universal values as the true test of creativity. Art must reflect life while also standing apart from it, and the artist must be a creator but also a critic of life. Their elaboration of this outline plunged the Humanists into controversy, for the search for standards required that they introduce moral and intellectual criteria into aesthetic considerations. It was a stance that won them little popularity. Almost alone among the critical movements of their own period, the Humanists looked mostly to eighteenth-century norms and sought by their revival to overcome the drift and confusion that was the heritage of the nineteenth century. This stance was crucial to their whole program and in the end depended on a successful application of their dualistic philosophy of man to a philosophy of art and criticism.

The New Humanists used a dualistic philosophy of man to set against the elements of change a principle of control and impose on the flux the idea of permanence. Intellectually, this was a matter of setting a higher reality, an enduring norm of moral and spiritual values against the particular, the individual, and the transitory. But this effort was above all a search for standards, and when applied to aesthetics it challenged the artist to use the objects of sense to adumbrate, to suggest by imaginative illusion a higher truth. Babbitt found this idea best expressed in the French critic Joseph Joubert. The best artist, Joubert said, is one who illustrates a sensitive perception of the flux of experience and joins this to an intuitive perception of the universal.[1] And this calling represented for Babbitt and More and their followers the supreme creative challenge. Properly conceived, art was the hope of the world, for true art was the successful unity of reason and imaginative insight and thus the basis of humanist culture. The perception and depiction of a higher reality was never completely a question of intellect or philosophy; in its successful form, it was always a matter of intuition and imagination.

In their outline of the aesthetic ideal, the Humanists were trying to fortify a rich tradition that had prevailed from the Greeks through the eighteenth century. Within the classical school Aristotle was more helpful than Plato, but even the latter, in asserting that poetry could not directly reflect the eternal and unchanging Ideas, realistically confined the aesthetic to the realm of experience. But once the transcendental ideals themselves are rejected, and the concept of universals confined to the empirical world, a new function for art emerges. Aristotle made clear the implications. In his *Poetics,* the successful poet extracts the form of things from the multiplicity of experience; he is thus the efficient cause for the creation or depiction of the universal. The mimetic theory, as M. H. Abrams has demonstrated, shaped the classical tradition and made the work of art, as opposed to the poet or the internal creative process, the central focus and concern of aesthetic inquiry. The artist under these standards was judged to be creative only by virtue of his imaginative portrayal of the universal experience of a uniform human nature.[2]

Romantic apologists have always found the cardinal elements in the

[1] Irving Babbitt, *The Masters of Modern French Criticism* (1912; rpt. New York, 1963), pp. 46, 56.

[2] M. H. Abrams, *The Mirror and the Lamp* (London, 1953), pp. 8–12, 34.

classical vocabulary—imitation, representation, norm, universality—
restrictive and mechanical when applied to the creative process itself.
But to the Humanists and their forebears such checks on emotional overflow and personal idiosyncrasies were by no means corruptive of true
genius, nor did they preclude a necessary and useful place for the local,
the particular, and the individual. That concern was emphatically put
in the epitome of English neoclassical criticism, Samuel Johnson's
Preface to Shakespeare, for here the creator incorporates elements that appeal
to the Elizabethan audience of his own time and to an audience of indefinite time and place, illustrating "those general passions and principles
by which all minds are agitated."[3]

Babbitt tried to come at this problem in a similar way. It was one of
his favorite sayings that the artist must combine opposite extremes and
occupy all the space between. The best art, that is, was recognizably
original, but representative as well. "Genuine originality," Babbitt said,
"is so immensely difficult because it imposes the task of achieving work
that is of general human truth and at the same time intensely individual."[4]
He and More related this theme directly to their own account of the human
condition. One may apprehend in great art, they said, the presence of "two
souls." One is that by which the work is seen to be unique. It represents that
part of the individual that responds to the materials of the flux, the sensations and emotions that affect his perceptions. The other is that by which the
work has permanent value; it is the exercise of the higher self that intuits
in the phenomena of change a common element of life and human nature.
It is the artist's disciplining of the flux to an apprehension of permanence
that liberates art from both a narrow subjectivism and an unreflecting realism and establishes its claim to universal recognition.[5] "Nothing can please
many and please long," Foerster wrote in quoting Samuel Johnson, "but
just representations of human nature." Babbitt in turn recalled Emerson's
comment that in reading the great classics of literature one senses
that they were all written by one "all-seeing, all-hearing," author.[6] So
in the broadest sense the central concern of art must always come back to an
elusive concept, yet one that was wholly real to the Humanists,
the ideal of universal man.

[3] Quoted ibid., p. 20.

[4] Irving Babbitt, *Literature and the American College* (Boston, 1908), p. 233.

[5] Babbitt, *Masters of Modern French Criticism,* pp. 75–76; Paul Elmer More,
Shelburne Essays: Seventh Series (1910; rpt. New York, 1967), pp. 264–66.

[6] Norman Foerster, *Towards Standards* (New York, 1930), p. 69; Babbitt, *Masters
of Modern French Criticism,* p. 346. Foerster, in exploring the major critical views of
nineteenth-century America, also used Emerson to defend the Humanists'

One of the central problems of the New Humanism lay in its efforts to deal with the revolt, and the legacy of that revolt, against the critical norms of classical aesthetics. The romantic movement was infinitely various, but one of the real values of Abrams's study is its successful delineation of several common and pervasive romantic themes. At the heart of the issue, he shows, was a clash of metaphors; the "mirror" of imitation was replaced by the "lamp" of expression. The second metaphor provided a central theme for discussions of art by Shelley, Keats, Byron, Wordsworth, Coleridge, and the Schlegels. Representation was still a concern but now assumed a significant new emphasis. "Poetry is representation of the spirit," according to Novalis, "of the inner world in its totality."[7] In the new creative function the internal is made external. "The romantic movement," Harold Bloom writes, "is from nature to the imagination's freedom. . . . The creative process is the hero of Romantic poetry, and imaginative inhibitions of any kind, necessarily must be the antagonists of the poetic quest."[8] The orientation of criticism now turns on the artist and on the elements of the work reflecting the state of mind of the creator. And that turn, the Humanists came later to see, was perilous to the defense of standards and taste.

The romantic turn was also allied with new directions in philosophy, of which the Kantian aesthetics, formulated in the *Critique of Judgment* in 1790 was the major statement. In this work Kant sought with great deliberation to separate the aesthetic world from the world of science, morality, and utility by confining aesthetic pleasure to "disinterested satisfaction." Kant, to be sure, was not making a plea for a doctrine of art for art's sake, nor even for a bold individualism, and he even appealed to the common sense of mankind as an ideal norm of art. But Kant clearly did initiate the transition from the late classical to the romantic period. The plea for aesthetic independence was then joined to the celebration of the individual. "Nature," "spontaneity," "selfhood" became more important to the vocabulary of the romantic period, and the new aesthetic ideal in Germany described a spontaneously unfolding self-conscious spirit. This ideal served as a point of contrast for the elder

---

aesthetics. Foerster could dispense with Emerson's transcendentalism and still find much merit in the Concord sage's appeal to a higher reality. Thus in a strictly empirical sense he could endorse Emerson's assertion that "the universal soul is the alone creator of the useful and the beautiful," and that to attain artistic distinction "the individual [mind] must be submitted to the universal mind" (*American, Criticism* [Boston, 1928], p. 68).

[7] Quoted in Abrams, *Mirror and the Lamp*, p. 50.

[8] "The Internalization of Quest-Romance," in Harold Bloom, ed., *Romanticism and Consciousness* (New York, 1970), pp. 6, 9.

Schlegel when he attributed the term *mechanical* to classical standards
and *organic* to romantic. The new spokesmen still adhered in a modified
way to the Kantian transcendental metaphysics and thus perpetuated
the notion of the universal in art; but they also appealed to the medium
of the self as the vehicle of poetic insight to this higher reality.[9]

The Humanists later saw in this new departure the roots of a movement
that reached monstrous proportions and far more dangerous extremes in
the twentieth century. But a review of their discussion of early romantic
aesthetics requires a few words of caution. In this matter, as in all others
that the Humanists confronted, they were of course less concerned with
exposition than with criticism, and selective criticism at that. Sensitive
to the influence of ideas and especially of those they saw writ large in their
own time, they tended to single out for emphasis one or a few parts of a
system as though these were the whole. Much in the ideas of the romantics
(Schiller's appeal to classical Greece, for example) was not entirely incompatible with Humanist ideas. But the Humanists were on their guard
to see whether others' views could be made complicit agents of any
anti-Humanist philosophy of life and culture and thereby linked with the
broader naturalistic and romantic traditions. Secondly, it will be clear
that within the Humanist group it was Babbitt who most frequently engaged
in philosophies of art and criticism. And this was so even though he was
much less the practicing critic than More or Sherman, who both wrote
less on the theoretical questions.

It was essentially a traditional classicism that the Humanists sought
to revive as the basis for a philosophy of art. But although they were
sympathetic to the eighteenth century, they were by no means uncritical;
it too had its own excesses. Too often the attention to precise rules and
standards rendered works formal and artificial. Babbitt often recalled the
story of the Frenchman who went to the theater but left in a state of vexa-
tion because he had not laughed "according to the rules." There was also
the man who complained of the stars in heaven that they were not arranged
in a symmetrical pattern![10] Babbitt therefore conceded a certain amount

---

[9] René Wellek, *A History of Modern Criticism,* Vol. I, *The Later Eighteenth Century*
(New Haven, 1955), pp. 227–30; William K. Wimsatt, Jr., and Cleanth Brooks,
Literary Criticism: A Short History (New York, 1957), pp. 368–77.

[10] Here again Babbitt felt that the heavy rationalistic emphasis of Descartes
and others had been injurious to the true classical spirit. By its concern for the
logical and mathematical, for that which alone was capable of empirical
demonstration, the rationalists undermined the sense of tradition and the illusion
of a higher reality. These limitations seriously restricted the aesthetic capacity
for creative imagination and for "the immediate insight into the universal" (Irving
Babbitt, *Rousseau and Romanticism* [Boston, 1919], pp. 27, 36, 56).

of good sense to the romantic protest, admitting that "no conventions are final, no rules can set arbitrary limits to creation." But on the other hand it was clear to the Humanists that the romantic reaction against a cold neoclassicism went too far. For the new partisans considered and celebrated life expansively, and, as Babbitt said of Madame de Staël, a person who conceives life expansively is less interested in form than in expression. Whatever useful might have come from that new emphasis was irreparably lost, the Humanists believed, when it was not subordinated to any higher norm or to any ethical center, thereby becoming its own end. "The partisans of expression as opposed to form in the eighteenth century," Babbitt wrote, "led to the fanatics of expression in the nineteenth and these have led to the maniacs of expression of the twentieth." Art thereby departed from its concern with the norm of humanity as an aesthetic value and began to cultivate the strange, the exotic, and the unique. Form and content both mattered less when the new concern was the liberation of the imagination to find its own vehicle of expression. This for the Humanists was the lasting legacy of the romantic rebellion. "An eccentricity so extreme as to be almost or quite indistinguishable from madness," Babbitt concluded, "is then the final outcome of the revolt of the original genius from the regularity of the eighteenth century." [11]

This problem of genius was itself central to the Humanist appraisal of early nineteenth-century culture. Babbitt believed that at the heart of the new romantic conception of genius was the idea of undisciplined imagination. "What the genius wanted was spontaneity." And to this extent he was in revolt against the classical ideal of imitation. For Babbitt, the romantic struggle signified the superiority of the spontaneous impulse over a discipline regulated by tradition and morality, and he held up for special blame in the new aesthetics the ideas of Kant. The latter's deficiency, Babbitt believed, was his inability to associate genius in art with the disciplining of the imagination to a purpose, an end or standard of value outside the artist himself. The "central impotence" of his system, that is, was his separation of outer authority and reason from the imagination. Once that alliance was broken, the imagination became the vehicle of the most extreme aberrations. Kant had opened the door, and with Schiller and others the way was prepared for "the worst perversions of the aesthete." [12]

It is not surprising that Babbitt utilized German sources more than English to document the excesses of the romantic movement. Friedrich Schlegel bears the romantic banner for Babbitt when he asserts that "the

---

[11] Ibid., pp. 46, 63, 68; see also Foerster, *Towards Standards*, p. 50.

[12] Babbitt, *Rousseau and Romanticism*, pp. 34, 37, 42–43.

caprice of the poet suffers no law above itself." In Germany music became
the queen of the arts because it was least correlated with the concrete and
the objective; it was most available as the medium of pure expression.
The musician, A. W. Schlegel believed, "has a language of feeling independent of all external objects."[13] When the unobjectified qualities
of music became the aesthetic norm for the other arts, the modern world,
Babbitt believed, inherited an impossible confusion.[14] But romanticism was
not entirely without restraints on limits to the free play of the imagination.
English critics usually preferred the lyric poem and criticized the lack
of determinate representation in music, but, even more important, the poetic
ideal often took the form of some transcendent universal. Platonic and
Kantian ideas were primary influences on many of the English poets and
critics, such as Coleridge, Carlyle, Shelley, and Blake, and did abate the
mere cult of individualism to a degree. When Shelley asserted that "a
poet participates in the eternal, the infinite, and the one," he used words
familiar to the classical and Humanist defense.[15] But Babbitt perceived
that the continuity of rhetoric merely obscured a fundamental change,
one that denoted a critical difference in the manner and use of the
classical and romantic imagination. That the British romantics could
appropriate the Platonic language and transcendental philosophy
served also to intensify the Humanists' dissent from the speculative
tradition in Western thought.

For Babbitt, the romantic quest for the universal did not in the least
compromise the cultivation of free expression. In the classical and Humanist aesthetic the concern for the universal norm also expressed a concern for the discipline of the individual; it had always something to do
with the expression of the higher self, not the natural self. The use of
the Platonic ideal by the romantics conspired only to fuel the egotistic outreach of the expansive self. The romantic's effort to link his soul to a
transcendent spirit, or to create in such a way, as Shelley described, as
to reflect the universal mind, was, we may suspect, too facile to win
Humanist endorsement. Babbitt saw the true meaning of the universal
perverted when it became linked to a grasping for the infinite and the
realm of freedom in the Kantian sense. Utilized in this way, it united with
the expansive temperament; the universal could no longer serve as a
disciplining ethical norm.[16] The Humanists' suspicions were further con-

[13] Quoted ibid., p. 241; quoted in Abrams, *Mirror and the Lamp*, p. 93.

[14] Hence the subtitle in Babbitt's *The New Laokoön: An Essay on the Confusion of the Arts*.

[15] Abrams, *Mirror and the Lamp*, pp. 91, 127.

[16] Ibid., pp. 127, 41.

firmed when they read the romantics' depiction of the creative process. Reading Keats's statement that "if Poetry comes not as naturally as the Leaves to a tree it had better not come at all," Babbitt and the others no doubt saw only self-abandonment and the loss of the *frein vital*. Shelley could endorse the Platonic universals and still believe that poetic composition is irresistible and automatic. "A great statue or picture grows under the power of the artist as a child in the mother's womb" was the organic metaphor employed, one that suggested a kind of spontaneity in the creative process that the Humanists distrusted.[17]

It was also necessary to make a similar distinction between the Humanist and romantic use of the past. In Germany especially the romantic movement showed a lively historical consciousness and looked backward, particularly to the Middle Ages, for inspiration. The Humanists themselves were spokesmen for tradition and the retrospectiveness of the Germans might suggest an affinity between the two groups. But in pointing out that the proper use of the past is its availability as a measure of judgment against the present, Paul More was calling for selection and discrimination. He and Babbitt wished to use the past as a check against the impressionistic and sensational reveling in the passion of the moment, as a restraint on the immediacy of the flux, and even as a check on individual spontaneity. But they sought also to discourage an uncritical reaction, and it was just this that the Humanists perceived in the cultivation of the Middle Ages and in the nationalistic dimensions of romanticism. Babbitt read in the German poets and the folklore revival a type of primitivism that he invariably associated with the romantic psyche. As the romantic in an individual sense worshipped the unspoiled innocence of the child or the ass, so in the nationalistic sense he worshipped the native sources of cultural expression in their primeval form. Here were to be found the cherished elements of an uncontaminated originality that flourished before their ruination under the confining restraints of civilized culture. For the Humanists the romantic recourse to the past transformed a properly disciplining activity into a form of escapism and emotional expansion intricately and dangerously linked to the cause of liberation.[18]

But the problem of aesthetic freedom assumed a different form later in the nineteenth century, even though the beginnings of the "art for art's sake" idea were partly suggested in Kant and to a greater extent in Cousin, Jouffroy, and Gautier in France. The later exponents followed some of the early pronouncements in separating critical judgments in art

[17] Quoted ibid., pp. 136, 192.

[18] More, *Shelburne Essays: Seventh Series*, p. 237; Babbitt, *Rousseau and Romanticism*, pp. 97–101.

from the standards of reason and intellect, morality and utility, but they now broke from the former in denying the attachment of art either to nature or to any transcendent order of reality. Like the Humanists, Baudelaire and others refused to be taken in by the celebration of innocence or the cult of the primitive in the romantic hankering for nature;[19] but the extreme aesthetic philosophies nonetheless drew from the Humanists a wholesale rebuke that ranged from their attacks on Walter Pater in the late nineteenth century to the advocates of the New Criticism in twentieth-century America. It included also their effort to undo the system of Croce and his disciple Joel E. Spingarn, and that quarrel itself was one of the more significant critical discussions of its day.

Impressionist criticism owed much to the work of Walter Pater, an English scholar of little influence today, who gained his reputation through his *Studies in the History of the Renaissance* (1873). To be sure, the Humanists probably understood Pater's comprehensive views as little as other critics and students, who have tended to center on a few quotable passages at the expense of the larger part of his work. Pater by practice was not a wholly impressionistic critic and never advocated with Anatole France the "adventures of the soul among masterpieces" as the appropriate method of criticism. But Pater did stand out clearly in his more extreme statements and was vulnerable to attack. His concept of poetry was consistently romantic and pastoral, and he tied his aesthetic views to a strong philosophy of the flux.[20] Pater rejected any appeal to a transcendent or higher reality and accepted what he considered a scientific view of life as a pulsating flux and flow of things. In one of his memorable lyrical passages Pater described the whirl of existence as "a drift of momentary acts of insight and passion and thought" within the breathing soul and the play of sensations without. The challenge to art was to make meaningful the immediate moment within this flux, and the highest value in life lay in this instantaneousness of aesthetic experience. "While all melts under our feet," Pater wrote, "we may well catch at any exquisite passion . . . that seems . . . to set the spirit free." The realm of art, then, lay in this single unit of reality, the reality of the moment and the experience of the individual in that fleeting fraction of time.[21]

If the Humanists concentrated on this aspect of Pater's aesthetics, it was

[19] Wimsatt and Brooks, pp. 476–77, 483.

[20] Wellek, *History of Modern Criticism,* Vol. IV, *The Late Nineteenth Century* (New Haven, 1965), pp. 383–92.

[21] Walter Pater, *Studies in the History of the Renaissance* (London, 1873), pp. 211–13; Ruth C. Child, *The Aesthetics of Walter Pater* (New York, 1940), p. 178; Wellek, *History of Modern Criticism,* IV, 389.

simply because they saw the effects of his views magnified in the art and
critical standards of their own day. Pater thus became a straw man for the
Humanists to attack, and in this way they held up to scorn much of what
they considered the new romanticism of the twentieth century. This in fact
was the critical issue, for behind the spirit of Pater the Humanists saw the
long legacy of Rousseauism. The cult of emotion as the good life, the
retreat to the personal as the single measure of truth, the escape from
standards and norms by the appeal to the immediacy of the present—these
were the symptoms of the hedonistic aesthetics that underlay the confusion
of standards and the chaos that plagued the creative life in the modern
world. More thus maintained that Pater's theory of art went against the
whole Humanist conception of life. It knew nothing of the search for value
and order, and in its grasping for the joy of the moment refused attachment to any norm outside the artist's own subjective temperament. The
new aesthetics, More asserted, "springs . . . from . . . an exasperated personality submerged in the ceaseless ebb and flow of things, and striving
desperately to cling to the shadows as they speed by." Impulses as Pater
utilized them, Munson said, furnish only the weakest material for art, and to
encourage their pursuit is but an invitation to live as unreflectingly and
mechanically as possible. Babbitt judged Pater the most flagrant of romantics and recoiled from the cultivation of whim and the pursuit of the
whirl that he judged the essence of Pater's aesthetics.[22]

Much more precise as statements of the "art for art's sake" idea were
the intuitional theories of the Italian philosopher Benedetto Croce and the
criticism of his American disciple Joel E. Spingarn. In 1902 Croce published his *Aesthetic*, a difficult and controversial work that went further
than any previous one in marking off the aesthetic life from the rest of
human activity, thereby striking a blow for the "purity" of art. Artistic
creation, Croce explained, was the work of an aesthetic faculty that he
called variously the "lyric intuition" or the "intuition-expression." It con-
noted for Croce a noncognitive, nonspiritual, nonmoral exercise. Aesthetic
intuition bore no special relationship to the beautiful or pleasurable as
such, so that Croce was going further than Pater or the earlier romantics in isolating the creative life. But it was to be understood also that the
intuition-expression was both intuition and expression; the former cannot
occur without the later, for the aesthetic experience is indistinguishably
an internal and external activity. But, as the basis of Croce's system, this

[22] Paul Elmer More, *The Drift of Romanticism* (1909; rpt. New York, 1967),
p. 114; Gorham B. Munson, "Our Critical Spokesmen," in Norman Foerster,
ed., *Humanism and America* (New York, 1930), pp. 241–42; Babbitt, *Masters of
Modern French Criticism*, p. 350.

view meant that art is essentially expression, and good or successful art is complete expression. Furthermore, in separating the lyrical intuition from the conceptual faculty, reason, and the intellect, Croce signaled that art was essentially autotelic. Art could not be linked to any notions of external beauty and was divorced from any connections with the natural world because these exist only in the conceptual realm.[23] One effect of Croce's system was to strike a blow for the freedom of the artist. In marking off the creative life with a kind of separate ontological identity, he removed art from all judgments respecting its practicality, its correspondence to intellectual truth, and its moral content. All these considerations, Croce suggested, involved an unwarranted introduction of rational thought and reflection into art, qualities fatal to the aesthetic instinct.[24]

It is hard to imagine a philosophy of art more remote from Humanist thinking, and Babbitt himself found the Crocean temperament to be one of the most menacing influences in the contemporary cultural confusion. Babbitt was not wholly critical, though, of a man he credited with "vast learning and intellectual brilliancy" who combined "numerous peripheral merits," above all, his antinaturalistic influence in criticism, with a "central wrongness" and a "central void." It was this void that was fatal to Croce's authority, Babbitt believed, for by reducing art to a "sort of lyrical overflow," Croce failed to relate his creativity to any external center or norm of judgment for either artist or critic. The Crocean fallacy was the romantic fallacy, and "nothing could be more romantic than Croce's cult of intuition in the sense of pure spontaneity and untrammelled expression." The central void in Croce's ideas derived from his inability to recognize the problems of the One and the Many, to seek for the unchanging amid all the changes and to use that as a check on individuality. There was in fact some sense to Babbitt's linking Croce to the romantic tradition, although Croce himself disavowed such ties. But Babbitt was on less sure footing in linking him with Henri Bergson and then in turn to the mechanical hedonism of the modern world. Babbitt read into the appeal to free expression in Croce and to the élan vital in Bergson the same undisciplined spontaneity that denoted the pleasure principle of the modern spirit, "the love of change and motion for their own sakes." For Babbitt, Croce and Bergson merely registered the "psychic restlessness" that was the equivalent in the inner life of the cult of speed and power in the outer.[25] By this

[23] Benedetto Croce, *Guide to Aesthetics,* trans. Patrick Romanell (Indianapolis, 1965), pp. 10–11; Wimsatt and Brooks, pp. 500–510.

[24] Croce, pp. 12, 16–17.

[25] Irving Babbitt, "Croce and the Philosophy of the Flux," *Yale Review,* NS 14 (1925), 378–81.

Humanist slight-of-hand two of the strongest opponents of scientific rationalism became complicit in the mechanical excesses of modern life.

The Humanists saw the reign of spontaneous overflow at work not only in the philosophy of art in Pater and Croce but also in their philosophies of criticism. Pater showed the implications of his aesthetics for criticism by insisting that creative reproduction is its essential function. The primary duty of the critic was to disengage the peculiar essense of each artist's work, "the special unique impression of pleasure" produced by the artist. But such analysis came in the end to mean a new and individual aesthetic experience. "What," Pater asked, "is this song or picture . . . to *me*? What effect does it really produce on me. . . . How is my nature modified by its presence and under its influence?" Croce also related his philosophy of art to criticism. By emphasizing the uniqueness of the aesthetic intuition, he removed the judgment of art from all moral, practical, and intellectual criteria. Criticism, then, became the dispassionate narration of what has happened in a work of art.[26] Finally, and much more important to the Humanist debate, creative criticism was given its strongest statement by Joel Spingarn in 1910. Spingarn, who received a Harvard degree at the same time Babbitt was launching his teaching career there, was later a student of George Woodberry at Columbia and then professor of comparative literature at that institution.

Like the Humanists, Spingarn sought to liberate the study of literature from the influence of science, and both he and Babbitt bolted from what they found to be the cold pedantry of the philological emphasis at Harvard. Spingarn then took up the banner of Croce in adhering to his philosophy of art as expression and particularly in carrying out the implications of Croce's ideas on criticism. If art is successful expression, then the artist has performed his function if his product bears the full imprint of his feelings, if it has successfully externalized the inner experience of the creator. To judge whether the artist has succeeded in expression is, then, the primary task of the critic. Such a view in itself obviously raised problems, but Spingarn nonetheless believed that if the critic became one in feeling with the artist, the critical act would be successful. Such an exercise meant that the critic must ultimately reproduce the work of art within himself in order to understand and evaluate it. Spingarn summarized his position by asserting that the essence of criticism was the identity of genius and taste. "It means," he wrote, that "in their most significant moments, the creative and the critical instincts are one and the same." Spingarn asserted these views, it should be noted, in a 1910 address, and expressed his philosophy in its rawest form. He elaborated on these thoughts much thereafter and

[26] Pater, p. viii; Croce, pp. 73–74.

repeatedly endeavored to clarify points of confusion, for there were many. But this clarification, according to Spingarn's biographer, was never successful, and the Humanists were not alone in approaching Spingarn in terms of the bare and rather simplistic outline of the 1910 statement.[27]

For many, and sometimes obvious, reasons the Humanists condemned impressionistic criticism as romantic excess. Impressionism, they believed, was an obstacle to the construction of objective standards for artist and critic, because although it preserved a sense of the individual and a tolerance of personal experience, it sacrificed all else in the way of these. Pater, according to Foerster, merely reflected the romantic notion that what is unique and important about an individual is his feelings; Pater then applied the same concerns to the critic. The value of the artistic product, consequently, lay in its ability to generate new thrills for the observer. Aesthetic appreciation was no longer a matter of experienced and considered judgment and appealed to no rules or standards beyond subjectivity. Impressionistic criticism, Foerster believed, simply encouraged an uncritical empathy on the part of the viewer while at the same time inviting him to embark on a new aesthetic experience of his own. Babbitt also saw the romantic fallacies writ large in the impressionistic vogue, especially in its obsession with expression as the essence of the aesthetic act. Holding this up as the single standard, Babbitt believed, was to ignore content, ideas, and moral values and thus to deprive the critic of his essential tools. For More, impressionism was a "surrender to luxurious revery" that replaced judgment with emotional indulgence.[28]

It was this "immemorial right to judge" that the Humanists sought to reclaim for the critic. "Criticism," Babbitt reminded, "is primarily judgment and selection and only secondarily comprehension and sympathy." In its failure really to concern itself with this matter, the Humanists believed, impressionism was not really criticism at all. It accepted works of art as the scientist examines the works of nature, as objects for study and enjoyment but not for evaluation by a moral standard or measure. Babbitt therefore charged the impressionists with irresponsibility. Spingarn's theory, he said, encourages laziness and conceit, and his exhortation to get rid of all restraints on expression was merely a call to follow the emotional line of least resistance—the easy path to "genius." Babbitt felt that Spingarn offered no standard that could limit the eager-

[27] Joel E. Spingarn, "The New Criticism," in Spingarn, ed., *Criticism in America* (New York, 1924), pp. 25–43; Marshall Van Deusen, *J. E. Spingarn* (New York, 1971), pp. 18, 76–77.

[28] Foerster, *Towards Standards,* pp. 46–55; Babbitt, *Masters of Modern French Criticism,* p. 10; More, *Shelburne Essays: Seventh Series,* p. 242.

ness of the creator to "revel in his own thrills" and left no measure of an artist's merit save his intoxication with himself. Here Babbitt recalled the remark that "every ass that's romantic thinks he's inspired" and demanded critical guidelines that would distinguish between the disciplined creator and the madman.[29]

Babbitt, More, and Foerster agreed that once the romantic movement succeeded in making the individual rather than the norm of humanity the prevailing frame of reference, the triumph of impressionism was assured. Babbitt referred to Joubert in reminding his readers that so long as we recognize that there is something unchanging in human nature, that there is a self that all persons share in common with others, then the standards of art are similarly unchanging. We need only ask to what extent any work of art combined individual uniqueness with an imaginative insight into the universally human.[30] But without that sense the critic had only to judge the artist's efforts at expression. "Intensity" and "vitality," the Humanists charged, became the key words that linked the creative process with the spontaneity of the natural man. More could then charge the impressionists with a dangerous inversion of priorities. In making emotion the essential aesthetic fact, the impressionist assigned an intrinsic value to the mere enjoyment of experience as an end in itself. More feared the worse for this effect and held up a statement from Pater as a kind of distillation of his whole philosophy: "Not the fruit of experience, but experience itself is the end. . . . To burn always with this hard, gem-like flame, to maintain this ecstacy, is success in life." Here, for More, was the uncritical hedonism of all romanticism. It was the pathway to "decadence."[31]

Nor did the debate end here, for much of this discussion was only peripheral to a larger issue, the question whether art could establish itself as an independent reality with standards and norms of its own, whether the aesthetic process was amenable to criticism only by rules of its own making, whether, as Friedrich Schlegel said, "poetry can only be criticized by poetry." The Humanists believed that so long as this idea persisted, individual temperament and emotionalism would continue to reign supreme; art would never transcend the realm of the subjective in either its creative or critical phases. Babbitt succinctly expressed the concern of his group. "There is a fatal facility about creation," he said, "when its

[29] Irving Babbitt, "Reply to Dr. Spingarn," *Journal of Philosophy, Psychology, and Scientific Methods,* 11 (1914), 328; Foerster, *Towards Standards,* pp. 54–55; Robert Shafer, *Paul Elmer More and American Criticism* (New Haven, 1935), pp. 13–14; Irving Babbitt, "Genius and Taste," in Spingarn, *Criticism in America,* pp. 163–65.

[30] Babbitt, *Masters of Modern French Criticism,* pp. 58, 346.

[31] More, *Drift of Romanticism,* pp. 109–15; see also Foerster, *Towards Standards,* p. 52.

quality is not tested by some standard set above the creator's temperament; and the same fatal facility appears in criticism when the critic does not test creation by some standard set above both his own temperament and that of the creator."[32] How then to check against the anarchy of subjectivism? The Humanists' answers to that question involved them in some of the most controversial aspects of their whole program; for in refuting the romantic separation of art from life, they sought to judge art by moral and intellectual criteria and to derive those criteria from the higher experience of the human race.

Their retreat to the moral function of art further confirmed the classical perspective in the Humanists' aesthetic. The eighteenth century was more inclined than the succeeding one to describe art in terms of its public function, a concern that had even motivated Plato's own evaluation of poetry and its place in the state. This in part explains the prevailing obsession with rules and the rigid formulas prescribed for artistic production. Art was to be pleasurable, but it was also to offer moral instruction, or, as the Scottish moralist James Beattie said, if poetry instructs it only pleases the more effectually. Under neoclassical standards, the poet often had a heavy burden. "It is always a writer's duty," said Samuel Johnson, "to make the world better." The moral emphasis supplemented the classicist's concern with selection. The poet does not copy nature or the real world, but "la belle nature," or "nature improved" by the abstracted higher qualities of experience. The quest for the norm of human experience was inextricably involved with the quest for meaningful standards and the ethical measure of life.[33] Any literature that transcended individuality and became representative, in the Humanists' sense, was then truly a literature of life and a moral literature as well. Stuart Sherman appealed to Matthew Arnold in upholding this view: "poetry," he quoted Arnold, "is at bottom a criticism of life. . . . A poetry of revolt against moral ideas is a poetry of revolt against *life*; a poetry of indifference to moral ideas is a poetry of indifference towards *life*." Any poetry that represents life adequately will always reveal an insight to the higher life. This was the basis of its fundamentally ethical nature.[34]

By interjecting a moral judgment that would link the two, Sherman was using Arnold to reply to those who honored the segregation of art from the ordinary life. Babbitt in turn defended the moral imagination as the most important quality for a work of art, a quality he saw desecrated by

---

[32] Babbitt, *Rousseau and Romanticism,* p. 65.

[33] Abrams, *Mirror and the Lamp,* pp. 15–16, 35–38. The quotation is on p. 20.

[34] Stuart P. Sherman, *Matthew Arnold: How to Know Him* (Indianapolis, 1917), p. 147.

the romantic assault. For it was the romantic break with the sterility of the classical past that set up emotion and aesthetic perception as the new ideals of the creative life. And in this way the romantics could bypass the moral considerations of art by seeking aesthetic experience as an end in itself, by establishing beauty as "its own excuse for being." But for Babbitt the divorce of the ethical and aesthetic was perilous. Whatever it might yield in its pursuit of the vivid and the picturesque (and Babbitt conceded here and there the occasional "recreational" value of romantic poetry!), in the end it meant that the beautiful was attached to nothing save the shifting pleasure of the individual within the relentless surge of the flux, the anchorless drifting of natural man. The Humanists therefore countered that beauty was most useful when at the service of the ethical imagination. "We should not hesitate to say," Babbitt wrote, "that beauty loses most of its meaning when divorced from ethics even though every aesthete in the world should arise and denounce us as philistines." Art, More added, cannot be judged on the standards of beauty alone; it must be subservient to ethics. Art that is merely recreative will seek the beautiful as the element of pleasure, but art that is highly serious will merge the ethical and aesthetic perception to capture imaginatively a higher reality. The critic too must above all employ the moral faculty in his judgments. More's essay "Criticism" scored Oscar Wilde's appeal to sympathy and tolerance as the essential critical guidelines and equated this liberality with a heedless escape from the "trammeling burden of moral responsibility."[35]

On the moral question the Humanists read the romantic literature selectively. One needs only to recall Shelley's *Defence of Poetry* to know that the true, the beautiful, and the good sometimes served as a trinity of value for the romantic aesthetic. Poems that are beautiful, Shelley said, are also moral. Yet it is easy to see why Babbitt could dismiss for naught this display of moral concern. For Shelley, poetry was the vehicle by which the poet reached out to other souls, it was "a going out of our own nature, and an identification of ourselves with the beautiful which exists in thought, action, or person, not our own."[36] The Humanists' fear of expansive emotionalism surely blinded them to the ego-restricting aspects of romanticism. What Shelley here described is the same temperament that Babbitt attributed to the Rousseauistic humanitarian. This was not a disciplining morality or check on the self; it merely conspired to energize the expansive tendencies of the romantic soul by bringing all of humanity within the orb of its indiscriminate benevolence.

[35] Babbitt, *Rousseau and Romanticism,* pp. 206–7; Paul Elmer More, *Platonism* (Princeton, 1917), p. 175; idem., *Shelburne Essays: Seventh Series,* pp. 234–37.

[36] Quoted in Abrams, *Mirror and the Lamp,* p. 331.

The burden that the Humanists sought to place on artist and critic was a moral and an intellectual one as well. The alienation of the artist that the Humanists attributed to romantic theories they now sought to overcome in part by connecting the world of art to the world of ideas. Babbitt's essay on Brunetière praised the French critic for preserving in the midst of the romantic assault the "antiquated notion" that "books exist primarily to express ideas"; we should turn to them for ideas rather than for "elegant aesthetic sensation." It was this kind of strong language that either numbed critics of Humanism or enraged them to equally strong retorts, and it served to show how great were the differences between the two camps respecting their use of art. That poetry should exist for mere enjoyment or delight, that it should merit value simply for its aesthetic qualities, seemed almost wholly alien to the Humanist mind. Babbitt could only assert that a literature devoid of "intellectual qualities" became a kind of "debauchery," a lazy emotional indulgence.[37]

These ideas were given special force when Babbitt confronted Spingarn directly in 1913 and 1914 after the latter reviewed, in the *Journal of Philosophy, Psychology, and Scientific Methods,* Babbitt's book *The Masters of Modern French Criticism.* Spingarn's review, it is worth noting, was not wholly critical of Babbitt, for he saw in his Humanism a welcome opponent of the philological current in American universities and a forthright opponent of the kind of materialism he detested in America. In fact, Spingarn even welcomed Babbitt's book for its breadth of outlook and interest in ideas. But the success of the work in these respects was also its ultimate failure as a study of criticism. While Babbitt excelled in the world of ideas, Spingarn said, he failed utterly to appreciate the life of art, the world of creative imagination. Spingarn could only wonder, he said, at a theory of literary criticism so inclusive as to find an interest in "every subject under the sun except imaginative literature." This failing was, of course, especially clear to one who followed the Crocean ideals. Babbitt could not be a good student of criticism, he said, because he does not have the "same kind of critical insight, as in the original operation of the critic in criticising poets and novelists." Babbitt, in failing to see the critical function as re-creative aesthetic experience, was in fact twice removed from the source of aesthetic genius in the original mind of the artist. Babbitt's rebuttal in turn showed only how far apart were the two men, for he hardly knew what Spingarn's charges were all about. The last thing that Babbitt looked for in criticism was aesthetic re-creation. He continued to defend the intellectual element in criticism, replying that both the literary critic and the artist were confronted by the same challenge as the philosopher in

[37] Babbitt, *Masters of Modern French Criticism,* pp. 304–8.

their need to find the elements of unity in life amid the flux of experience.[38] In the end it was clear that the Humanist, while protesting against the merging of the creative and the critical functions in the romantic movement, was yet forging such an alliance in a different way. But whereas the impressionist looked for creative reenactment on the part of the critic, the Humanist sought the incorporation of the critical function into the creative process. The shift was important, though it left the parties so remote from each other in their values that when confrontation did take place there was hardly any meaningful exchange of ideas.

The nineteenth-century revolt against the classical past was a two-sided affair that included a romantic protest and a scientific and naturalistic rebellion. The Humanists, as we shall see, would find themselves fighting a two-front war, but it is worth noting here that they had in this campaign one nineteenth-century figure whom they could use as a constant ally against both enemies. The New Humanism found inspiration in a variety of sources but none so influential as Matthew Arnold. The English spokesman for culture and criticism received Humanist recognition everywhere. He was the subject of Sherman's first book, the central figure in More's essay on criticism, and the title of Babbitt's most succinct statement of the whole Humanist point of view.[39] Nor is it difficult to see why Arnold was so often made the standard-bearer of the Humanists. He was an apostle of culture, above all of the classical tradition. His recourse to the ancients expressed the call to his own generation to concern itself with the "permanent problems" of human life and to check the cult of contemporaneousness and the "present import" in an age celebrating mechanical progress. It was the Greek writers that best displayed for Arnold, as for the Humanists, the balance of the total man united under the "imaginative reason," and it was to the Greeks that Arnold looked for the source of that "self-restraint" that would curb the exuberance, the expressiveness, and the "attractive accessories" of the English romantic poets.[40]

One can find in a dozen of Arnold's essays passages that might have easily come from the pens of Babbitt, More, or Sherman. His famous "Sweetness and Light," for instance, set the struggle for perfection against the contemporary cult of individualism and "our hatred of all limits to the unrestrained swing of the individual's personality," and appealed

[38] J. E. Spingarn, rev. of *The Masters of Modern French Criticism*, by Irving Babbitt, *Journal of Philosophy, Psychology, and Scientific Methods*, 10 (1913), 693–96; Irving Babbitt, "The Modern Spirit and Dr. Spingarn," ibid., 11 (1914), 215, 218.

[39] More's essay appears in *Shelburne Essays: Seventh Series*, Babbitt's in *Spanish Character and Other Essays* (Boston, 1940).

[40] Wimsatt and Brooks, pp. 437–38; Wellek, *History of Modern Criticism*, IV, 155.

to the "moral development and self-conquest" of the old English Puritans against the comfortable ease of the "mechanical and material civilization [now] in esteem with us." Or, turning to Arnold's "The Function of Criticism at the Present Time," one finds a forestatement of the Humanist demand for the merging of the moral, the intellectual, and the aesthetic. In literature, Arnold believed, "the elements with which the creative power works are ideas. . . . in modern literature no manifestation of the creative power not working with these can be very important or fruitful." Poetry too must have a "great critical effort" behind it. And, most famously, criticism must know "the best that is known and thought in the world" and apply it against the shifting and practical interests of the day. But, these affinities notwithstanding, the identity of Arnold and the Humanists was by no means absolute. Arnold did not always write from a consistent intellectual viewpoint; a dualistic philosophy similar to the Humanists' was often quite apparent though less steadily applied than that of the Americans. More himself was sensitive to this want in Arnold and said that he lacked a philosophy that would "tie together [his] moral and aesthetic sense."[41] On the other hand Arnold surely exhibited an aesthetic sense or sensitivity that was quite lacking in the Humanists, and that is in itself a critical point of difference. Babbitt and More in fact never turned to Arnold's poetry when seeking the help of their English predecessor in aiding their own cause. Nonetheless, a selective use of Arnold made him invaluable to the Humanists whenever their attention turned to the subjects of art and criticism.

The nineteenth century, as the Humanists knew, was not singly a triumph of romantic ideas. Important new directions in criticism came from the influence of science and materialist culture and introduced new approaches to the study of literature. Nor were the romantic and materialistic movements unrelated, for it was a kind of naturalized Hegelianism that gave the initial thrust to the new historical process by defining its evolution as the progress of Spirit, the self-realizing Absolute. Such a view was subject to a national twist as seen in the writings of Herder, who preceded Hegel, and the Russian Belinski, who was influenced by him. Literature then became a measure of the historically developing national spirit, a vehicle of description that could offer a means of judgment as well: the great authors were those who identified with the community and its evolution and captured its spirit in their work. The function of criticism in turn was to elucidate the movement of history by making clear

[41] Matthew Arnold, *Culture and Anarchy* (New York, 1883), pp. 13, 21; idem., *Essays in Criticism* (Boston, 1865), pp. 4–6, 17–19; More, *Shelburne Essays: Seventh Series,* pp. 233–34.

its hidden meaning, to illustrate to a people their peculiar national identity. This emphasis could induce a kind of scientific study of art by using works as historical documents, and even in the eighteenth century Thomas Warton had urged the study of old forms of poetry as an index to the style, manners, and customs of another period. The historical perspective could thus assume both a spiritual and materialistic form. It could also make art the vehicle of propaganda. Under the influence of French socialists and positivists and, in succeeding generations, of Marxist critics, art was urged to assume a new didactic function, instilling a special consciousness or furnishing a kind of documentary evidence of the ills of modern society. The new social novel that proclaimed scientific objectivity in a realistic depiction of modern life could also be the means of political reform. For a number of reasons the Humanists saw in Zola and others a naturalistic variety of romanticism, a "romanticism on all fours." But one critical difference was most important. The spokesmen for the historical method stood clearly apart from the romantic concern for individual expression and turned from the spirit of the author to the spirit of the age as their primary consideration. They both sought and established a union of art with life in its totality that the romantic movement had done much to write out of aesthetic criticism.[42]

To expose the fallacies of the historical school, Babbitt, and the other Humanists to a lesser extent, concentrated on the French historian and literary critic Hippolyte-Adolphe Taine, whose *History of English Literature* appeared in 1864. Taine was the most renowned of his school, and his work was a colorful and graphic history that successfully executed the author's intention to show that literature is "not a mere play of the imagination" but the product of "race, environment, and epoch." Taine sought to use literature as a means of access into the special characteristics of national life and times. He was offering a secularized model of Hegel, an early influence on his thinking, and from the perspective of history as the objectification of spirit, he became interested in art less for its own sake than for its usefulness as a measure of cultural evolution. Babbitt also saw Taine later combining with this emphasis a Darwinian ingredient that substituted a naturalistic content for the spiritual. Specifically, art now gained significance not as the expression of the individual or his culture in participation with the Absolute, but simply as the manifestation of the primordial energies of the human animal. Placing man with the other species in the web of nature, Taine reduced his activities, including the artistic, to the deterministic interplay of instinct and environment.[43]

[42] Wimsatt and Brooks, pp. 456–61, 526–27.

[43] H. A. Taine, *History of English Literature* (New York, 1879), pp. 17–35; Babbitt, *Masters of Modern French Criticism*, p. 225.

Babbitt's critique of Taine posed a Humanist dualism against a natural-istic conception of human nature. Taine denied the existence of any con-trolling human faculty above the flux of phenomena, Babbitt charged. The soul existed in Taine's view as a mere point of convergence of the forces that prevailed in the external world, with no separate reality apart from them. There was some force to that judgment, and Babbitt might have noted that the use of the biological or organic metaphor, as first employed by Herder, coincided with the emerging expressionist theories of art in the German romantic movement. Herder's essay *On the Knowing and Feeling of the Human Soul* has been called a "turning point in the history of ideas," for it indicates the rising importance of the life sciences, as opposed to the physical, at the end of the eighteenth century. The creative artist is now compared to an unconsciously growing plant, but this organic metaphor does no violence to the romantic ideal of spontaneity and expression in the creative process. Immersed in the milieu of nature, the artist and his creation alike grow from the soil of their time and place. Babbitt criticized the use of this metaphor by Taine, for it blurred the "two souls" that denote effective creation. This loss of distinction ren-dered the aesthetic effort the mere work of a mechanical energy, the artist reacting as a machine to electric current. The Humanist argued, therefore, that Taine had no sense of the inner check that could restrain and direct vital energy. The French critic, he said, had "endless comparisons to suggest how inevitably human faculties unfold and how little they are a matter of individual choice and volition."[44]

For Babbitt and his group Taine's views could only be judged one-sided and antihumanist.[45] Like the romantic, the historical or scientific critic failed to see art as the product of the "two souls" that Babbitt and More insisted always denoted successful creative efforts. If the romantics ignored the elements of a common human nature, the other school ignored the place of the individual genius. For inevitably in the creative process there was the unaccountable force of the individual. "In the most commonplace personality," according to Babbitt, "there is a fraction, however infinitesi-mal, which eludes all attempts at analysis." More defended that point in an essay on Hawthorne. It would be easy to explain Hawthorne's works by reference to environment and heredity, he said. But though this method might have some use, in the end it could explain little. For behind the

[44] Abrams, *Mirror and the Lamp,* pp. 204–5, 231, 238; Babbitt, *Masters of Modern French Criticism,* p. 231.

[45] The Humanists found this antihumanist influence especially strong in the American universities and made it a central issue in their discussions of higher education. See chapter 5.

greatness of Hawthorne "was the daemonic force of the man himself, the everlasting mystery of genius habiting in his brain." Art would always express its age and the best art would transcend its age to attain a higher universality; but as the creative re-creation of universal nature, art would always require the individual genius.[46]

But it was also the Humanistic tendency to place its enemies in the same camp, and even if the romantic and the naturalist differed fundamentally in many ways, they were always seen in a common league against usable standards of judgment. This double assault was no less apparent in the problems of art and criticism. It mattered not that the impressionist defended artistic freedom and the historical critics qualified it, for both in fact deprived the critic of his. Each side reduced the critical function to some form of elucidation that bypassed judgment as the central emphasis. While the exponents of aestheticism sanctioned the elaboration of feelings and personal experience, historical criticism sought to describe the external forces affecting the creation and reflected in it. But neither exercise, the Humanists hastened to indicate, left the critic free to judge and evaluate, save perhaps the impressionist, who held up the impossible criteria of successful expression. The Humanists' own search for universal standards may have been just as elusive, but they were correct nonetheless in charging that their opponents placed a premium on passive reaction at the expense of critical assessment. The historical critic, like the scientist, need not pretend that one phenomenon was better than another; his job was to analyze and explain artistic documents as they passed beneath the objective eye. As a further charge, the historical and romantic schools both were judged insensitive to the constant and universal elements of great art. To the historians, literary works served only to illustrate the special uniqueness that differentiated one civilization and one epoch from another. But it was the truly significant artist who transcended the spirit of the age to reflect the spirit of the ages, transcending both himself and his environment to offer imaginative insight to a common humanity that constituted the Humanists' ideal. This achievement required that the artist work through, and even against, his own emotions, and against the limitations of his own time and place, to attain a higher vision than those alone afforded. Such an effort would require a critical and selective use of the past and the present. For the Humanists that was art's achievement and its enduring gift to civilization, and in this way especially the good artist will always exercise more influence than he reflects. Historical criticism and the scientific ethos constituted a betrayal of Humanist

[46] Babbitt, *Masters of Modern French Criticism*, p. 247; Paul Elmer More, *Shelburne Essays: First Series* (1904; rpt. New York, 1967), p. 50.

standards, for they never required that creator or critic look beyond the limiting conditions of time, race, and place. [47]

The close identity that the historical school forged between life and art, history and creation, was a descriptive norm that could also become a value in itself. Art in the marketplace, art and politics, art and the common man—all of these expressions suggest a kind of lowbrow contempt for aestheticism and a protest against the esoteric nature of art that inhibited its usefulness to the society at large. Much of Marxist criticism has exhibited such prejudices, but in a purer sense the emphasis on art as social communication and the judgment of art by its relevance to the whole community was vigorously defended by Leo Tolstoy in *What Is Art?* (1898). Tolstoy's little volume, though taken with little seriousness today, stemmed from honest democratic and populist sympathies. In its strongly anti-aesthetic posture, it demanded that art be returned to the community, that poets be "accessible to their age and common to the entire people." Tolstoy ridiculed the fashionable salons and art schools, the "decadence" of high culture that he saw infecting an enfeebled modern society. Against this effeminacy he offered the "unperverted tastes" of the sturdy country peasants as the safest repository for artistic judgment. This for the Russian novelist was the surest way to overcome the dehumanized and isolated character of art in the modern world and to assure that art would fulfill its essential role as a "means of union among men." [48] Certainly the Humanists could be in sympathy with some of these feelings, and Stuart Sherman on the liberal side of Humanism tested them out in his own criticism. Even Babbitt and More might see a useful antidote here against the special pleadings of the aesthetes and a healthy curb on the subjective anarchism of the romantic aesthetic. But although the Humanists also looked for a means of integration for the artist and society, they could never accept it on Tolstoy's terms. Tolstoy may have tried to discredit the romantic notion of art for art's sake, but the Humanists were not fooled. The Russian had all the romantic infections of a Rousseau, and the Humanists were quick to read into Tolstoy's celebration of the common man the Arcadian idyllicism and primitivism of the romantic's longing for the unspoiled simplicity of precivilized society. But if men were to come together in any meaningful way, the Humanists rejoined, they must not do so on the level of their ordinary selves; they must not "descend to meet" as Babbitt believed was the way of romantic humanitarianism. The whole effect of Tolstoy's sympathy, More said, was to bring the "battle

[47] Babbitt, *Masters of Modern French Criticism*, p. 248.

[48] Wimsatt and Brooks, pp. 462–68; Wellek, *History of Modern Criticism,* IV, 280–84.

of the books" to the man in the street and reduce the creative life to its lowest common denominator. The true spiritual insight that always made great art the Humanists now saw yielding before the noise and clamor of the crowd. Nor were Babbitt and More unfair in charging a romantic legacy in the modern democratic aesthetic. "Where are we to find the best measure [of human nature]?" Wordsworth had asked. "I answer . . . by stripping our own hearts naked, and by looking out of ourselves to[wards men] who lead the simplest lives, and most according to nature; men who have never known false refinements, wayward and artificial desires . . . effeminate habits of thinking and feeling." We must "descend lower, among cottages and fields, and among children." But a true aesthetic discipline would always lift the creator above the immediate and shifting circumstance of the common life. Great art, More said, addressed itself to the universal higher self of man and spoke with meaning to persons in any age or civilization; it did not depend in the least for its enduring achievement on the judgment of the Russian peasant.[49]

It remains to see how the New Humanism related to other critical movements of the twentieth century. That effort must be selective, for the Humanists showed parallels with several groups and persons of importance.[50] Certainly there was in twentieth-century criticism an anti-romantic movement that included not only the Humanists but several other parties as well. T. S. Eliot for example, although he was critical of Babbitt in many ways, was nevertheless influenced by his Harvard teacher. Eliot, of course, was associated with Ezra Pound in trying to establish an impersonal art and criticism. Poetry, Eliot believed, could not be the direct vehicle of private emotion, but must seek an "objective correlative" as the mediator of communication between poet and reader. This required the poet to find the appropriate external symbols as the means of transmitting sensory experience, of objectifying the private and personal. Eliot, in fact, assumed an extreme position in contending finally that poetry is an "escape from emotion" and an "extinction of personality." The

[49] More, *Shelburne Essays: First Series*, pp. 210–16; Babbitt, *Masters of Modern French Criticism*, p. 23. The Wordsworth quotation is in Abrams, *Mirror and the Lamp*, p. 106. It is instructive to note the coincidental appearance in 1930 of both *Humanism and America* and Ortega Y. Gasset's *The Revolt of the Masses* in Spain. Not only was the latter a ringing denunciation of mass taste in art—"The masses crushed beneath [them] everything that is different, everything that is excellent, individual, qualified, and select" (quoted in Wimsatt and Brooks, p. 472)—but Ortego also elsewhere condemned the exclusiveness and withdrawal of the artist in his search for a private vision. The result he called "The Dehumanization of Art."

[50] T. E. Hulme and F. R. Leavis in England, Yvor Winters, Henry Seidel Canby, and the Neo-Aristotelians in America.

Humanists as a whole were reluctant to go so far in the directions of an antiromantic revolt, and only G. R. Elliott in their ranks equaled Eliot's impersonalism. " 'Poetry' and 'individualism,' " Elliott contended, "are in reality opposed terms." When the artist executes his work successfully, he ceases to be an individual and extends his experiences to a wider whole, repossessing them "in a new and impersonal way." But perhaps the most important identification of the Humanists and Eliot was their merging of the critical with the creative process. Poetry, as a process of expunging and refining personal emotions, was also for Eliot a process of criticism that must have access to some form of external standards. These for Eliot included the tenets of the Christian religion, and they gave to his critical ideal a moral and intellectual character very similar to the Humanists. [51]

Also like the Humanists, Eliot was willing to add a critical exercise to creativity, but warned against adding aesthetic experience to criticism. He was clearly opposed to impressionism ("aesthetic" criticism) and believed that Pater's views appealed only to "lazy and enfeebled minds," wholly confusing the true function of the critical act. [52] Like true art, successful criticism was for Eliot an impersonal experience. The imperfect critic, like the ordinary person, will always take his private life to be the ultimate reality and will be unable to distinguish the poetry he reads from the emotional response that it elicits from him. But for Eliot, "the end of the enjoyment of poetry is a pure contemplation from which all accidents of personal emotion are removed." Criticism then will be more a "labor of the intelligence" than emotional reaction, and never the mere satisfaction of "a suppressed creative wish." With this point the Humanists were in sympathy. Where they and Eliot parted company was on the issue of moral criticism. Eliot called More and Babbitt "imperfect critics." While he allowed for a moral factor in the creative process, Eliot was mostly willing, it seemed, to let the finished product exercise an autotelic function.

---

[51] T. S. Eliot, *The Sacred Wood* (London, 1920), pp. 47, 53; G. R. Elliott, *The Cycle of Modern Poetry* (1929; rpt. New York, 1965), p. 146; Walter Sutton, *Modern American Criticism* (Englewood Cliffs, N.J., 1963), pp. 104–5.

That Eliot's views should come from one of the twentieth century's most renowned poets has struck many as rather curious. Paul Elmer More could not make sense of the apparent contradiction between Eliot's philosophy of poetry and his writing of poetry. He wrote to Babbitt in 1928 after a visit with Eliot: "What strikes me about [Eliot] is the difficulty of reconciling his own damnable practice as a poet with his . . . critical views. There is something almost uncanny in this discrepancy" (Nov. 18, 1928, in the Paul Elmer More Papers, Department of Rare Books and Special Collections, Princeton University Library, Princeton, N.J.).

[52] Quoted in Wellek, *History of Modern Criticism*, IV, 381–82.

The Humanist mixing of the moral and the aesthetic in criticism was, in Eliot's judgment, fatal to the critical function. He wrote with respect to More that to be a moralist was "a worthy and serious thing," but it did not foster good criticism.[53]

Eliot's influence in America was also apparent in the New Criticism of the 1930s and afterwards, although he himself was by no means entirely in agreement with it. With respect to John Crowe Ransom and Allen Tate, that school has considerable affinity with the New Humanism.[54] Ransom, Tate, and the Southern Agrarian movement that they helped to lead shared with the Humanists a conservative and traditional social philosophy and were outspoken critics of modern materialist culture (see Epilogue). Here it seems safe to say that if the Humanists were sensitive to the depths of the romantic movement in modern culture, they were less sensitive to the reasons why it occurred or why it had to occur in the manner it did. The New Criticism was the long legacy of a critical division in the Western consciousness that emerged in the early nineteenth century. With the rise of the empirical sciences, poetry was under attack. Poetry, Bentham said, is a corruption of reality, a distortion of fact. Thomas Peacock denounced the aesthetic imagination; it employs an ornamental and figurative language and arouses the emotions at the expense of objective truth. The defense of poetry assumed many forms, even the claim that art has nothing to do with truth and falsehood at all. But at least two other defenses were also possible. Art, it was claimed, provides a special and different access to truth; hence Carlyle's belief that the poet "penetrates into the sacred mystery of the Universe," that art supplies an insight into a realm of truth that is not accessible to the rational and cognitive faculties. Or art might be a different realm of truth altogether. "I am certain of nothing," Keats wrote to Benjamin Bailey, "but of the Holiness of the heart's affections and the truth of Imagination—What the imagination seizes as Beauty must be truth."[55] The New Critics continued the critical break that was emerging here, the contention or the suspicion that the advance of science is incompatible with the advance of art, that it corrupts the imagination, restricts the ability to think in terms of symbol and myth. For the Humanists the general outcome of this bifurcation was lamentable. That reason, observation, judgment, discipline, and control, should be judged accepted tools of the scientist exclusively and the free imagination the prerogative of the poets was a wholesale

[53] Eliot, *Sacred Wood,* pp. 2–5, 13–14, 37–38.

[54] Cleanth Brooks, Yvor Winters, R. P. Blackmur, Robert Penn Warren, and I. A. Richards are also identified with this group.

[55] Abrams, *Mirror and the Lamp,* pp. 299–327. The quotations are on pp. 313, 315.

violation of priorities. The New Critics feared the scientific encroachments, and, like the Humanists, were antiromantic; but they were also very much concerned with establishing strictly aesthetic standards.

The New Critics' aversion to modernity led them to an aesthetic retreat that was much more emphatic than the antinaturalism of Babbitt and More. The New Critics particularly wanted to cultivate a poetic language different from that of science, insisting that poetic knowledge is a distinct and separate kind not accessible to the cognitive tools of science. Ransom carefully defended this ontological dimension of poetry. Poetry, he believed, can treat "an order of existence, a grade of objectivity, which cannot be treated in scientific discourse." Tate further explained in 1941 in "The Present Function of Criticism" that criticism's main role should be to "maintain and demonstrate the special, unique, and complete knowledge which the great forms of literature afford us."[56] But Tate was also a moralist, and like most of the Agrarians he sought to oppose naturalistic philosophies by shoring up the fundamentals of the Christian faith. In this respect the Agrarians shared more with Eliot than with the Humanists, whose dualism was avowedly empirical (see chapter 7). But even in this respect some critical differences remain. For Tate the aesthetic absolutes could not substitute for, or even combine with, religious and intellectual functions as Eliot insisted. Tate, then, adhered to an extreme aesthetic criticism that carefully segregated the realms of the moral, the intellectual, and the aesthetic. It was Paul More whom he cited for the worst offenses in mixing these together. As a critic More suffered from the moral demands he made on the artist, subordinating those to any consideration for the techniques of poetry and its peculiar aesthetic qualities. The result, Tate felt, was a "moral mechanism" that made "morality for morality's sake" More's critical rule of thumb.[57]

Tate certainly touched here on one of the difficult problems of the New Humanists' criticism. Humanists were always quick to deny that they were defending a didactic poetry, though their opponents were equally ready to label them "moral monsters." The Humanists no doubt hopelessly entangled the moral and aesthetic, and for this reason their usefulness as critics and appreciators of art suffered. But in 1938 G. R. Elliott tried to set the Humanist position straight and dissociate his group from the charges of a narrow didacticism. He insisted that great art is not so because it is moral, but that "it is moral because it is great. It does not strive for moral values; it attains these incidentally while striving for more

[56] Quoted in Sutton, pp. 100, 124.

[57] Alan Tate, "The Fallacy of Humanism," in C. Hartley Grattan, ed., *The Critique of Humanism* (New York, 1930), pp. 54–59.

inclusive forms of experience."[58] The moral should be seen as an adjunct of the normal and representative in human experience, a postulate that assured the Humanists that the quest for the universal was also a means of ethical insight.

On several points the Humanists' aesthetic was vulnerable and merited the criticism it received. But on other issues it received only a smug dismissal from the modern aesthetes. The Humanists were clearly correct in instructing the moderns that the individualistic cult had deprived criticism of meaningful standards. And the question of standards was worth a hearing, especially in an age of triumphant relativism. For a considerable time in America the Humanists were the only group that was willing to raise this question. They sought above all to distinguish what was valuable in art, what was permanent and of universal appeal, from what was not. The impressionist critics were inadequate to that task, for to ask only whether an artist succeeded in expressing himself was to utilize a merely quantitative measure that knew not the difference between a work of genius and a baby's cry. The Humanist criteria at least made it possible to insist that art do more than register the temperamental anguish of the private soul and to demand that the critic tell us more about the work of art than about his own experience with it. Nevertheless, the Humanist aesthetic was itself clearly inadequate as a solution to the problem. Although Babbitt and More were not so insensitive to the individual personality in the creative life as their opponents accused, they were little concerned with the creative process itself, were much more concerned with results. Probably they tried too much to contain art in a formula. Their demand that art reflect an interplay of the individual and the universal, the permanent and the flux, could indeed serve as a useful standard for the critic, but it was not much help to the artist. Furthermore, Humanist opponents were largely right in denying the usefulness of emotional self-denial and restraint to the individual creator. This is a difficult question, but surely a position so categorical as the Humanists', or T. S. Eliot's for that matter, was insensitive and extreme. Many would go so far as to say that the notion of self-denial was the very extinction of the artist's existence, and it is hard not to be sympathetic to Henry-Russell Hitchcock's proclamation that "the Artist calls for bread and the Humanist offers him the stone of renunciation."[59] It could be argued too that the Humanists were too narrow and selective in their aesthetic criteria, that they were insensitive to the variety and diversity of aesthetic experience. Opponents also over-

[58] *Humanism and Imagination* (Chapel Hill, N.C., 1938), p. 15.
[59] Henry-Russell Hitchcock, "Humanism and the Fine Arts," in Grattan, p. 229.

stated this weakness, but one does miss in the Humanists a zest for the merely pleasurable and imaginative, and this lack was to show in their own approach to modern literature. They had little use for a Poe, or for a Balzac who could capture vividly the life and color of a particular time and place. These deficiencies nonetheless do not wholly disqualify the Humanists' attempt, coming at the end of a decade or more of aesthetic protest, to reverse the tide of criticism in favor of the representative and universal as meaningful standards of judgment.

Part II

HUMANISM AND MODERN AMERICA

CHAPTER FOUR

The Battle of the Books

I love few pictures, few operas, few statues, and few poems, and yet I am a great lover of the arts.

—Joseph Joubert

The basic problems of contemporary literature are, for the thoughtful and responsible writer, manifold in appearance but in essence simple: How to present a view of life both wise and brave, answering to experience as well as to desire, serviceable in art or in the daily walk. Single in essence, in appearance they are manifold: How to give pleasure without corrupting the heart, and how to give wisdom without chilling it. How to bring into play the great pleasures of men without unchaining the beast. How to believe in Darwin and the dignity of man. How to recognize the role of the nerves in human action without paralyzing the nerve of action. How to admit the weakness of man without debasing his heroism. How to see his acts and respect his intentions. How to renounce his superstitions and retain his faith. How to rebuke without despising him. How to reform society without rebelling against it. How to laugh at its follies without falling into contempt. How to believe that evil is fleeting forever before good, but will never be overtaken and slain. How to look back upon a thousand defeats, and yet cling to the fighting hope.

—Stuart Sherman

FOR THE HUMANISTS the aesthetic question was not a narrow theoretical issue. Rather it was a practical question that shaped their own role in the critical warfare of the early twentieth century and engaged the younger members of their group in one of the liveliest of the contemporary literary debates. And though it must be admitted at the outset that the Humanists showed little more than contempt for the new efforts in prose and poetry, it is also difficult, even in retrospect, to say just why this reaction was so strong. Humanist criticism was often vague and generalized, showing little attention to individual differences among novelists and poets and all too ready to dismiss the lot of them with the wave of a hand. It was quick to scent symptoms of naturalism and romanticism as though these sufficed in themselves to discredit the new efforts. Given the imprecision of their analysis, one is often left to conclude that much of the Humanist reaction was a matter of style. Their case against American literature was so interwoven with their case against modern American life that literary and social criticism became hopelessly mixed. The new American letters suffered because it was so close to home, so reflective of the real and unpleasant world outside. And in the face of this contemporaneousness, Sherman and More retreated to the American literary past to find the models of excellence and literary sobriety that eluded them in their own day.

The first outlines of a Humanist movement appeared at a time when realism had become the major tradition and style of American literature. Realism had succeeded in sweeping away the overripe idealism and gentility of an earlier day and joined with a new spirit of honesty and moral fervor in America at large to get at the facts of American life. But it is important to note also that the New Humanism was growing to maturity precisely at a time when a new style and a new shift in perspective were occurring within realism itself. As Warner Berthoff has indicated, a second generation of American realists, born after 1869 and coming to maturity around 1900, was now influencing literature. Significantly, the members of this group were most often the second-generation sons and daughters of the mass migratory movements from Europe to the United States (Theodore Dreiser, Gertrude Stein, Carl Sandburg) or they were products of the internal disruptions and fluidity of American life itself (Jack London and Sherwood Anderson). This group seemed to show little of the sense of certainty and control, the mastery of events of the first generation. Much of the new literature was a response to the drift, the uncertainty, the flux of American life. The effect very often was to throw the writers back upon themselves in an effort to discover first the truths of private experience amid the confusion without. Furthermore, this perspective helps to explain much of the new naturalism in the United States and its particular style in this country. The Humanists were partially correct in seeing in American literature a mixing of naturalism and romanticism, the fatal combination that signified to them the central decadence of modern culture. As John McCormick has suggested, American romanticism, as evidenced by Emerson and Thoreau, had always illustrated a certain discipline of fact, an attention to detail. There is a continuity of style, then, in the heavy documentation of American life, the new world of cities and factories, that coexists with the romantic quest for self and the intimate truth of personal experience in the new writing. The realistic perspective, furthermore, permitted novelists to demonstrate the working of a purposeless and mechanical universe, the forces of a Darwinian chaos, which in turn lent drama to the search for individual truth in a world without ultimate meaning.[1]

[1] Berthoff, *The Ferment of Realism* (New York, 1965), pp. 220–23; McCormick,

It was not the Humanists alone who were sensitive to the new style. Henry Seidel Canby noted that a marked subjectivism persisted in the new literature along with the scientific obsession with fact and detail. What Canby called the "new romanticism" differed from the melancholy of a Byron or the enthusiasm of a Wordsworth. Canby believed that although most of the new writers were romantic in mood, they were realistic in their contact with life. "It has been the hard realism of an unfriendly world," he wrote, "that has scraped them to the raw, and they retaliate by describing all the unpleasant things they remember." Canby believed this retreat was a kind of romantic escape into self and attributed the pattern, much in the fashion of the Humanists, to the loss in the modern age of a central philosophy of life, to a core of unity or body of general truths that transcended individual experience.[2] Here too it was the question of style that bothered the Humanists, and Sherman especially was anxious to explore the American tradition in letters to rediscover what had been lost in the confusion of the modern age.

This theme helps to explain part of the Humanist reaction to modern literature, but there were other factors as well. A different kind of rebellion was under way in the years before the First World War, and as Henry F. May has shown, its roots were various and complex. Some of it drew inspiration from the French poetic revolt of the late nineteenth century, from the amoralists Baudelaire, Verlaine, and Rimbaud, who rejected modern civilization in pursuit of the exotic and who became defenders of a new aestheticism. With the same spirit American experimenters in verse, Ezra Pound, Eliot, Amy Lowell, and later E. E. Cummings, made their appearance. The new poetic celebrated free individual expression and cultivated spontaneity and subjectivism. Even before the war the small towns of the drab American interior sent young literary rebels to Chicago, New York, and to the older eastern universities where they conducted an aesthetic reaction against the inherited nineteenth-century values of material progress. New products of the aesthetic retreat won considerable attention: the *Literary Review,* the *Chicago Evening Post,* the *Smart Set,* the *Seven Arts.*[3] Thus at the same time that Irving Babbitt's *Masters of*

The Middle Distance (New York, 1971), pp. 9–12. The review here, and what follows, is not intended to comprehend all the new developments in American letters. The Humanists themselves were barely cognizant of many of the changes, and often then in only a superficial way. The general outline here mostly anticipates the Humanists' criticism, considered below.

[2] Canby, *Definitions: Essays in Contemporary Criticism, First Series* (1922; rpt. Port Washington, N.Y., 1967), pp. 153–59; idem., *Definitions: Essays in Contemporary Criticism, Second Series* (1924; rpt. Port Washington, N.Y., 1967), p. 155.

[3] May, *The End of American Innocence* (London, 1959), pp. 193–94, 216, 241, 249–74.

Modern French Criticism was offering a vigorous defense of classical principles in art, much of the literary community in America was becoming indifferent or hostile to traditional values.

Whether the early literature of the twentieth century was a matter of poetic retreat from life or a wholesale immersion in the world of experience, many of the critics felt that literature itself was not the only question that counted. "What is the use of criticizing modern literature," Canby asked, "unless you are willing to criticize modern life?" Nor was he the only one to see the issue in this way. There was a sense of urgency about criticism in the postwar period, an urgency that linked novels and poems to the wider questions of politics, economics, society, and morals. Another prominent critic, Ludwig Lewisohn, spoke to this issue: "It was profoundly if not always consciously understood," he said, "that criticism cleaves deep and that the battle joined . . . between Stuart Sherman and Henry Mencken, was no squabble between rhetoriticians, but a philosophical warfare over all that men hold dearest and over the future of our civilization itself."[4]

Critical rivalries were sharp and clearly drawn, often so much so that antagonists, sensitive to their differences, ignored shared sympathies. Indeed, this is one of the striking facts about the whole series of critical debates that took place. Babbitt and More especially had serious differences with the writers and critics of their age, but there was much that they shared in common. The New Humanists, no less than H. L. Mencken or Van Wyck Brooks, were part of an important phenomenon of their day, the celebrated "revolt of the highbrow." No matter how liberal or conservative their own temperaments, the intellectuals of the postwar period often denounced with one voice an America they judged a spiritual failure. They saw in their country a people that had waxed rich and powerful by trading on their material and practical skills, but failed to give breathing space to their writers and artists. In dozens of novels, from Floyd Dell's *Moon-Calf* to Ben Hecht's *Erik Dorn,* the flight from democracy and the blight of a business civilization was a common theme.[5] An America that offered the picture of open and unrestrained pursuit of physical comforts on the one hand and a conformist mentality and organized fear of ideas on the other was more than an amusing contradiction; for the intellectuals it was the source of their disaffection and the object of their abuse. The Humanists shared in that condemnation.

The chief foe of many intellectuals was a carefully constructed symbol

[4] Canby, *Definitions, First Series,* p. 128; Lewisohn, *Expression in America* (London [1932]), p. 426.

[5] Frederick J. Hoffman, *The Twenties* (New York, 1949), pp. 27, 30.

of their own making, the American Puritan. On his shoulders was laid the blame for the spiritual failures of a moralistic and aesthetically numb America. He was the prohibitionist, the censor, the preacher, the member of the local PTA. To Randolph Bourne, a democrat and socialist, the Puritan was a public menace; to Mencken, an elitist and defender of capitalism, he was also a public nuisance. Both saw in their Puritan model an avowed "will to power" that had become a powerful agent of repression and conformity in the community and a threat to free thought and creativity. Mencken, for example, traced the modern Puritan to his historical ancestor. The early Puritan, he said, exercised a profound concern for the salvation of his soul and kept his eyes focused on heaven. But with the decline of the religious spirit a national and secularized Puritanism emerged. Now, Mencken said, the American Puritan became concerned not only with the rescue of his own soul but felt as well "an irresistible impulse to hand salvation on . . . to ram it down reluctant throats, to make it free, universal and compulsory." For Mencken the modern Puritan was a self-righteous moralist who, in the things of the mind, feared the new and different. The result was "comstockery," "a sinister and ever-present menace to all men of ideas." Mencken followed the impact of Puritanism through the literary past and saw also the toll it exacted on modern literature. The greatest hindrance to good writing, he felt, was the national dread of free inquiry—the final upshot of Puritanism.[6]

The anti-Puritan crusade was part of a wider rebellion: the revolt against traditional America. Much of it was caricature, such as Mencken's jibes at the rural and fundamentalist South and Midwest in his *American Mercury* and in his essays. But elsewhere the discontent was deep and serious. It was symbolized in part by the predominance of small-town refugees in Chicago, New York, and Parisian expatriate circles. These literary rebels offered intensely personal accounts of the small towns and villages of the American heartland—the endless boredom of their lives and their own revolt from spiritual impoverishment. The documentation appeared in the antimidwestern novels that were introduced in the decade following the war: Glenway Wescott's *The Apple of the Eye* and *Good-Bye Wisconsin*, Carl Van Vechten's *The Tattooed Countess* and *A Preface to Life*, Edith Wharton's *Hudson River Bracketed*, and Sherwood Anderson's *Winesburg, Ohio*.[7]

A similar mixture of protest and escape entered into the treatment of sex, which became virtually a new theme in American literature. The

---

[6] H. L. Mencken, *A Book of Prefaces* (Garden City, N.Y., 1917), pp. 235–39. See also Randolph Bourne, "The Puritan's Will to Power," *Seven Arts,* 1 (1916–17), 634–36.

[7] Hoffman, *The Twenties,* pp. 49, 371–77.

emphasis here merged with the vogue of Freud and copied the psychoanalytic technique of self-revelation, the raising of suppressed truth to the surface of consciousness. But it fitted also the general mood of freedom from repression and the liberation of the individual from a restrictive social code. Sex was prominent in many of the popular novels: Fizgerald's *This Side of Paradise;* Ben Hecht's *Erik Dorn, Gargoyles,* and *Humpty-Dumpty;* Floyd Dell's *Moon-Calf* and *Janet March*; Sherwood Anderson's *Windy McPherson's Son, Many Marriages,* and *Dark Laughter*; Waldo Frank's *The Unwelcome Man* and *The Dark Mother*; Maxwell Bodenheim's *Blackguard.* The heroes in these works were usually outcasts by choice, and their personal resistance to established mores dictated their behavior. Literature became one manifestation of the anti-Puritan protest.[8]

By temperament and doctrine the New Humanists were defenders of tradition. The sense of the past and the search for the best within it offered one of the surest restraints against the appeal of the moment; this could provide a more useful frame of reference than the romantic whim of the original genius. Against drift and confusion Babbitt prescribed a reawakened sense of the literary past. He and More particularly looked to the great classics and were less inclined than Sherman to give a national content to this quest. But they too knew that America needed a revitalization of its own traditions. Sherman began his examination of the American literary past on the wave of patriotic fervor that he carried from the war. He urged writers to look to the past for the source of a new cultural renaissance in America and for its liberation from the constraints of the present. We grow dull and unadventurous, not because we are traditionalists, but because we have ceased to feel the formative spirit of our traditions. But this was not the sole motivation in Sherman's turn to the past. "I conceive of literature," he said, "as a partner of politics, religion, and morals." Literature must be important to the average man and woman, it must promote democratic Humanism, and Emerson, Whitman, and Twain could be useful weapons in that effort. His, and, in fact, all the critics' examinations of the American past in letters were selective ones. Each found materials to fit his model for the present.[9]

There was no quarrel, then, with Van Wyck Brooks when he wrote that the past yields "only what we are able to look for in it. And what people find in literature corresponds precisely with what they find in life."[10] Both

[8] Ibid., pp. 236–37.

[9] Irving Babbitt, "Are the English Critical?" *Nation,* 94 (1928), 311; Stuart P. Sherman, *Americans* (New York, 1922), p. 26; Jacob Zeitlin and Homer Woodbridge, eds., *Life and Letters of Stuart P. Sherman* (New York, 1929), II, 680.

[10] Quoted in Richard Ruland, *The Rediscovery of American Literature* (Cambridge, Mass., 1967), p. 7.

Sherman and Brooks were students of Babbitt at Harvard; but whereas one became for a while a faithful disciple, the other was a wayward son. Brooks's *The Wine of the Puritans* (1908) and *America's Coming-of-Age* (1915) established him as the leader of the "young critics" and placed him in the center of the quarrel with the Humanists.

Brooks joined his assault on the American past with a wider attack on Puritanism in general. He found in the culture of the Puritans the dominant force in all American history and traced to it the cultural failures of the nation. Brooks recognized that America began as a country pioneering in material enterprises and that the overwhelming demands on its physical resources created a culture that was suitable only to commercial and material interests. Puritanism, Brooks argued, suppressed the creative or aesthetic energies to assure that the practical and physical energies were available for the business at hand—the physical development of the nation. All things here conspired to guard against purely intellectual and artistic pursuits; these were thwarted and redirected into other channels. Puritanism was "a complete philosophy for the pioneer." It made contemptible the purely aesthetic joys of life and thus "cleared the decks for practical action." Whatever there was of intellect and culture was wholly divorced from the workaday world. The "fine eternal ideas" of Puritan theology threw no light on the Puritan's business affairs; nothing, at least, to moderate the catchpenny opportunism that quickly became America's all-consuming passion. [11]

The divorce between what Brooks called the "highbrow" and the "lowbrow"—the artist and the philistine—began with Puritanism and persisted thereafter. Brooks found that fact reflected in nearly every major American writer from Edwards, to Emerson, to Hawthorne, and to Poe. Walt Whitman was the only exception to this tradition. In the great poet of democracy, Brooks felt, "we have the rudiments of a middle tradition." Whitman was valuable because he put his idealism to work and never lost it in mere sentimentality. Alone of the American poets he could touch the hearts and lives of the average person, combining action, theory, idealism, and business into "a fresh democratic ideal." [12]

But there was an important ulterior consideration to Brooks's condemnation, and he spoke frankly in writing that "if my soul were set on the accumulation of dollars not one of [these American writers] would have the power to move me from it." That was the whole point. American literature

[11] Van Wyck Brooks, "The Critics and Young America," in Joel E. Spingarn, ed., *Criticism in America* (New York, 1924), p.121; Brooks, *America's Coming-of-Age* (New York, 1915), p. 9.

[12] Brooks, *America's Coming-of-Age*, pp. 112–18.

was a failure because it had not prevented the emergence of a society that the socialist Brooks disdained—a society that was individualistic and capitalistic. But the blame was not to rest with the writers alone. Brooks's attack indicted the American experience itself. Its literature failed because Americans wanted it that way. The American soul, Brooks said, did not want to be moved from the accumulation of dollars. "The immense, vague cloud-canopy of idealism which hung over the American people during the nineteenth century was never permitted . . . to interfere with the practical conduct of life." [13]

Brooks thought that his account of the American past helped to explain the plight of the artist in the twentieth century. He still found the creative pursuits under heavy repression. From childhood, he said, the American is taught to repress anything that conflicts with the material welfare of the race. The American environment itself, Brooks thought, was so depleted of all that might nourish the imagination that artists were unable to turn upon it and infuse it with a spiritual content. Brooks did see a new generation of writers emerging in the United States and hailed their advent. But he observed also that they were wholly unprepared for the tasks they had set for themselves. There was a new but wasteful outpouring of emotional energy, for the American writer had no tradition worthy of emulation and no spiritual quarters in a business world. The result was confusion and incoherence. "Our society," Brooks warned, "is rapidly breeding a race of Hamlets the like of which has hardly been seen before." [14]

The American literary tradition was under attack from the Right as well as the Left. Both H. L. Mencken and Brooks elaborated the Puritan myths, and Mencken too charged that the Puritans feared the aesthetic life as a distraction from more compelling matters. Mencken, however, coupled this criticism with his utter disdain for American democracy, and it too became his whipping boy. He believed that democracy had ruined the arts in America, subjecting the canons of taste to a "commonwealth of peasants and small traders," a whole nation of philistines that wielded as much power in matters of taste as they did in the voting booth, and with equally disastrous effects. He appraised America's literary tradition in a manner similar to Brooks's. "One is conscious [in that tradition] of no brave and noble earnestness," he wrote, ". . . no generalized passion for intellectual and spiritual adventure . . . no organized determination to think things out." Mencken was left to wonder with Brooks whether it was the fate of Americans to develop only the practical skills, "the wood-hewing and

[13] Ibid., pp. 44–45.

[14] Brooks, "Critics and Young America," pp. 133–34, 147, 143–44.

water-drawing of the race," and live forever under a pious and sentimental morality that passed as literature.[15]

But here again the ultimate responsibility for failure rested not with the artists themselves but with the larger national society. Mencken could find no real tradition in the American past, only the rebellion of individual suffering souls against the mediocrity of American life. If there was any tradition at all it was that of the abused and misunderstood artist who was forced into rebellion or retreat. That view fit suitably his whole contempt for democratic culture. Democratic life meant the domination of the small man and the reign of the herd. The hallmark of its society was bigotry, intolerance, and a perverse fear of the new and unknown. "The one permanent emotion of the inferior man . . . is fear. . . . What he wants beyond everything else is safety. His instincts incline him toward a society so organized that it will protect him at all hazards, and not only against perils to his hide but also against assaults upon his mind." The absence of a civilized aristocracy was the greatest source of spiritual failure in America, and against the democrat the artist had no chance. The intellectual audacity and passion that Mencken found so weak in the American literary past could thrive only among an aristocratic class secure in its position and animated by an intellectual curiosity superior to the timidity and sentimentality of the mob. The Puritan and the democrat in their national character set Americans to turning all aesthetic endeavors into moral questions that denied the individual the right to stand on his own merits as an artist.[16]

The defense of the past undertaken by the Humanists imposed a considerable job of reconstruction. Stuart Sherman decided that iconoclasm had gone too far. It was imperative to reverse the tide of criticism and meet the enemy head-on with a vigorous defense of Puritanism. Sherman joined his Humanism and his nationalism and labeled Puritanism the American principle in life and letters. He would make his model acceptable by outfitting him in new clothes. The Puritan that became a Humanist was then shorn of the bigotry and narrow-mindedness that led to his ostracism among the intellectuals. Sherman defined his Puritan as an individualist motivated by his concern for self-perfection. "The revolt of the Puritan," he said, "is always inspired by his zeal for improvement, by his passion for perfection." For the Puritan did not revolt out of sheer love for rebellion. His path led to self-discipline and the higher life, never to

---

[15] H. L. Mencken, *Prejudices: Second Series* (New York, 1920), pp. 16, 20; idem., *Book of Prefaces*, p. 210; Ruland, p. 132.

[16] Ruland, pp. 130–31; Mencken, *Prejudices: Second Series*, pp. 69–77; idem., *Book of Prefaces*, pp. 226–27.

the complete break with all restraints sought by the moderns. "Puritanism, rightly understood, is one of the vital, progressive, and enriching human traditions."[17]

It was clear that the Puritan of Brooks and Mencken was not the Puritan of Sherman. But the models were useful nonetheless. When Sherman defended Puritanism he defended all that comprised the "national genius." Sherman's defense, then, was not a mere endorsement of an historical figure but wholesale support for the American tradition in general, and its most vital expression in literature. Sherman knew, as did the others, that his review of the past would arm him for his own campaign for modern America, that the American classics would yield the spiritual content of his "religion of democracy" and "the profound moral idealism" that he judged to be the strength of the American character. In varying degrees the other Humanists joined in Sherman's resurrection of the American tradition, but the "usable past" would reveal sharp differences among the Humanists too.

In Emerson, Sherman found his favorite model—a humanist and democrat. He concurred with Matthew Arnold's assessment of Emerson as a "friend and aider of those who would live in the spirit." To many a lonely individual, Sherman said, Emerson has come to the rescue, "as with the sound of a magical trumpet, shattering the dungeons of fear." We think rightly of Emerson "when we think of him as a humanist bent upon liberating and developing . . . all of the properly human powers." Sherman prepared his own case against contemporary literature by comparing Emerson as a rebel in his own time with the revolt of the young artist that Sherman witnessed in his. Against the "emancipation" declared by the modern set, Sherman posed the restrained and critical protest of Emerson. The moderns, Sherman charged, discarded outworn clothes, but then preferred to go naked rather than seek new raiments. But the best of man seeks not the freedom of the beasts; he advances upward rather than outward. Here Emerson was the better model. He was critical toward the past, but determined to preserve the best of it as reform of the present. The true liberator, Sherman advised, does not set the ship adrift; he gives it new direction.[18]

Emerson's optimism and faith in the common man appealed to Sherman the democrat, and his critical and discriminating respect for standards to Sherman the Humanist. For the Emerson that Sherman defended was

[17] Sherman, *Americans*, pp. 136–37; idem., "The Belligerent Young," *Literary Review*, 2 (Jan. 14, 1922), 1–2; idem., *The Genius of America* (New York, 1923), p. 53.

[18] Sherman, *Americans*, pp. 73–74, 120, 107, 76–77.

neither a blind romantic nor a leveler. Emerson was not prepared to submit matters of taste to the mob, and recognized that along with the political reforms of the day the improvement of human society must rely on the moral and intellectual regeneration of men. Here was Emerson the Puritan, a battler against the external forces and materialism of his own day that hindered spiritual advancement. All these qualities won Sherman. He believed that Emerson had done more than any other man to establish the right notion of a "good American." And that was the most important kind of influence any writer could exert.[19]

Babbitt was frankly appalled at Sherman's "panegyric" on Emerson and told him so. He thought that his former pupil's democratic enthusiasm had run away with his Humanism and led him to what the mentor considered a dangerously distorted appraisal of the Concord sage. Babbitt himself considered Emerson a dangerous man. He conceded only that Emerson had done some good in emphasizing the need for selection, but he was guilty nonetheless of encouraging those who were anything but selective, who were undisciplined and untraditional. Perhaps it was the fault of Jonathan Edwards, Babbitt wrote, to overstate the power of sin in. the human breast. But that was to err in the right direction, for Edwards was only exaggerating facts. But Emerson and the Rousseauists (and there was the vital link), by denying the "intrinsic evil in human nature," were repudiating facts. Emerson's divine expansiveness and exaltation, Babbitt feared, might lead the naive to believe that the reality of evil may be charmed away by a sort of emotional intoxication. Emerson's call to plant oneself squarely on one's instincts was lethal. It is all too likely that the man who plants himself squarely on his instincts will plant himself squarely on "his own crudity." Babbitt saw Emerson as a departure from the Puritan tradition, not as an essential link with it as did Sherman. Babbitt too defended that tradition and believed that in the face of the romantic and naturalistic decadence of the present, it was only the "capital of moral energy inherited from Puritanism" that kept the nation from going off the deep end.[20]

In his *Shelburne Essays* Paul Elmer More gave much attention to the early American literature that he saw as the fruition of a refined and wholesome Puritanism. Never as ardent in defense as his younger friend Sherman, More nonetheless considerably strengthened the Humanist case for the Puritans. When More considered "The Spirit and Poetry of Early New England," he found in the art of the Puritans "that sense of something

[19] Ibid., pp. 100–105, 113, 72–73.

[20] Irving Babbitt, *The Masters of Modern French Criticism* (1912; rpt. New York, 1963), pp. 354–61; idem., *Spanish Character and Other Essays* (Boston, 1940), p. 166.

central and formative in man, of character as distinguished from the mere portrayal of unrelated passions." The moral quality of the earlier literature and the sense of fire and hearth that lingered in it both appealed to More. His own personality blended strongly in his admiration for one of its constant motifs—"the peaceful affections of home, the cool and quiet places out of the turmoil of the world's contentions." If there was a dearth of love poetry then, the "erotic Muse" had more than made up for it since. More in fact admitted that he still preferred James Russell Lowell's *Under the Willows* to the "self-advertised passion" of a contemporary poetess who bore the family name. He saw the strength of the Puritan literary tradition coming out of crude but healthy beginnings in Michael Wigglesworth and Anne Bradstreet and growing rich and live in Cambridge and Concord later. The "fragile beauty" that runs throughout was "the fairest thing this country has produced." "At its best the poetry of New England is one of the very desirable possessions of the world, and not to appreciate it is to prove one's self dulled and vulgarized by the strident conceit of modernity."[21]

Though More was a confirmed admirer of Emerson, he shared reservations similar to Babbitt's. He too, as the title of his essay showed, was concerned about "The Influence of Emerson." Emerson's divine light, he feared, had attracted a lot of bats and insects of the night. He was "mischievous to weak minds," dynamite in the wrong hands. The Emersonian influence, unfortunately corrupted, was raising havoc in American life. It had wrought in religion, politics, and literature, "a perilous dizziness of the brain." Emerson's terms for personal salvation and spiritual uplift were too easy. "If we may believe him," More said, "a man shall walk out under the open sky and breathe the sweet influences of the spirit as cheaply as he inhales the untainted breeze." Emerson failed to condition his spiritual therapy on some discipline of the emotions and the reason and drew to his philosophy many who were incapable of these restraints. But More did not want to lay at Emerson's door "the whole evil of a faded and vulgarized transcendentalism." He considered himself "a lover" of Emerson and believed that, properly read and followed, Emerson remained an enduring source of spiritual strength.[22]

The Emerson of Brooks and Mencken bore scant resemblance to that of Sherman, and that of Sherman to Babbitt's and More's. Each let his view of the present influence his vision of the past. Mencken clearly ex-

[21] Paul Elmer More, *A New England Group and Others* (1921; rpt. New York, 1967), pp. 7, 24–25, 31–32.

[22] Paul Elmer More, *Shelburne Essays: First Series* (1904; rpt. New York, 1967), pp. 76–79, 72.

hibited that habit in this judgment of Emerson's writings: "I can imagine nothing better suited to the spiritual needs of used-car dealers, trust company vice-presidents, bath-fixture magnates, and the like, gathered together in the sight of God to take cheer from one another and shove the Republic along its rocky road." Mencken therefore could see in Emerson only what he saw in modern America, "a philosophy made for soaring American business men."[23] Again the clash served to illuminate the points of contention between the opposing factions.

On his retreat to Shelburne, New Hampshire, in 1903, More wrote the first of his essays that bear its name. His subject was Thoreau, whom he read in a secluded setting not unlike that of Walden Pond. More was sympathetic to Thoreau, more than he was to his transcendentalist friend, and his appraisal of Thoreau was one of the strongest defenses of the American literary tradition. More was struck particularly by Thoreau's treatment of nature. He might have expected to find in his prose and poetry much that was typical of a romantic age's worship of nature and the natural man. But he saw in Thoreau none of the "self-abandonment" of a Keats, or the "unearthly mysticism" of a Shelley, or the revolutionary fervor of a Byron. Thoreau abstained from any "effeminate" pantheistic reverie or forest daydreaming in his confrontation with the natural world. Nature to him was something quite different from the traditional conception of the romantic. "We have not seen pure Nature," More quoted Thoreau, "unless we have seen her thus vast and drear and inhuman." "Nature was to him," More wrote, "a discipline of the will as much as a stimulant to the imagination." Thoreau would, in his own words, "combine the hardiness of the savages with the intellectualness of the civilized man." Furthermore, Puritan tradition gave to Thoreau's writing a moral quality that further recommended it to More. That element, he felt, saved Thoreau from the "moral dissipation," the renunciation of standards and the undisciplined revolt against traditional values characteristic of the romantic.[24]

Both Sherman and More found in Hawthorne the literary mind at its best in America. Sherman credited Hawthorne with the same qualities that More found in Thoreau. Hawthorne was also a close observer of nature and external fact. But by background and personality Hawthorne was led to the visible world as the sphere of the spiritual and moral. To these he gave "reality, importance, and supreme interest." External nature was above all symbolic, and Hawthorne's involvement with it was conscientiously a search for ulterior meaning and spiritual significance, the moral realities

[23] Quoted in Ruland, p. 125.

[24] More, *Shelburne Essays: First Series,* p. 20.

that a lingering Puritanism perpetuated in the author's sense of life. Hawthorne surpassed most of the contemporary writers whom Sherman saw wallowing in the muck and mire of their flaunted "realism," those who compiled endless details from the sordid side of life with no ability to see beyond these to a higher reality. Hawthorne, though, exhibited "a certain disdain . . . for the immediate gross reports of the senses." He put his imagination to work to contrive an escape from the "vulgar and humdrum" and catch a glimpse of a transcendent meaning in life. Hawthorne for Sherman was both Puritan and American. He agreed with the judgment of Henry James that *The Scarlet Letter* sprang from the American soil and belonged to the national genius.[25]

More too called on Hawthorne to testify for the viability of the Puritan tradition, "the distinct mark of the American temperament," in the national letters. But it was the sense of sin and solitude, a sense that More saw drained from the modern world through its unreflecting hedonism, that confirmed Hawthorne's usefulness to him, for the Puritan Hawthorne recognized the war in the cave as an immovable reality. "All the intensity of the Puritan nature remained in him, and all the overwhelming sense of the heinousness of human depravity." More saw throughout Hawthorne's writings the constant theme of the isolated individual, separated from the community of his fellows by the oppressive weight of sin. His characters play out their lives against that force in a pattern of tragedy that makes Hawthorne's art comparable to that of Aeschylus.[26]

Not surprisingly, though, it was Walt Whitman who offered Sherman the most help in his defense of the American character. His democratic enthusiasm, his nationalism, and his spiritual vision made Whitman a vital cornerstone in Sherman's reconstruction of the American past. The Whitman that Sherman defended was no noisy braggart, no poet of the common and humdrum. Whitman was the veritable ethos of the American people, "the poetic interpreter of their political and social ideals." That was the high quality that Sherman was anxious to hold for modern writers. For Whitman recognized that there is only one way by which a poet can win the permanent interest of the American people. He must help them unfold the meanings and fulfill the promises of their democratic traditions. Whitman did that by establishing as the imaginative and emotional theme

[25] Sherman, *Americans,* pp. 126–27, 145. Here in fact Sherman saved Hawthorne from the realistic tradition, but he did so by finding in Hawthorne qualities that were in fact possibly romantic in their tendencies. On the other hand, in More's assessment, which follows here, the effort is to exonerate Hawthorne of any romantic affiliation.

[26] More, *Shelburne Essays: First Series,* pp. 23–40, 45 (the quotation).

of his art a "sublime and serious Religious Democracy." He had the vision that could raise the democratic potential to new heights, the spiritual vigor and strength that Sherman saw as modern America's greatest need.[27] Here the liberal side of Humanism merged with the critical rebellion of Brooks.

Babbitt's assessment of Whitman, on the other hand, revealed how fully the Harvard professor was out of touch with the American tradition and the extent of his breach with Sherman. The "primitivistic revery" of Whitman left Babbitt cold, and he contrasted the discipline and self-control of the genuine spirituality of a Buddha with the shallowness of Whitman's mystic meandering. He saw in Whitman a general dissipation that had relaxed his grip on the hard realities of life and blinded him to the qualitative distinctions that distinguished a meaningful spiritual quest from romantic dizziness. Whitman was something of an American Rousseau and emerged in Babbitt's judgment a mere "cosmic loafer." And these offenses were compounded by Whitman's humanitarianism. Here was another romantic corruption. Like Rousseau, Babbitt charged, Whitman tried to balance his individualism and self-worship with a benevolent kiss for all mankind. But both emotions were only the expansive instincts unleashed and "the explosion of egoism" that fathered a "fraternal anarchy" after it was only the usual romantic escape from discipline.[28]

Finally, around Mark Twain the entire debate about the past was joined. Nothing better registered Sherman's democratic inclinations than his warm endorsement of Twain. Sherman admitted finding little of the Humanist elements of discipline and the higher life in Twain, but he championed Twain nonetheless as one of the most valuable writers for Americans. Twain, Sherman said, does not give us much help toward realizing our best selves. "But he is a rock of refuge when the ordinary self—'the divine average' is in danger." Sherman stated the difficulty of living always at "the highest level," a fact that perhaps More and Babbitt knew but were reluctant to allow. "The divine average" was indeed a live concern to Sherman, and he looked to the wholesome strength and character of Twain to raise it. Sherman called Twain a bulwark against the insidious forces that threatened to corrode the American fiber—"anaemic refinements, cosmopolitan decadencies, Teutonic heresies, imperial lusts, fraud and corruption." Against these, Twain is a reminder of our wholesome better selves and a booster for the democratic spirit. "We are grateful," Sherman wrote, "even for the firing of a national joke heard round the world."[29]

[27] Sherman, *Americans,* pp. 158–59, 167.

[28] Babbitt, *Spanish Character,* p. 166; idem., *Masters of Modern French Criticism,* p. 329.

[29] Stuart P. Sherman, *On Contemporary Literature,* 6th ed. (New York, 1931),

But it was not Twain the funnyman that appealed to Mencken or Brooks. Mencken regarded the Sherman view of Twain as typical of the American habit of taking the artist from the man and making of him an innocuous democrat. To Mencken, Twain was "the first genuinely American artist." But it was the later Twain, the pessimist, who won Mencken. Twain, he felt, might have been a truly great artist; but the "American" qualities that endeared him to Sherman ruined him for Mencken. "His nationality," Mencken lamented, "hung around his neck like a millstone; he could never throw off his native Philistinism." For Twain, unfortunately, was as "American as Prohibition," and he never became the artist he could otherwise have been.[30]

That was the conclusion also of Brooks's remarkable and controversial study *The Ordeal of Mark Twain*. The real Twain that Brooks discovered was tortured by conscience, by self-accusations and self-contempt, by "morbid feelings of sin." And to that bitterness Brooks attributed "a certain miscarriage in his creative life, a balked personality, an arrested development." Brooks looked for the sources of conflict and found the first clue in the character of Twain's mother, Jane Clemens. She was, Brooks said, "the embodiment of that old-fashioned, cast-iron Calvinism" which had proved so favorable to the life of enterprising action but which perceived the scent of the devil in any expression of the aesthetic life. Twain absorbed part of that spirit from his mother and from his age. It was the spirit that set him to riverboat piloting and mining in Nevada; he would fulfill his promise that he would be a faithful and industrious man like his father. But Brooks found too that Twain at an early age had shown himself to be "the born, predestined artist," that his whole nature manifested a tendency toward creativity. And throughout his life the two sides of Twain's personality warred fitfully against each other. Twain's America allowed ample room for the practical man in him but thwarted continuously his artistic instincts. "In all his environment . . . there was nothing to assist in the transformation of an unconscious artistic instinct, however urgent, into a conscious artistic purpose." "His unconscious desire," Brooks wrote, "was to be an artist, but this implied an assertion of individuality that was a sin in the eyes of his mother and a shame in the eyes of society." Here,

---

pp. 44–45. This essay shows better than any other how precariously related were Sherman's democratic enthusiasm and his Humanism. Emerson could clearly hold both together for him, but with Twain the alliance was strained, and, as Sherman's essay makes plain, the democratic hope was unquestionably the stronger force. The result, strangely, was a kind of Wordsworthian enthusiasm for the plain and common against the refined and cultured, and Babbitt and More were right to perceive in it a dissipation of their own variety of Humanism.

[30] Mencken, *Book of Prefaces*, pp. 203–5.

Brooks said, was one variant of the "eternal dilemma of every American writer."[31]

Twain, then, could not fulfill his real artistic genius; so he compromised his warring factions by becoming a humorist. That won him a modicum of pubic toleration and enough wealth to enable him to face his mother with self-respect. But Twain knew that circumstances had thwarted his best talents. He wrote to a friend: "I am demeaning myself—I am allowing myself to be a mere buffoon. It's ghastly, I can't endure it any longer." This dilemma furnished Brooks's explanation of *Huckleberry Finn* as the only work that showed Twain's potential realized. In Huck, the illiterate and mischievous youth, Twain felt free to let himself go. Anything the rapscallion said would pass the censor freely, and because he was a little boy he would not be expected to know anything about morals and Puritan habits. Twain, Brooks said, was free at last. The raft and the river were more than material facts. "His whole unconscious life, the pent-up river of his own soul, had burst its bonds and rushed forth, a joyous torrent!"[32]

There was much in the Humanist position that was well-taken and needed.[33] Undoubtedly Sherman's democratic dizziness reached indiscriminate proportions, as in his approach to Twain, and the whole discussion was marred by the usurpation of literary criticism by ulterior motives and standards. On this issue Mencken and Brooks were hardly less offensive than Sherman, and the mixing of literary with social criticism makes one yearn for the aestheticism of the New Critics. It surely makes their reaction understandable. But what was wrong with the cultural past, in spite of the popular debunking spirit, was its neglect by the present. One need not fall into philistinism or a narrow nationalism in pleading for the rediscovery of literary influence, and it was not implausible to suggest that Emerson might serve as an antimaterialistic presence in the contemporary culture. How precisely that was possible, the Humanists failed to demonstrate, though Sherman and More gave it a good try. To a great extent the problem for the Humanists was to show how the "in-

[31] Van Wyck Brooks, *The Ordeal of Mark Twain* (New York, 1920), pp. 14, 35, 39, 80.

[32] Ibid., pp. 84, 195–96.

[33] I have not attempted here a complete exploration of this theme. Within the Humanist circle Paul Elmer More especially included much in his criticism that did not follow merely from a direct application of Humanist principles to literature. I have selected for this study that material which most clearly illustrates the general positions of the different critics. The Humanists' critiques alone could be greatly extended, for their discussion also examined authors not included here. For a fuller study of the critical warfare over the American literary past, see Ruland.

fluence" they wished to recover could be extracted from the past apart from the entire cultural and social context that gave it birth. Somehow that influence would have to utilize materials from the present, the present from which Babbitt and More were thoroughly alienated.

Thus the Humanists and their opponents joined in heaviest battle when the critical act centered on the contemporary literary revolt itself. H. L. Mencken celebrated the naturalistic turn in literature and used Theodore Dreiser as the model of his defense. Mencken found in the novels of Dreiser what he had failed for the most part to see in America's literary past—a realistic involvement of art in the affairs of men, art devoid of pious morality, blissful innocence, and sentimentality. Dreiser pictured life as essentially tragic, a ceaseless and ultimately meaningless struggle. In Dreiser's view, Mencken wrote, life "is gratuitous and purposeless. There is . . . no grand ingenuity, no skillful adaptation of means to ends, no moral . . . plan in the order of the universe." Mencken himself endorsed that view and attributed its presence in Dreiser to the influence of Huxley and Spencer. Dreiser himself referred to his own "sense of life as a complex biological phenomenon, only dimly comprehended," and Mencken endorsed that vision as the basis for great art. "This conviction that human life is a seeking without a finding," he wrote, "that its purpose is impenetrable, that joy and sorrow are alike meaningless, you will see written largely in the work of most great creative artists."[34]

Dreiser appealed to Mencken as a rebel against conventional, moral America, but he was also a first-rate artist with a penetrating vision of the human condition. Mencken in fact defended Dreiser in terms familiar to the Humanists. His novels, he said, deal with the most important things in human existence. They confirm that "this life is a bitter fight between the animal in [man] and the aspiring soul, between the flesh and the spirit . . . between what is base and what is noble." For Dreiser, Mencken felt, was a tragedian. His aim was not merely to tell a tale. "His aim is to show that vast ebb and flow of forces which sway and condition human destiny." The intention is to awaken and stir his audience to a greater sense of life. There was more to the stories of Dreiser's characters, Mencken argued, than seduction and abandonment. "The tragedy of [Sister] Carrie and Jennie [Gerhardt], in brief, is not that they are degraded, but that they are lifted up, not that they go to the gutter, but that they escape the gutter and glimpse the stars." To each there comes eventually "an awakening of the finer perceptions . . . an increased capacity for loving and living." Dreiser was also an American writer who captured for Mencken the throbbing heart of civilization in the United States, the feverish ambitions,

[34] Mencken, *Book of Prefaces,* pp. 89, 85; quoted in Ruland, p. 15.

the wretchedness and despair of the "muddled, aspiring, tragic, fate-flogged mass." Dreiser's art did not fall into piety or fade in a cloud of moral idealism. It was the healthiest sign of a new American literature.[35]

Predictably, what Sherman found in Dreiser was something radically different from the inspiration Mencken received. Sherman was convinced that the artist who best expresses himself and his society will express the "profound moral idealism of America," the idealism he found in Emerson, Whitman, and Twain. In America "the artist who does not in some fashion concern himself with truth, morals, and democracy, is unimportant, is ignoble." Sherman's nationalism thus weighed heavily on his criticism. He sought a vital cultural unity for America and called on the artist to promote it. It was for the painter, the poet, the musician to draw out meaning and purpose from a half-articulate land. They would give vitality and purpose to the national faith and lift us "above the vulgar practice of the hour."[36]

By this measure Dreiser was a failure. Sherman sneered at Mencken's efforts to present Dreiser as a realist and as an acute interpreter of American life. He rejected at the outset all art that pretended to be a "slice of life." The true artist was not akin to the photographer who caught wild animals in their natural habitat. Sherman scorned the pretensions of the realist to capture what appears to the senses and reproduce it. Such objectivity had questionable value in itself and belied Sherman's convictions that the artist cannot wholly remove himself from his subject or fail to reveal some aspects of his personality and beliefs. That made Sherman look at the reasons for Dreiser's literary use of "his physical eyes and ears," his capturing of the noise and the rabble of the city streets and tenements. Here Dreiser's naturalism excelled, but his spiritual and moral insight were woefully deficient. For only by a deliberate "suppression of evidence" was Dreiser's indifference to the moral forces of American life conceivable. Dreiser saw only the jungle side of existence because he himself was immune to the higher qualities of life and their unmistakable presence in America.[37]

But Sherman saved his heaviest rhetoric for Mencken—"the man midwife of the naturalistic fiction which makes its bed in the parlor window." Sherman's essay "Mr. Mencken, the Jeune Fille, and the New Spirit in Letters" was an exercise in vindictive sarcasm equal to Mencken's own. Whatever appreciation for good literature Mencken might once have possessed, Sherman charged, he had lost "in protracted orgies of literary

[35] Mencken, *Book of Prefaces,* pp. 137–38, 97, 110–13.

[36] Sherman, *Genius of America,* pp. 25–28, 31.

[37] Sherman, *On Contemporary Literature,* pp. 88–89. See also idem., *The Main Stream* (New York, 1927), pp.137–39.

'strong drink.' He turns with anguish," Sherman wrote, "from the pure and simple flavors that please children as the first gifts of nature, and that delight great critics as the last achievements of art. His appetite craves a fierce stimulation of sauces, a flamboyance and glitter of cheeses, the sophisticated and appalling ripeness of wild duck nine days old." Not only did Mencken "empty dishwater" over the whole American tradition in letters; he was now threatening to poison the American atmosphere with strong doses of his crude Teutonism. Sherman pictured Mencken, spattered with mud, riding into town on horseback. He stables his stud in the church, shoots the priests and professors, burns the library and university, and, amid the ashes, founds a new school of criticism on German principles. Thus did Sherman convey the threat posed to America's native strength and culture by Mencken and his "hunting pack of horny-hearted super-men."[38]

Mencken did not take this abuse quietly. Sherman to him was the worst of the American species—"the moralist turned critic." The American could never view a work of the imagination without injecting a moral judgment on it. Sherman came to represent all that Mencken had seen in the American past, the smothering of the pure artist by the Puritan and the democrat. These forces, Mencken felt, had ruined Sherman as a critic. For what offended Sherman, Mencken charged, was not Dreiser's shortcomings as an artist, but his deficiency as a Puritan and American. He charged that Sherman could not accept even Shakespeare without proving first that he was an Iowa Methodist, a member of the local chamber of commerce, and a Wilsonian. "Sherman is . . . honestly American . . . but the trouble with him is that he is *too* American. The Iowa hayseed remains in his hair; he can't get rid of the smell of the chautauqua."[39]

Sherman was left to do most of the fighting for the Humanists in the battle of the books. He read voraciously and joined eagerly in the critical warfare of the postwar years. Babbitt and More were conspicuous for their absence in this part of the literary debate. Save for an occasional journey into the wilderness, both remained aloof from the contemporary scene, offering only a wide critical framework for their young disciples to apply against current movements in art and literature. Babbitt and More indulged rarely in modern works. More wrote to his sister in 1926 that he was chastising himself for promising an editor an essay on modern American fiction. To read the Greeks in the morning, he said, and then to pass the

[38] Stuart Sherman, *Critical Woodcuts* (1926; rpt. Port Washington, N.Y., 1967), pp. 238–41; idem., *Americans*, pp. 9, 5.

[39] Mencken, *Prejudices: Second Series,* p. 22; idem., *Prejudices: Third Series* (New York, 1922), p. 177.

evening wrestling with Dreiser, Anderson, and Cabell "is a soul- and body-wracking distraction." When a rare venture into one recent work produced from More the description of Dos Passos's *Manhattan Transfer* as an "explosion in a cesspool," More's enemies jumped all over him. From contemporary lietrature More selected only detective stories. Here, he commented, there was no playing tricks with the Ten Commandments. Murder was still murder, adultery still adultery, and there were no romantic or naturalistic apologies for the facts.[40]

Babbitt was equally uninvolved. He wrote one essay on Mencken, but none on a contemporary writer. Babbitt found his own sentiments expressed by the French critic Joubert. "The great drawback of the new books," said Joubert, "is that they keep us from reading the old ones." What was true for Joubert in 1820 was true for Babbitt a hundred years later. With justice, then, Edmund Wilson accused Babbitt and More of having a blind spot for contemporary literature. He believed that if they looked closely and honestly they would see that many of the modern writers they condemned shared views similar to their own respecting the sordid state of American life. "It is not objected," R. P. Blackmur wrote, "that they admire Racine [or the classical literature in general], but that . . . they prevent themselves in advance from reading Dos Passos and Dreiser."[41]

G. R. Elliott detected both romantic and naturalistic symptoms in the new literature. He found in much contemporary poetry only "an imagistic snatching at the emotional surface of life" and little of the genuine insight that marks true poetic vision. Passion and fury alone could not place one at the core of human experience. Elliott felt also that science had made a noticeable impact on modern literature. Thus while Mencken defended Dreiser as a tragedian, the Humanists argued that the scientific temper had reduced tragedy to naturalistic fatalism. Elliott maintained that great artistic impulses spring from the sense of man's struggle with himself. But the obscuring of human duality destroyed the capacity for tragic portrayal. Responding to the same concentration of matter that permeates all life, we yield before the inexorable pressure of environment or to the irresistible force of our impulses. Human lives become part of a mechanical series devoid of moral content, against which the older war in the cave is meaningless. The scientific outlook, Elliott said, "blurs those mighty oppositions in our nature" around which the best art revolves.[42]

[40] Quoted in Arthur Hazard Dakin, *Paul Elmer More* (Princeton, 1960), p. 249; Paul Elmer More, *The Demon of the Absolute* (Princeton, 1928), pp. 63, 99.

[41] Babbitt, *Masters of Modern French Criticism,* p. 39; Wilson, "Notes on Babbitt and More," in C. Hartley Grattan, ed., *The Critique of Humanism* (New York, 1930), p. 56; Blackmur, "The Discipline of Humanism," ibid., p. 251.

[42] G. R. Elliott, *The Cycle of Modern Poetry* (1929; rpt. New York, 1965), pp. 72,

The Humanists also saw the influence of science in the psychological novel and particularly in its wide use of sex as a theme in literature. They identified this trend too as a variant of the romantic search for the intensely personal and the turn inward for the only verifiable truth. The stream-of-consciousness technique appeared to follow both the romantic and the naturalistic tendency to go below the rational level of consciousness, dissolving the world, as More put it, into a "Protean flux of meaningless change." Sherman added that the modern writer had been taught to shun all repressions, to open up his naked soul, and to examine it frankly and fully. The Humanists saw the vogue of Freud as but one variant of the romantic theme, now joined to the naturalistic and resulting in the abandonment of discipline and restraint in the vigorous pursuit of the natural man. Sherman called the Freudians "tragically wrong." Like the Rousseauists, they were holding forth the promise of liberation that generations of experience had proved a mere illusion.[43]

The treatment of sex in modern literature also disturbed the Humanists. Their discussion expanded their thoughts on the place of the imagination in the creative life and brought forth their insistence that if the imagination did not work in the service of a higher reality, it would be fuel for the natural man. Sherman linked that point to his own criticism. If art, or the pursuit of beauty, he said, did not concern itself with "truth, morals, and democracy," it will go to some other less valuable end. He saw that very occurrence in the new writers. Having "liberated" beauty from its denotation of spiritual realities, he charged, they were preoccupying its new leisure with sex and placing it at the disposal of "sensual gratifications." Babbitt too saw that development, citing the "dangerous" use of illusion by the moderns. It had made madness and lust appear beautiful, he said, and was responsible for the "phosphorescent slime" of the new decadent art and literature. American writing, Elliott charged, had become "a smoky imagery of sex, soft, acrid, and voluminous," serving only to conceal "the trivial fire of passion in the green veins of our authors."[44]

92, 153. On this point, shared by all the Humanists, their movement joined the New Critics' case against the impact of science, which the latter group saw despoiling the possibility of purely aesthetic experience.

[43] Paul Elmer More, *On Being Human* (Princeton, 1936), pp. 92–93; Sherman, *Genius of America*, pp. 224–25.

[44] Sherman, *Genius of America*, pp. 16–17; Irving Babbitt, *The New Laokoön* (Boston, 1910), p. 104. Hence Babbitt's contention that naturalism was only "romanticism going on all fours" (*Rousseau and Romanticism* [Boston, 1919], p. 104); G. R. Elliott, *Humanism and Imagination* (Chapel Hill, N.C., 1938), p. 49.

There is a frustrating and superficial generality about all of these statements and no reference to specific authors or individual works. The criticism was impressionistic and unanalytical.

Stuart Sherman demonstrated his sudden rapprochment with contemporary literature shortly before his death when he spoke before the American Academy of Arts and Letters in December 1924. He entitled his speech "The Emotional Discovery of America" and hailed the many pioneers engaged in the literary exploration of the country. Most significant of these efforts was what Sherman called "the new pessimistic literature" coming from those writers who were giving vent to their dissatisfaction with the spiritual limitations of the nation. Sherman regarded this new restlessness as the first sign of a wholesale invigoration of American democracy, a significant step that might match in cultural achievements the obvious material success of the country. "The most fascinating aspect of American life today is the ascent into articulate self-consciousness of that element of our people which Emerson called the 'Jacksonian rabble.' " Sherman associated that element particularly with his own Midwest. An area earlier addicted to a crude materialism and most affected with the vulgarism of the philistine Sherman now saw reexamining its values in a healthy quest for the qualitative improvement of its democracy. [45]

As the best exemplar of this movement Sherman selected Sherwood Anderson. Anderson, said Sherman, was conscious of all that was shoddy and vile in American life, and he filled his stories with broken lives and lost souls. But there were qualities in Anderson that lifted him above the level of the naturalists, and Sherman gave much attention to these. Though his characters cry out, "Oh, I feel so queer!" and though they can say only "I'd like a drink" or "I want a woman," Sherman refused to see in their animal expressions the mere naturalism that he perceived in Dreiser. Now he sensed in Anderson's characters "a passionate eagerness to be washed and made clean," a search "for some mystical union with the spirit of life." In what Babbitt and More would certainly have labeled a naive confusion, Sherman attributed to Anderson an articulation of the average American's spiritual quest that distinguished that author from the persistent barbarism of Dreiser. For one thing, Sherman defined Anderson as "tremendously American and . . . glad of it." For another, he saw Anderson as a "passionate seeker for . . . the inmost meaning and purpose, in this driving, noisy, smoky, ugly, hungry, monotonous, wearying civilization in which we welter." These two qualities established Anderson's value. "We should approach Mr. Anderson," Sherman said, in a manner reminiscent of his endorsement of

---

[45] Sherman, *Critical Woodcuts*, p. 244; idem., *Genius of America*, p. 218. Sherman's views, interestingly, were close to those expressed by Harold Stearns, who also thought the rebellion of the disaffected the most hopeful sign of a revolt against America's spiritual bleakness (*Civilization in the United States* [New York, 1922], p. 150).

Whitman, "as the impassioned interpreter of day-dreams, the day-dreams of common people . . . the great masses of the plain people, in their occasional hours of revolt against . . . the destiny of most men: 'leading lives of quiet despair.' "[46] There was the vigorous inward struggle, the groping for a meaningful spiritual ascent, that Sherman credited Anderson for making available to the nation, the spiritual ascent that Mencken found, but Sherman refused to acknowledge, in Dreiser.

But Sherman clearly was casting a wider net. His expanding sympathies greatly moderated the hostility of his earlier *On Contemporary Literature,* and he found that the Humanist framework he still used could include more of the moderns than he earlier believed. Willa Cather, whom he called "one of the true classics of our generation," was another favorite. In her stories of pioneer life Sherman found scenes that paralleled the naturalistic settings of Dreiser's cities. The primitive struggle with nature was paramount: "just not to perish; just to hold one's own on the hard bedrock of existence." Here too was the Darwinian world illustrated. But Cather's heroes struck Sherman profoundly, and he distinguished them from Dreiser's. The former rally all their moral strength for spiritul resistance to the material world. The challenge of life calls forth "one's best and one's utmost." Cather's world, then, was no mere blueprint of the naturalist scene, where man and woman struggle blindly with a meaningless existence. Alexandria, the heroine of *O Pioneers!,* rallies her inner resources enough "to shape a little the terms of her struggle for survival, to make of it a big thing, an inspiring and rewarding activity."[47]

Both Cather and Ellen Glasgow presented a view of the world as a moral order and illustrated effectively the duality of the human condition that defies the natural order and makes life durable and worthwhile. Referring specifically to Glasgow's *Barren Ground,* Sherman pointed to the same motivating forces that governed Cather's characters: "the indomitable fighting spirit . . . the passion for progress and mastery, the determination to bite through to some faint sweetness in the fruit of life." Glasgow's people lived in a world that ostensibly bore the marks of Dreiser's, full of the same primitive forces. The difference in portrayal stemmed from the "observant ethical spirit" that dominated Glasgow as an artist. It enabled her to capture the sustaining forces of life, family, group, and community. She was the true realist, well in the tradition of American writers of the past, who objectified in their work the profound moral idealism of the American character.[48]

[46] Sherman, *Critical Woodcuts,* pp. 12–17. The quotations are on pp. 17, 16.
[47] Ibid., pp. 41–42.
[48] Ibid., p. 74.

In 1921 Sherman nominated Sinclair Lewis's *Main Street* to the Academy of Arts and Letters as the best novel of the year. Sherman did not endorse all of Lewis's work, and he pointed to the difference he saw between *Main Street* and *Babbitt* to illustrate a major point in his criticism. While many of the modern realists and naturalists had done much toward identifying the blight of America's civilization, the most useful literature, Sherman believed, must go beyond diagnosis to therapy. Thus the reader of a perceptive writer will gain from his efforts a greater insight into his own state or society's in general and perceive a solution to the dilemmas depicted. Sherman urged Lewis to include in his next work a spokesman for his own views. In *Main Street* he had done that, but not in *Babbitt*. [49]

The Humanists' role in the battle of the books indicated how difficult it was to apply the Humanist aesthetic against the current of contemporary literature. Sherman gave it an enthusiastic try but ran into trouble. Probably there was inherent in Sherman's early criticism a dangerous tension between his antinaturalism and his democratic idealism. In the end Sherman could find the new Whitmans, the poets of the democratic ideal, only among those who explored the seamier side of American life. When the aspirations of struggling, confused Americans were articulated by the new novelists, Sherman had to conclude that the struggle was heroic, the effort spiritually uplifting. He was, however, not wholly unsuccessful in preserving these two values in his judgments, and with his sensitivity to both he was able eventually to develop a measure of tolerance. The same cannot be said of Babbitt and More. The smug dismissal of the new literary efforts by the two major Humanist minds was patently irresponsible. Their culpability was two-fold. Babbitt and More genuinely believed that the Humanist prescription was capable of qualitatively improving American life, even if they never expected a thorough Humanist renovation. There was much in Babbitt's and More's philosophy of art that was valuable, but they rendered it ineffective by failing to apply it to the contemporary literary scene. One may choose not to blame the Humanist leaders for slighting Dreiser, Lewis, and Dos Passos; certainly they had their limitations as artists and were very often provincial and limited in their range of vision. But naturalists and realists demanded a

[49] Stuart P. Sherman, *Points of View* (New York, 1924), pp. 216–17. Lewis, incidentally, read Sherman's review and replied to him by letter. "I think you may perhaps like to know," he told Sherman, "that in [my] new novel [which was to be *Arrowsmith*] I shall, to some extent, do what you suggest . . . use a central character, a person whom I really like and genuinely admire: an investigative scientist . . . who fights commercialism, but without any sentimental propaganda, and certainly no sobs about 'commercialism' under that name" (Dec. 11, 1922, Sherman Correspondence, University of Illinois Archives, Urbana-Champaign).

Humanist critique, and when Sherman compromised there was no one left to deliver it. Those who wondered how a Humanist literary revival might emerge from the new aesthetic disaffection in America simply did not get an answer. Secondly, More and Babbitt—and Sherman, too, on this count —read the new literature too narrowly. Dreiser's America was not classical Greece, though Mencken thought he saw some aspects of genuine tragedy in *Jennie Gerhardt* and other works. Had the Humanists looked closer they might have found elements there of the spiritual struggle and the search for self-perfection that they themselves endorsed. But when these aspirations centered in the crude democratic masses that Babbitt and More disdained, their reaction was naturally stronger than Sherman's and they turned their heads. In the end the battle of the books did successfully elaborate Humanist values and prejudices, and certainly it demonstrated how remote Babbitt and More were from the cultural directions of American life. But that fact, unfortunately, meant that the battle, for these Humanists, was a lost opportunity to give some substance to the Humanist program.

CHAPTER FIVE

Liberating Education

A university emphasizing everything emphasizes nothing.
—Norman Foerster

THE AMERICAN CAMPUS was the center of the New Humanist movement. Twelve of the fifteen Humanists who contributed to Foerster's *Humanism and America* in 1930 were involved in some way with an American college or university, while only two of the thirteen contributors to *The Critique of Humanism* were similarly placed. The alignment reflected a major orientation of the New Humanism and explains the frequent charge that the movement was strictly an academic one with little relevance to society at large. The Humanists in turn were ready to draw the battle lines for their program in the American college, for they hoped to make it a major bastion of defense against the materialistic and humanitarian-democratic forces in America—forces they saw bringing heavy assault even against higher education itself. The real struggle of the day, Babbitt thought, would be in education—"the one altruistic activity of the humanist."[1] He and his collaborators prepared a weighty defense, and the educational issue emerged as the only one on which the Humanists spoke with a large number of other critics, joining with them to encourage a counterrevolution in higher education that would reverse the trends set by a half-century of major changes.

By the second decade of this century the American university bore little resemblance to its predecessor, the old-time college. The Humanist critique of higher education took place against the background of change that had substituted for "discipline" and "piety," the emblems of the older schools, a concern for scholarship and research, vocational and professional training, and public service. These became the new ideals of the American university. This redirection arose with an academic movement away from an earlier emphasis on the passing on of an acquired tradition to a concentration on new knowledge for its own sake and for the service of society. The old-time college had established as the necessary function of education the discipline and training of the mental and moral faculties. Greek and Latin, mathematics, science, and philosophy were seen not only

---

[1] Irving Babbitt, "Humanism: An Essay at Definition," in Norman Foerster, ed., *Humanism and America* (New York, 1930), pp. 50–51.

as valuable increments of culture but also as tools to sharpen and train the reasoning powers and the intellect. These could not be trusted to develop on their own, a fact that governed the required curriculum and teaching methods of the institution. Mental exertion was good in its own right, and rote memorization and classroom recitation were the pedagogical keynotes of the old-time college. As Noah Porter, Yale's stalwart president and one of the last giants of the older ways, said: "The college course is preeminently designed to give power to acquire and to think, rather than to impart special knowledge or special discipline."[2]

The New Humanist movement arose after the first quarter-century of a remarkable transformation of American higher education that brought about the modern university. New forces and new values promoted the change. A demand for practicality and utility, the elective system, the democratic thrust of the new state universities, and the emulation of the German university's concern for research and the advancement of new knowledge—all these factors broke the narrow curriculum of the past and gave new definitions to higher learning. The leaders of the new education—Eliot, White, Jordon, Gilman, and others—may have differed on specific questions, but it was clear nonetheless that by the time Babbitt and More were writing, apologists for traditional culture had been forced into a defensive position. And as the Humanists' own program made apparent, one salient fact—and the most regrettable fact in their minds—was most decisive: American higher education reflected all the shortcomings of American culture and was itself one of the indices of the nation's spiritual failure. The American college had ceased to stand for the perpetuation of the classical and humanistic past and was succumbing to all the expansive forces of the age. The colleges and universities had enslaved themselves to popular tastes, to the prevailing commercialism, and to the leveling egalitarianism of American democracy. But education too was a matter of "first principles," and the Humanists made the cause of counter-revolution a central object of their program.

Collectively, the new forces in education had at least one common effect, the Humanists believed. They all violated the essential purpose of education—to link the cultural past to the present. The new course then became in their eyes a major symptom of an age trying desperately to find itself and not knowing where to go. The ideals of service, utility, individualism, and the cult of learning for its own sake merely signaled the abandonment of any effort to rediscover the permanent in the human condition and betrayed the modern fallacy that a greater involvement

[2] Laurence R. Veysey, *The Emergence of the American University* (Chicago, 1965), pp. 21–25. The quotation is on p. 24.

with the present will uncover the principles needed to resolve its problems. But especially in a nation such as the United States, Babbitt believed, this first principle of education needed a stentorian defense. Nowhere else had the fact and ideal of newness been more completely a principle of living than in this country. Here stood no Pantheon or Notre Dame "to make a silent plea for the past against the cheap and noisy tendencies of the passing hour." America had always been lured by concepts of the perfectibility of man and by evolutionary notions of progress. It had come to believe that each new decade was a gain over the last. The result was a kind of tyranny of the present. The emancipation from this tyranny, Babbitt insisted, was the chief benefit to be gained by a humanistic education that reflected the continuities of history. More also endorsed this defense of liberal education. Rightly directed, he said, education could help the individual grasp in his imagination "the long course of human history" and distinguish "what is essential therein from what is ephemeral." The college graduate of the present, More believed, received a training that merely left him "prey to the prevailing passion of the hour," saturated by courses that prepared him only for the pressing and momentary tasks of the day, and insensitive to the permanent and unchanging in the human condition. At its best, then, education would be a liberation from these limiting experiences. This concern of course made Babbitt and More sympathetic toward the older tradition. The curriculum of the old-time schools, Babbitt said, "embodied the seasoned and matured experience of a multitude of men, extending over a considerable time." By their pliantness to popular whim and the demands for material gain, the modern institutions suffered in contrast.[3]

But the pedagogical efforts of the old tradition could be defended too on strictly practical grounds. The very conditions of rapid change in the modern world argued all the more strongly, the Humanists believed, for liberal, as opposed to special, education. "What today seems an education for efficiency," Foerster wrote, "may turn out to be merely fixation in maladjustment." A narrow ad hoc education might stifle one into eventual uselessness and hinder the acquisition of other talents because it had ignored the training of all the other faculties. Foerster pointed instead to the value of a liberal education that had as one objective the cultivation of the mind in general. He looked for the development of intellectual excellence itself, in preference to the acquisition of specific "useful knowledge." Judgment, wisdom, perspective were the proper goals of a sound

[3] Irving Babbitt, *Literature and the American College* (Boston, 1908), pp. 166, 118, 82–84; Paul Elmer More, *Aristocracy and Justice* (1915; rpt. New York, 1967), pp. 36–37.

educational program. Foerster and the Humanists in fact were not at all
unsympathetic to the old "faculty psychology" and the discipline and
training of the mind.[4]

Their admiration for the ancient classics above all showed most strongly
the affinity the Humanists shared with the older tradition in American
higher education. Here their attitude was almost wholly uncritical, for
they were willing to emphasize that body of learning quite at the expense
of the modern fields, including sometimes contemporary literature. More
insisted that so much economics and sociology in the colleges had the effect
of "isolating the student from the great inheritance of the past." Contemporary education, he charged, toiled excessively to drag the student
through these academic "slums" and gave little effort to making him feel at
home "in the society of the noble dead." More defended the classics both for
their pure intellectual discipline and for their ability "to mold character
and to foster leadership in a society much given to drifting." He called for
"a return, if possible, to pure classical tradition and discipline."[5] He and
Babbitt both valued the classics over modern literature, for which they
had virtually no appreciation, as essential elements of the useful curriculum.
Babbitt expressed his faith in the classics as relevant guides for the
present and argued that modern literature merely made a cult of the sensations and promised only "a purely personal and sensuous satisfaction from
life." It was wholly devoid of the assimilative qualities of ancient literature and "so deficient in certain qualities of sobriety and discipline as to
make us doubt its value as a formative influence upon the minds of the
young." He appealed again to classical literature for its power to lead one
away from personal instincts "to the service of a high, impersonal reason."
The *Iliad* and *Odyssey*, More believed, "have a beauty and humanity that no
modern epic poet has ever touched."[6]

[4] Norman Foerster, *The American State University* (Chapel Hill, N.C., 1937),
pp. 201–3. Faculty psychology viewed the human mind in terms of its various
faculties—will, reason, imagination, sensibility—and by an analogy to the body's
muscles prescribed the growth to full potential of each of these through careful
discipline and training. The famous Yale Report of 1828 furnished the classic
American defense of this pedagogical emphasis: "the two great points to be gained
in intellectual culture are the *discipline* and *furniture* of the mind; expanding its
powers and storing it with knowledge." The Report insisted that the different
components of the college curriculum be selected according to their usefulness
in training and strengthening the mental powers. See Frederick Rudolph, *The
American College and University: A History* (New York, 1962), pp. 132–33. Paul More
virtually echoed the Yale Report: "Without discipline the mind will remain
inefficient just as surely as the muscles of the body, without exercise, will be
flaccid" (*Aristocracy and Justice*, p. 46).

[5] More, *Aristocracy and Justice*, pp. 37, 45–46, 49, 67, 88–89.

[6] Babbitt, *Literature and the American College*, pp. 135–36; More, *Aristocracy and*

Generally the problem of education for the Humanists was the familiar one of breaking the romantic and naturalistic traditions by renouncing both extremes and adhering to the humanist center. They were quick to identify an education for utility and service with a philosophy of man which emphasized only his need to adjust to the circumstances of his environment and which thus confirmed the naturalism in contemporary culture. The romantic notion was equally apparent. A system that promised only to follow the inclination of the student and develop to their fullest his natural instincts valued only the unique in the individual over the attributes that he shared in common with a consistent human nature. Foerster explained that the Humanists were concerned with the individual as much as were Dewey or Rousseau, but sought to offer the educational content that would promote an awareness of the higher self over the natural self. While they hoped therefore to avoid the mere cult of the whim, they wished to preserve individual integrity as well. Theirs was not a call for a complete return to the old curriculum. The main problem in education, Babbitt said, was the same as in art or in government: the balancing of the elements of freedom and restraint, individuality and proportion. To go to either extreme was easy, but a judicious combining of the two was the most difficult task of all. "The task of assimilating what is best in the past and present," he wrote, "and adopting it to one's own use and the use of others, so far from lacking in originality, calls for something akin to creation."[7]

One clear instance of the combining effects of romantic and naturalistic culture that the Humanists perceived was the course of action taken at Babbitt's own institution and universally emulated. Harvard's elective system sprang both from a faith in the maturity and ability of the average student and from a conviction that no grounds existed for distinguishing the merits of one course or field of knowledge from another. And so long as utility and self-expression were measures of value there was little ground for imposing a uniform or required course of studies against one responding to the natural instincts and native abilities of the individual. The

---

Justice, p. 91. Here the impersonalism of the Humanist aesthetic paralleled the educational emphasis. Not the least important value of the classics for Babbitt was its appeal "to our higher reason and imagination—to those faculties which afford us an avenue of escape from ourselves, and enable us to become participants in the universal life" (Babbitt, *Literature and the American College,* p. 173).

[7] Foerster, *American State University,* pp. 200–201; Babbitt, *Literature and the American College,* pp. 72–73, 101. But with the indiscriminate diffusion of the curriculum it was clear to Babbitt that the B.A. degree had become a largely meaningless certificate, more a quantitative measure of accumulated educational units than any assimilated body of knowledge (*Literature and the American College,* p. 97).

Humanists saw in the appeal of the elective system both a democratic blindness to distinctions and quality and a lingering romantic notion of individual uniqueness and personal whim. On both practical and philosophical grounds they condemned it. Merely to view the products of the elective system, Shafer felt, sufficed to indict it. He listed such courses as Administrative Problems of the High School Cafeteria and Public School Plumbing Equipment as two among many of the new curricular absurdities.[8]

But the Humanists also insisted that the elective system sprang from serious misconceptions about the essential function of education. Above all, that function was not, More said, "to confirm the young mind in its natural temperament" or "in its tendency to pursue the present and easier pleasure." To leave education to the elective system was to expose it to prevailing pecuniary ambitions and to the whim of the moment. The result would be a meager and enslaving education at best. On the contrary, the truly educated man, More said, is he who has been trained to know "that highest and most enduring pleasure" that comes from the great books "selected and approved by the verdict of tradition." Only a liberating education of this kind could free the individual from his own limitations and personal inclinations to which he was otherwise captive.[9]

At Harvard, Babbitt viewed Eliot's elective system with dismay. He commented that Eliot had indeed provided a rich and costly banquet of electives for eighteen-year-olds. But the system was working only to indulge students in their natural inertia. A few large and notoriously easy courses were flooded with students; few of them were working strenuously along their chosen paths. Nine men in ten, Babbitt maintained, are as lazy as they dare to be, and the vast majority of students was winding its way through Harvard along the lines of least resistance; the elective system was making America the laziest nation in the world. But Eliot was laboring under a more serious misconception still. Babbitt identified Eliot's faith in the ability of the freshman to decide for himself with the same thinking that led Rousseau to find the worth of a man in his individuality and uniqueness. "Every youth of eighteen," Eliot said, "is an infinitely complex organization, the duplicate of which neither does nor ever will exist." Babbitt labeled that notion a dangerous half-truth, which, when made the basis of an educational program, was simply incompatible with the survival of humanist standards. For Babbitt recognized in Eliot's reasoning a covert denial of the element of sameness in man so central to the Humanist credo.

[8] Robert Shafer, "University and College: Dr. Flexner and the Modern University," *Bookman*, 73 (1931), 232.

[9] Paul Elmer More, *The Demon of the Absolute* (Princeton, 1928), pp. 26–27.

Babbitt now saw the ideal of the norm of humanity, measured through civilizations and their past achievements, yielding to an indiscriminate individualism and a new hedonism in education. He summarized the whole upshot of the elective system thus: "The wisdom of all the ages is to be as nought compared with the inclination of a sophomore."[10]

The new naturalism that the Humanists judged pervasive in higher education was associated mostly with state universities. But opinions here were by no means uniform. Foerster accused the state systems of a perverse materialism and leveling democracy, but Sherman found their idealism wholly compatible with Humanist principles. Foerster hailed the beginnings of the state-university ideal under the sane auspices of Thomas Jefferson and spoke with favor of the plan for the University of Virginia and Jefferson's hopes that it might be a model for the rest of the states. The ideal of a natural aristocracy had led Jefferson to conceive an elaborate system for screening students that would allow the most talented to develop their fullest potential through an education subsidized by the government. A well-ordered republic, Jefferson believed, must provide for "separation of the *aristoi* from the *pseudo-aristoi*, of the wheat from the chaff. . . . Worth and genius would thus have been sought out from every condition of life." But that spirit, Foerster explained, did not prevail; it yielded instead to the stronger impulses of Jacksonian democracy, which did not, like the Jeffersonian variety, seek to preserve an aristocratic principle within a democratic framework. While one insisted on the rule of talent, virtue, and intelligence, the other appealed to the numerical majority and flourished in a philistine atmosphere replete with contempt for "book learning." These anticultural forces came to exercise greater influence on American institutions, and the state universities especially "imaged with startling vividness the materialistic society which they served."[11]

However, the state universities received a different reading from Sherman, who provided an enthusiastic defense. The spirit and ideals of the expanding public institutions appealed greatly to Sherman, for they combined elements of cultural progress and democracy that were so compatible with his own beliefs. He expressed his feeling in a letter to a friend. " 'Out' here, as you Easterners say, we think the line of state universities extending from Ohio to California is about the most significant and hopeful thing that the country has been engaged in for some years." Sherman, who turned down offers from Amherst and Yale, was sensitive to the criticisms made against the state schools, many of them by other Humanists.

[10] Babbitt, *Literature and the American College,* pp. 52–53. Eliot is quoted on p. 47.
[11] Foerster, *American State University,* pp. 7, 21–23, 60.

These usually argued that the public institutions had contributed to raising the farmer's yield per acre through scientific and technological research but had contributed little to the cultural life of the nation. They had expanded their enrollments to spread education as widely but also as thinly as possible and were forced to go to the public for support in return for a promise to double the earning power of its citizens.[12]

Sherman conceded some truth in the "stock criticism" of the state universities. But he charged that opponents had failed to capture or appreciate the spirit behind their programs. Sherman did not despair, like Babbitt and Foerster later, of improving the general quality of American life, and he was therefore unwilling to trust culture to a small elitist minority. The health of American democracy, he argued, required some enlightenment at all levels of society so that an educational program that exposed the future farmers and merchants to some culture was the surest prescription for democratic stability. He then did not condemn a program that offered literature and history and vocational training.[13]

For Sherman the lesson behind the state universities was the democratic truth that if the people are going to govern, one had better educate the governors. While the other Humanists shared that concern, they failed to recognize that the assumption of political office by the natural aristocracy would also require a wisdom in the people to identify and support that group. No elitist system of education could achieve that condition, Sherman believed. He reviewed an article by a Yale professor who maintained that since the state schools were so hopelessly locked in the quest for better fertilizers and stronger rails, America should entrust to them the care of the nation's body, while the eastern schools looked after its soul. Sherman would have none of this; the whole notion was antidemocratic and impractical. Moreover, Sherman was correct in replying that the state universities had not wholly yielded to base popular passions and predicted that in the long run they would do much to raise the cultural and intellectual level of the nation. That was the sum of his faith in democratic education and his case against what he considered the elitist education of the East. He refused to let culture become the possession of the rich but sought to combine it with the occupational life of the fields and factories.

[12] Jacob Zeitlin and Homer Woodbridge, eds., *Life and Letters of Stuart P. Sherman* (New York, 1929), II, 385; Stuart P. Sherman, *The Genius of America* (New York, 1923), pp. 149–51.

[13] Sherman, *Genius of America*, pp. 52–53. Thus Sherman, despite his disagreement with Babbitt and More in other respects, strongly defended the classics. They supplied "a masculine vigor and seriousness, which are altogether too frequently lacking in the lopsided educational programs of our day" (ibid., p. 254).

"You have preserved your idealism in glass jars," he told the supporters of the private colleges; "we have not lost ours by putting it to work in the bread of life."[14]

Sherman thought that the idealism of the new democratic education would moderate its materialism. Babbitt and Foerster believed the two went hand in hand. In an age that was both sentimental and materialistic, it was no surprise to them that its education evidenced the same traits. The gospel of service was only naturalism, if one took off the sheep's clothing and exposed it for what it was. Eliot's program for "power and service" merely showed how compatible were the two ideals. Babbitt saw in Eliot and other exponents of the service ideal the faith that science and technology, if put to use in as wide an area as possible, would assure continued progress for all. But the forces that created the modern world's problems, Babbitt insisted, could not be the forces to solve them. The service ethic betrayed the naturalistic faith that human happiness derives from the adjustment of the human species to its environment. To that extent it was a surrender to the flux and thus defiant of the very purpose of education. But it did serve as a rationale for the modern university. Each new course would satisfy a specific want and bring to the country the fruits of the new learning by putting it to use in the facilitation of living.[15]

Many educators, who, like the Humanists, saw only corrupting influences in the new educational realism, carried a different banner and defined the true university as an institution for the disinterested pursuit of pure knowledge through research. These ideas never became as honored in this country as in Germany, although the establishment of the Johns Hopkins University in 1876 symbolized their growing influence. The

[14] Stuart P. Sherman, "The University of Illinois," *Nation*, 105 (1917), 226–27. More again rose to challenge Sherman's idealism, for he considered his argument here utterly implausible. He wrote to Sherman: "Do you really believe the people—that is the great, busy majority—have any magnanimous desire for pure education? Do you see any signs of that in the kind of journalism they ask for, the kind of books that sell, or in anything else? . . . Higher education always has been and always will be the desire and reward of a comparatively few men. If the people support an institution of higher learning which has no practical value, they will do so because in one way or another they have been cajoled into it" (Arthur Dakin, *Paul Elmer More* [Princeton, 1960], pp. 141–42).

[15] Foerster, *American State University*, pp. 30–31, 43, 56; Irving Babbitt, "President Eliot and American Education," *Forum*, 81 (1921), 2–3. Babbitt may have correctly detected elements of romantic and naturalistic perspectives in Eliot's views, but in fact Paul More, recognizing Eliot as a champion of American liberalism and a Spencerian at heart, may have more accurately read the elective system as an offspring of the individualistic doctrine of laissez-faire (*Shelburne Essays: Seventh Series* [1910; rpt. New York, 1967], p. 256). More's own opposition to that doctrine is presented in chapter 6.

Humanists' dissent from this course, as well as from the vogue of utility, enhanced their alienation from the contemporary academic scene. For a narrow intellectualism, though a limited place might be allowed it in the universities, was a betrayal of collegiate principles and the education of the "whole man." Despite the protestations against utility, the Humanists charged, the pure research ideals reflected the indiscriminate obsession with the new that characterized an expansive society. The university to this extent simply mirrored the popular fallacy that the latest is the best. "There is a craze," Frank Mather wrote, "not to prove something valuable, but merely to prove something." Foerster noted that scholarly journals eagerly opened their pages to the intellectual minutiae of the new scholarship, and in the universities doctoral candidates scrounged for a third-rate poet still without a biographer. Quantity, in short, was the spreading standard of academic life in all departments and scholarly production the single path of academic advancement. As early as 1908 Babbitt wrote that "the uncritical adoption of German methods is one of the chief obstacles to a humanistic revival." He himself could not view the endless "German theses" that sprang from the universities without a sense of "intellectual nausea." [16]

The Humanists were particularly concerned with the impact of this pedantry on the teaching of the humanities in the colleges and illustrated their grievances with reference to the study of literature. Babbitt at Harvard warred endlessly with the group he called the "Philological Syndicate," the professors whose approach to literature emphasized textual criticism and documentary examination as opposed to the spirit and ideas of the works. [17] The study of literature, Babbitt and More felt, had ceased to be a humanistic enterprise, and both of them chose not to pursue the doctorate themselves. Mather actually took a doctorate in philology at Johns Hopkins, emerging from "the mill," he confessed, "with much of the juice squeezed out of me, but with enough left to know that I had been squeezed." He and Babbitt talked much together about education, agreeing that the specialization emphasis was threatening to reduce

---

[16] Frank Jewett Mather, Jr., "Higher Education Made in Germany," *Nation*, 72 (1901), 334; Norman Foerster, *The American Scholar* (Chapel Hill, N.C., 1929), pp. 43–46; Babbitt, *Literature and the American College*, pp. 136, 134. Because the modern scientific spirit in education and the romantic spirit in art both conspired against a view of life that insisted on seeing things whole, Babbitt again placed the prototype of each in the same camp: "The scientific pedant who is entirely absorbed in his own bit of research is first cousin to the artistic and literary pedant who is entirely absorbed in his own sensation" (*Literature and the American College*, p. 234).

[17] William F. Giese, Jr., in Frederick Manchester and Odell Shepard, eds., *Irving Babbitt: Man and Teacher* (New York, 1941), p. 15.

learning to "mere pedantry, while encouraging sheer dilettantism in the field of taste." [18]

Foerster elaborated on Babbitt's general objection in stating that in the study of literature more emphasis focused on historical explanation of works than on the human content of the literature itself. Here was another indication of the corrupting influence of romanticism. For there the concern was historical relativity, the unique or special qualities of other times and places. One looked, then, not for identity, permanence, and universality in the literature of the past but for difference, change, and development. Literature, one of the surest and most valuable records of enduring human experience, had become, Foerster thought, a field of scientific study that recognized only objective data. Too often it was read only as an indication of the spirit and history of the time and less as an expression of the universal dimensions of the human condition. [19]

Invariably the Humanists had to confront the question, Who should receive a college education? The state university, Foerster said, was taking on the character of "a commercial home study institute," trying to find some means of appealing to the increasingly diverse interests of American society on the assumption that every young man or woman has a right to a college education. He conceded that even the slowest minds might pick up a little culture on the way through, but that was a small return for the toll exacted on the superior students. Foerster charged that "the very atmosphere of the university seems oppressive with the weight of concern for helpless mediocrity, as if it were an intellectual sick chamber," and More lamented the reorientation of the curriculum to the needs of the "intellectual proletariat." [20]

[18] Frank Jewett Mather, Jr., in Manchester and Shepard, pp. 42–43. Babbitt even called for the establishment of a degree different in kind from the present doctorate, one that would stand for a "discipline in ideas, and not merely for a discipline in facts." He headed a department committee at Harvard that tried to win adoption of an "AM with Honors" that placed primary emphasis, "not upon original research, but upon assimilative reading." The proposal was defeated (*Literature and the American College*, pp. 131–32; copy of the minutes of the Division of Modern Languages, Feb. 10, 1930, Babbitt Correspondence, Harvard University Archives, Cambridge, Mass.).

[19] Foerster, *American Scholar*, pp. 9, 13.

[20] Foerster, *American State University*, pp. 85–88, 177–78, 184 (the quotation); More, *Aristocracy and Justice*, pp. 58–59. Babbitt had concurred entirely. The B.A. degree had become watered stock, victim of the humanitarian's effort to take whatever measures he could to bring the degree within the reach of the widest number. But Babbitt entertained no illusions that one could make "Greek scholars" of the majority of modern youth. The average student entered college with his attention already dissipated by the American newspaper and relaxed by the modern erotic novel (*Literature and the American College*, pp. 78–79, 175).

But the Humanists continued to plead for the redeemable few. The natural aristocracy of Thomas Jefferson remained their model. The college above all would be the breeding ground for a leadership class, and for this it would have to abandon its democratic pretensions. The purpose of the college, Babbitt wrote, "is not to encourage the democratic spirit, but on the contrary to check the drift toward a pure democracy." American education must serve neither the democratic mass as a whole nor an unmixed aristocracy, but "a blending of the two—an aristocratic and selective democracy." More argued that the college must become "a breeding place for a natural aristocracy"; if it did not, it would either be an apprentice school for young mechanics or a pleasure resort for the idle rich. Both characteristics were already paramount and boded ill for American democracy. The nation must produce its natural aristocracy and draw from it a group of disciplined and learned leaders, or it would fall under the weight of its own pervasive mediocrity. Foerster felt that concern enough to endorse again the Jeffersonian practice. He urged the state governments to spare no effort to seek out at as early an age as possible the youth among them who showed the most promise for intellectual growth and achievement. It would support at public expense the training of that group as much and as long as necessary. The returns to democracy would be immense. [21]

Irving Babbitt's *Literature and the American College* (1908) was the first major criticism of the course American higher education had followed since the Civil War. By the 1920s the kind of protest he was making had swelled considerably; America was ready for a humanistic counter-revolution in education. The first signs were apparent at Harvard itself, where after forty years of Eliot, the new president, Abbott Lawrence Lowell, hinted at a reversal of the tide. He suggested that Harvard graduates were neither as intellectually nor as socially rounded as they ought to be. Others, like Nicholas Murray Butler of Columbia, sensed that something had been lost in the training once provided by the older colleges for "the simple profession of gentlemen" and for the "generous and reflec-

---

[21] Babbitt, *Literature and the American College*, p. 80; More, *Aristocracy and Justice*, p. 45; Foerster, *American State University*, pp. 187–96. By this means, it would appear, Foerster sought to circumvent the democratic electoral process itself and democratic controls as well. This statement anticipates the problem of leadership considered in chapter 6, and, as it is made in connection with the subject of higher education, it elaborates the role the college must play in establishing an aristocratic principle within the democratic framework: "Once we have sound leaders," Foerster wrote, "we may safely trust to them the administration of our economic, political, and social arrangement. If our present arrangements are defective, they should be altered by the wise and not the foolish" (*American State University*, p. 232).

tive use of leisure" that seemed to have disappeared with the advent of football, the automobile, and with what Babbitt called "that strangest of all anomalies, the hustling scholar." More and more people were convinced with Babbitt that the college, which used to be the "quiet and still air of delightful studies," had become a madhouse.[22]

More serious yet was the sense among many educators that something central and formative in the content of education had disappeared during a half-century of change. That concern became increasingly articulate from the time of Babbitt's early protest to the issuing of the Harvard report on general education in 1945. Alexander Meiklejohn of Amherst and later of Wisconsin wrote in 1922 that the central problem of higher education was the restoring of unity and cohesiveness to its academic program. He denounced the "fallacy of the scholar," the belief that since all knowledge is good, all parts of knowledge are equally good. Proponents of this faith have conceded that "they have no guiding principles of selection in their arrangement of studies, no genuine grasp of the relationship between knowledge and life." Meiklejohn was especially critical of the elective system for this reason. The willingness to let students wander about in the college curriculum was indicative of a certain "intellectual agnosticism, a kind of intellectual bankruptcy." The later Harvard report stated that "a supreme need of American education is for a unifying purpose and idea."[23]

Shortly after the First World War these feelings were realized in a great many efforts to restructure the curriculums of the colleges and universities. The first program to draw attention was Columbia's in 1919. It was one of many general education programs initiated thereafter, and advanced as its rationale the proposition that "there is a certain minimum of . . . [the Western] intellectual and spiritual tradition that a man must experience and understand if he is to be called educated." The program began as a required course in the problems and values of Western civilization and was extended later to cover two years of related studies. Most significant of the new programs was that undertaken at Chicago by Robert Hutchins and explained in his book *The Higher Learning in America* (1936). Hutchins believed that the central purpose of education was cultural enlightenment, the connecting of the past with the present, the linking of the

[22] Rudolph, pp. 450–51, 447; Babbitt, *Literature and the American College,* pp. 246–49.

[23] Alexander Meiklejohn, "The American College and Its Curriculum," *New Republic,* 32 (1922), 2–3; idem., *The Liberal College* (Boston, 1920), p. 41; *General Education in a Free Society: Report of the Harvard Committee* (Cambridge, Mass., 1945), p. 43. Another earlier criticism along these lines was Abraham Flexner, *Universities: American, English, German* (New York, 1930), pp. 130–34.

minds of men. This objective could not be trusted to the elective system for its fulfillment. "If this is the aim of education," Hutchins wrote, "it cannot be left to the sporadic, spontaneous interests ... of undergraduates." And the university, he also believed, needed to move away from the commercial and utilitarian spirit that had infested it. The rapid advance of knowledge had given modern man a false sense of confidence in breaking with the past. The material circumstances of our contemporary life were so sharply in contrast to those of past generations that we have ceased to believe that ages gone by can speak to modern man with any relevance. Hutchins's own program at Chicago prescribed the "single-minded pursuit of the intellectual virtues" and consisted of "the greatest books of the Western world." Hutchins intended to turn from science and utility, seeking an order and value in the great classics that he believed the modern university had neglected to its peril. He shared the Humanists' concern for turning education away from purely individual tastes and narrow specialization and maintained that the best program would seek the universal in man's experience. Hutchins added that the program for general education sought to "draw out the elements of our common human nature." We are interested, he said, "in the attributes of the race, not the accidents of individuals." Education then would pursue its own ends, indifferent to the passions and styles of the moment. "The heart of any course of study designed for the whole people," he said, "will be ... the same at any time, in any place, under any political, social, or economic conditions."[24]

Norman Foerster's own work at the University of Iowa was the most direct effort to put Humanist ideas into practice. Foerster assumed the directorship of the School of Letters and Science in 1930 and began immediately to restructure it. He attacked first the departmental rigidity of the college, which he felt to be in part responsible for the narrow specialization that prevailed in the liberal arts. Bringing the departments of English, German, Classics, and Romance Langages into the new structure of the school, Foerster placed himself at the administrative head of all of them. He then worked for a humanistic revival in the curriculum. New courses appeared, including Greek Drama in Translation, Roman Literature in English, Readings in the History of Humanism (taught by Foerster), and Theory and Practice of Literary Criticism. Foerster also created the American Civilization major at Iowa.[25]

[24] Rudolph, p. 455; Richard Hofstadter and Wilson Smith, eds., *American Higher Education: A Documentary History* (Chicago, 1961), II, 901–2; Robert Maynard Hutchins, *The Higher Learning in America* (New Haven, 1936), pp. 71, 24–27, 66–73; see also *General Education in a Free Society*, pp. 44–45.

[25] Frances Mary Flanagan, "The Educational Role of Norman Foerster," Diss. University of Iowa 1971, pp. 105–15, 234.

Secondly, Foerster's innovations with the doctoral program won attention and probably best registered the Humanist reaction against the German ideal. Like Babbitt and More, Foerster believed that successful completion of the standard form of doctoral dissertation was no indication that one had acquired a humanistic education or was qualified to teach literature. Foerster's reforms sought to undo the effects of the pedantry he believed emanated from doctoral pursuits. In 1931 the school announced that it would accept "imaginative or critical writing" in place of original research as satisfactory fulfillment of one of the requirements for the degree. Even a fifty-page standard research paper would suffice, for Foerster maintained that a brief, publishable article could establish a student's qualifications as well as the longer work. Foerster's radical departure here continued directly from Babbitt's earlier 1908 protest against the death of humanistic education and pursued a recovery of imagination and critical judgment over scientific neutralism in the exploration of culture. The new alternative for critical writing attracted students and in 1939 led to a separate program, the noted Writer's Workshop at Iowa. [26]

But at Iowa too the whole modern war over education had to be fought. Foerster's reforms met opposition from the very beginning. Many who were at Iowa before him had no sympathy for the new course, and department heads resented Foerster's authority over them and resisted it. The issue with the Classics Department became especially acute, for Foerster considered a classical revival central to his program. But that department, he felt, was appointing dry, dull persons to teach, men whose education was characterized by a "rudderless scientism." Foerster cared little for strict erudition on this count and looked for scholars and teachers "who by their example, show the profound civilizing effect of the classics." Opposition to Foerster spread after 1941 when Harry K. Newburn became dean of the College of Liberal Arts. Newburn was a former high school principal who received his doctorate in education and was partial to the "progressive education" values of Dewey's followers. Newburn more and more assumed the leadership of the forces determined to undo Foerster's program. He called for ending most required courses and for liberalizing the program to fit individual needs. He also sought earlier and greater specialization in opposition to Foerster's broad general education. Foerster fought vehemently against the new movement, and he and his supporters, including twenty-eight graduate students who signed a petition in support of him, defended the broad humanistic course. Personality conflicts flared, for Foerster, it must be admitted, lacked tact and diplomacy in carrying out his reforms. The "educationists" he regarded

[26] Ibid., pp. 108, 148–49, 235; *Daily Iowan*, Mar. 26, 1931.

almost beneath contempt and apparently showed it in his personal relations with them. In the end Foerster lost, and in July 1944 he submitted his resignation with a ringing denunciation of the new "reactionary" liberal arts program.[27]

Foerster and others who supported the counterrevolution in American higher education found that they could win a partial victory at best. Indeed the very length of their continued protests, extending over four decades to its last major attack in 1945, was itself an indication that American institutions responded but slowly to their calls for change. Moreover, that response did not really reverse the tide; it only moderated it to the point that the humanities and liberal culture recovered from neglect. The democratic ambitions of the state universities, and of others, have not abated; they have accelerated, both in the efforts to bring into the university's confines a wider number of persons and to satisfy these with an infinite array of available subjects.[28] Nor has the research syndrome subsided, as scholarly productivity, allegations to the contrary notwithstanding, remains, in the universities and many colleges, the essence of professional advancement.

The Humanists' discussion of education indicates as well as any other subject their alienation from the American mainstream. Their aspirations in education were elitist and aristocratic in the face of the democratic tide. Babbitt, More, and Foerster could never see what Sherman recognized as true: that no effective democracy can ignore the broad mass of its people. The two older Humanists knew that democracy is inevitably a compromise with the highest standards but resisted the fact by entrusting the survival of culture to the intellectual elite. At the same time, then, that they railed against a democratic philistinism in America, they were ready to assign the majority to a narrow vocationalism. In the end their efforts were self-defeating. Moreover, one cannot avoid the conclusion that the Humanists were largely ignorant of the demands of a technologically advanced society. Science was affecting every area of American life, from the kitchen to the farm to the factory. The nation needed technical experts and would get them, for the commitment to material progress was a national faith as well as a legitimate national need. The Humanists were largely insensitive to this concern, and their reaction demonstrated their alienation from the pluralistic dimension of American life. The central fact of American education was its immense diversity. Combined with its democratic aspira-

[27] Flanagan, pp. 129–44, 193–94; *Des Moines Sunday Register,* Feb. 21, 1944; unidentified newspaper clippings, Norman Foerster Papers, University of Iowa Archives, Iowa City.

[28] Rudolph, pp. 462, 465.

tions, this condition pointed higher education not to one end but to several. At best one could realistically hope, and expect, that liberal culture would at least receive a place next to science and utility.[29]

But even with these shortcomings the Humanist protest cannot be ignored. It is hard to read More and Babbitt and Foerster without sympathy and even admiration. They early perceived a danger in an education that responded only to the demands of the present and the whim of the hour. They feared greatly for the survival of cultural values under such conditions, raising this fear even before later generations would ponder the effects of a generation of youth with minds dazzled by television. At a time also when educators fretted over individual tastes and self-expression, the Humanists reminded their age that society needs to preserve its elements of cohesiveness, unity, and cultural tradition and that discipline may yield a measure of self-discovery more effectively than indulgence. The Humanists also effectively exposed much of the romantic naiveté that later educators perceived in the use and abuse of Eliot's elective system. Even today it is already apparent that such modern innovations as pass-fail credits register not the supposed disinterested pursuit of learning that justified their origin but a mere minimum effort to achieve a passing grade. The short-comings of the new directions in education became apparent, of course, to New Humanists as well as others, but the Humanist critique derived from a precise conception of man and a wider set of values. In this way their judgments acutely perceived the interplay of romantic and naturalistic culture, and their dualistic philosophy provided a new measure of defense for the humanities. Unfortunately, it was undoubtedly that perspective that made the Humanists indifferent to the most fruitful academic achievements of the new university, the social sciences. For it was their concentrated focus on the higher self that blinded the Humanists to the value of studying human nature in its social, economic, and political interactions with the world. Furthermore, the Humanists might have profited from the utilization of this perspective in their own efforts to explain the emergence of the modern university and might have found in Thorstein Veblen's imaginative suggestions about the influence of business enterprise on the American University (*The Higher Learning in America*, 1918) further evidence for their own indictment. It was not simply the cultural symptoms of the romantic and naturalistic traditions that were responsible for the demise of the old curriculum, but inexorable social forces. The American university was becoming part of a complicated social matrix, including political, business, and professional interests, that we have only recently begun to examine and understand.

[29] See ibid., p. 481.

And yet it is still possible to speculate whether a humanistic recovery in American higher education can occur without a simultaneous recovery of the kind of philosophy of human nature that the Humanists endorsed. The demise of Scottish philosophy at the end of the nineteenth century brought into disrepute the faculty psychology and its associated values of mental discipline. These in fact had never adequately sustained the true spirit of the classics and the humanities and were more conducive to a dull pedagogical routine. It is suggestive, therefore, that the major leaders of the revolt against the academic revolution, from Meiklejohn to Hutchins to Conant, have defended general education with a philosophical outline similar to, but less amplified than, that of the New Humanists. These have recognized with the Humanists that it would be obviously hopeless to look to a unifying religious culture, such as that which gave much unity to the curriculum of the medieval universities, to provide educational direction in the modern world. But after the middle twentieth century at least two facts about American higher education were fairly clear. The humanities were again on the defensive and persons entrusted with their transmission were often noticeably reluctant or ill-prepared to justify their existence or their usefulness for life. Also, the American university itself was increasingly plagued by doubts about its own purposes and functions. The loss of confidence found academicians without criteria for deciding what the university should or should not teach and without defense against the pressures from without. The proliferating curriculum virtually announced to the world that there was room in the university for every passing fad and every public interest. At times it seemed that declining budgets alone could compel institutions of higher learning to make discriminating choices or invoke standards of inclusion with respect to the business in which it was engaged. The role of the modern university is necessarily multifaceted, but many quite legitimately insist that the university preserve itself as the trustee of the inherited culture. If we ask on what intellectual basis we can defend that responsibility, then a dualistic philosophy of human nature, with its corollary of the higher self and the universality of human experience, is a useful and even necessary proposition.

CHAPTER SIX

The Democratic Dilemma

Were all men free in themselves, the perfect form of government would be an absolute anarchy. As the world is, the freest society is that in which custom and law impose the least restraint on the man who is self-governed, and the greatest restraint on the man who is not self-governed.

—Paul Elmer More

THE HUMANISTS' VENTURE into political and social comment brought the movement into its most troubled waters. More and Babbitt's undisguised criticism of democracy, their defense of property, and their acknowledged aristocratic presumptions jeopardized the appeal of their position on other matters not directly related to the political and social. Many found it easy to read into the Humanists' position on literature and criticism a conservative political program that was not in fact implicit in it. Van Wyck Brooks, for example, who himself often merged social and literary criticism, charged that More's literary opinions were a disguise for other interests. Turning from More's philosophical and literary essays, Brooks said, one sees immediately how More "lets the cat out of the bag" when he enters upon social and economic discussions.[1] Actually, the Humanists, as others noticed, really had no program for society; in application, theirs was a program for individuals only. Sherman's remark about Emerson, that he was not a political man and paid little attention to political theory or practical politics, was true of Sherman and the Humanists as a group. For politics, "the art and science of governing masses," as Emerson defined it, engaged the Humanists not at all in a practical capacity, and only Babbitt and More in a theoretical one.[2] The Humanists were, like Emerson, far more concerned with the art and science of governing oneself, and rarely did their reflections on social problems leave the realm of the individual; rarely did they confront the difficult and sophisticated task of implementing programs that would realize their

---

[1] Van Wyck Brooks, "Our Critics," *Seven Arts*, 2 (1917), 107–8; see also John Chamberlain, "Drift and Mastery in Our Novelists," in C. Hartley Grattan, ed., *The Critique of Humanism* (New York, 1930), p. 261; Malcolm Cowley, "Humanizing Society," ibid., p. 68.

[2] Stuart P. Sherman, *Americans* (New York, 1922), pp. 96–97.

general values. But the Humanists were by no means indifferent to these matters. They faced the problems of American democracy with the same concern they brought to literature, education, and religion.

Babbitt and More consistently linked their political ideals and their general Humanist philosophy by moving from a philosophy of the inner life to a philosophy of the state. More took this step by placing the central problem of government in the form of the question, How may the people be saved from themselves? So defining the political problem, he linked the issues of restraint and liberty, the most important ones for the individual, to society at large. His and Babbitt's critique of democracy revolved entirely around this major concern and registered its harshest judgment against democracy as its inability by itself to supply the needed controls against the natural expansiveness of human nature. Both Babbitt and More were convinced that democratic theory rested on certain erroneous and misleading assumptions about the nature and character of man. So the political question too was one of first principles and extended directly from observable facts about the human condition.

For both leaders of the New Humanism the political question was bound inextricably with the problem of dualism. Every one of the political forces they saw vying for power in the modern world exhibited to them a basic violation of that one essential fact of the human condition. The theory of absolute democracy, as More pointed out, depended for its reasonableness on the assumption that the will to refrain, or the inner check, might assert itself in all men if they were left free from external checks. It required therefore, a dualistic principle, in opposition to a romantic theory of democracy that trusted the natural goodness of man and then dispensed with the inner control. This concern assumed a greater importance when measured against the Humanists' own loss of faith in a romantic and naturalistic age. For the successful functioning of any society required some form of discipline and restraint. They were anxious most of all to provide these strictures for the individual, but believed that a society in which individuals themselves were uncontrolled must counter an excess of liberty with external controls. The modern age, now witnessing the fulfillment of the romantic and naturalistic traditions, was by that very fact unable to give its members the needed internal restraints. As a system for the government of men, therefore, democracy loomed all the more precarious.[3]

Even Sherman recognized that fact in his wartime essay "American and Allied Ideals" and sought to link democracy with Puritanism. The latter he defined as the principle of inner restraint, the essential companion of

[3] Paul Elmer More, *The Drift of Romanticism* (1913; rpt. New York, 1967), p. 283.

the democratic principle of external freedom. Babbitt endorsed Sherman's point, although he and More had none of Sherman's confidence that Puritanism or any other force could easily contain the expansive tendencies of an antihumanist culture. More and Babbitt supported Edmund Burke's contention that people are qualified for civil liberty in proportion to their willingness to put moral chains upon their natural appetites. A naturalistic and romantic age offered no encouragement of that exercise, however. Though each believed that the fewer the restrictions men placed upon themselves, the more there must be from without, they feared also the possibility of totalitarian excess from the latter direction. The danger thus was two-fold, and both Babbitt and More found in Burke a clear perception of the dilemma. "Society cannot exist," Burke had written, "unless a controlling power upon will and appetite be placed somewhere, and the less of it there is within, the more there must be without. It is ordained in the eternal constitution of things, that men of intemperate minds cannot be free. Their passions forge their fetters."[4]

Here in essence was the challenge that democracy posed for the Humanists: the pragmatic necessity of finding the source of control needed for social stability. Democracy, a system born of the faith in natural man, could not by itself supply the restricting elements. It was compelled to inevitable excess by the assumptions under which it labored. Its machinery worked only in the one direction of finding more efficient methods of implementing the will of the majority and hence of removing all obstacles to the immediate actualization of prevailing sentiment. But exponents of democracy, Babbitt charged, have always failed to indicate any way of preventing the sovereignty of the people from becoming a kind of absolutism in itself. The common cry of the day, as More heard it, was "the cure of democracy is more democracy," a plea that he renounced outright. "It is a lie, and we know it is a lie," he answered. That cry had always paved the way to anarchy or despotism, for one or the other was the certain product of democracy unrestrained.[5]

Nonetheless, neither More nor Babbitt abandoned a democratic framework. "The cure of democracy," More said, "is not *more* democracy, but *better* democracy." The political solution, for both Babbitt and More, required not the abandonment of this system but the implementation of checks within it. These the Humanists called the aristocratic principles, which needed

[4] Stuart P. Sherman, "American and Allied Ideals," U.S. Government *War Information Series*, No. 12 (Feb. 1918); Irving Babbitt, *Democracy and Leadership* (Boston, 1924), pp. 251–52, 110; Paul Elmer More, *Aristocracy and Justice* (1915; rpt. New York, 1967), pp. 26–27. The quotation from Burke also appears at the beginning of Babbitt's work.

[5] More, *Aristocracy and Justice*, pp. 28–29; Babbitt, *Democracy and Leadership*, p. 61.

to be exercised within the democratic framework. "In the final analysis," Babbitt wrote, "the only check to the evils of an unlimited democracy will be found to be the recognition in some form of the aristocratic principle."[6] Babbitt and More credited the founding fathers with a keen perception of this need and believed they had rightly constructed checks against the immediate registration of the public will. But both Humanists, as their political views took shape against the rising Progressive movement, saw an erosion of these restraints and a drift toward what Babbitt called a democracy "of the radical type." The referendum, the recall, the initiative, the primary, the direct election of Senators—in these landmarks of the Progressive Era Babbitt and More saw the spirit of democratic excess, a determination to break down all barriers against the instantaneous registration of prevailing opinion. Such a course was possible only under the assumption that wisdom resides in a popular majority at any given moment. But that notion, Babbitt wrote, "should be the most completely exploded of all fallacies." Society, no less than the individual, must find some assurance that mere emotion and whim will not propel it off the deep end.[7]

If the social problem derived directly from the individual, then why, the Humanists asked, were the moderns so completely ignoring the essential ingredients for human progress? The answer lay again in the impact of romanticism and naturalism, or, more precisely, in the complementary influence of the two. Translated onto the social platform, the romantic fallacy became the humanitarian fallacy, and no group of twentieth-century thinkers more thoroughly inveighed against this ethic than the New Humanists. Their attack won them few friends and raised louder the cry of their critics that the Humanists were remorselessly negative. But the latter believed they knew why an age that celebrated science along with sympathy was at the same time materialistic and destructive.

Babbitt was careful to distinguish the humanitarian from the humanist. The difference was fundamental. While one looked ultimately to the perfection of the race, the other looked to the perfection of self. The difference in emphasis was possible only because the humanitarian, partly a product of the romantic movement, had obliterated the war in the cave and posited evil in a source outside himself. The shift was critical, for the struggle to win one's own soul had been the central preoccupation of the earlier religious and humanist periods. Babbitt said of the new perspective that gained consent in the ideas of Rousseau and the romantics,

[6] More, *Aristocracy and Justice*, p. 29; Babbitt, *Democracy and Leadership*, p. 61.

[7] Babbitt, *Democracy and Leadership*, pp. 263–64, 306; More, *Aristocracy and Justice*, p. 23.

"Inasmuch as there is no conflict between good and evil in the breast of the beautiful soul he is free to devote all his efforts to the improvement of mankind . . . by diffusing the spirit of brotherhood." The result was the new religion of humanity, one of the most fundamental changes in the history of ideas over two centuries. Modern man had transferred his allegiance to this new deity while preserving all the elements of service and worship proper to a religious age. But whereas the earlier fear of God had directed man's attention inward against the evil inherent in his own condition, the new humanitarianism drew him outward to the service of his fellows. Conscience had become an emotion, an expansive feeling of sympathy and benevolence. As an emotion it was worthy of cultivation for its own sake, and an unstable element of the flux. The romantic conscience then abandoned standards and judgment for a general feeling of good will for all the world. Babbitt and More believed that this development had grown in force up to the present and wholly obliterated the older dualism. "For the conscience that is felt as a still small voice [of God] and that is the basis of real justice," Babbitt wrote, "we have substituted a social conscience that operates rather through a megaphone."[8]

The Humanists found in humanitarian excess one of the clearest examples of the dangerous conspiracy of romanticism and naturalism against humanist values. For humanitarianism needed the naturalist to see the wrongdoer as the victim of his environment and the romantic to extend him moral consolation and sympathy. The American public, Babbitt believed, consisted largely of persons who have either "set up sympathy for the underdog as a substitute for all the other virtues" or who "hold that the criminal is the product of his environment and so is not morally responsible." Here as elsewhere there was cooperation between those who mechanize life and those who sentimentalize it.[9]

The cooperation of romantic and naturalist was apparent in another way. Humanitarianism promised to save the race by enhancing its physical comforts. Deprived of the guidance of the inner check, which it had left to stagnate, the humanitarian could seek only a happiness that required adjustment to external conditions. Here Foerster pointed out that the word *comforter* used to denote the Holy Spirit but had come in the modern age to signify a blanket. Humanitarianism was in fact "a materialistic

[8] Irving Babbitt, *Rousseau and Romanticism* (Boston, 1919), pp. 131, 180; idem., *Democracy and Leadership*, p. 200; Paul Elmer More, *A New England Group and Others* (1921; rpt. New York, 1967), pp. 251, 254; see also More, *Aristocracy and Justice*, pp. 211–12.

[9] Babbitt, *Democracy and Leadership*, pp. 254–55; see also similar remarks by More, *Aristocracy and Justice*, pp. 194–97.

world-view" that found intolerable any form of physical discomfort, and Foerster protested the one-sided emphasis that had prevailed since the humanitarian movement's ascendance. "A civilization based on the avoidance of suffering and discomfort," he said, "is negative and hollow." [10]

Babbitt, More, and Foerster, it must be said, bore to the humanitarian a distrust that bordered on obsession. The stereotype they contrived represented to them the very worst of the human species, a combination of the meddling and self-righteous do-gooder, the charlatan, and the hypocrite. The most reprehensible trait of the day's reform style, Foerster thought, was the character of the reformers themselves. Intemperance, intolerance, and a misguided sense of justice described their usual personalities. From Rousseau to Robespierre and on, he said, reform had seldom meant the improvement of oneself, but always the improvement of others. Resorting to impassioned haranguing or intimidation, the reformer was ready to use extreme means to vague and even dangerous ends, while all his actions increasingly unveiled "the imperialistic egoist masked as a benevolent brother." Babbitt himself thought the humanitarian type the worst product of the romantic revolution. "The transformation of the Arcadian dreamer into the Utopist," he said, "is a veritable menace to civilization." Loosed from the veto power in his own personality, he was free to project the vague ideal of his private dreamworld onto the real world before him and to struggle to make the two fit. Without the inner restraint and propelled by an all-consuming emotion, the character of the humanitarian was likely to be marked by a basic instability and intolerance that rendered him an object of suspicion. More issued this caveat: "If you hear a man talking overmuch of brotherly love and that sort of thing . . . you are pretty sure that here is a man who will be slippery or dishonourable in his personal transactions." For the humanitarian, while championing his ability to regulate others, was demonstrably inexpert in managing himself. Those most eager to serve us, Babbitt said, are also those most eager to control us. [11]

[10] Norman Foerster, *The American State University* (Chapel Hill, N.C., 1937), pp. 39–40.

[11] Ibid., pp. 42–44; Babbitt, *Rousseau and Romanticism*, p. 377; More, *Aristocracy and Justice*, pp. 143–44; Babbitt, *Democracy and Leadership*, pp. 287–88. Woodrow Wilson was the chief target of the Humanists' antihumanitarian barbs. More attributed Wilson's military intervention in Mexico to "a group of obstinate humanitarians in Washington," whose idealism, and that of the president, plunged America into a "hypocritical" war for service. Babbitt charged that the intervention was "an unwarranted attack on [Mexico's] sovereignty." In Wilson the country found a president whose zeal for international service disregarded established constitutional restraints and grasped for "unlimited power" to pursue its pious objectives. As for Wilson's plan for a League of Nations, it

Clearly the Humanists dangerously universalized the humanitarian personality and failed to distinguish its various types. Humanitarian concern was not by any means incompatible with the Christian humility or self-restraint they themselves celebrated. Sometimes, however, their perceptions were acute. They rightly saw that those who are benevolent in their ideals are often anything but benevolent in their actions. Radical movements of the late 1960s were profuse both in their confessions of love and idealism and in their physical destructiveness. Their own intellectual framework also enabled the Humanists to analyze the reform efforts in terms of its softer emotional side and its harder material side. But the diagnosis here also demonstrated that this framework alone was inadequate. The Humanists seldom spoke of specific issues; and they ignored the social and economic factors that underlay the evils to be attacked. Without this consideration Humanists could see only the romantic and naturalistic principles as the generating forces operative in reformism, and they were left to ignore the physical causes of social decay, turning, as we shall see, to inner regeneration as the only sure course. Perhaps this is why so many of their critics found the Humanists' prescription irrelevant and futile. Like many others, Malcolm Cowley misunderstood the Humanists' emphasis, but his lament was typical: "And what," he asked, ". . . has Humanism to do with the scene outside my window: with the jobless men who saunter in the dusk, or the dying village, or the paper mill abandoned across the river—this mill whose owners have gone South where labor is cheap?"[12]

A misdirected idealism was only one danger of the romantic and naturalistic alliance, less sinister in its long-run effects than its political counterpart in socialism. For socialism was only a bastard humanitarianism pushed to further excess. The blind benevolence of the humanitarian might sometimes be innocuous enough and suffer only from misdirection and a confusion of standards; but the inordinate will to power that Babbitt and More detected in the humanitarian personality too often led directly to political action and to a vicious egalitarianism that defied every distinction of merit and ability. Here the Humanists turned the issue toward the crucial question of leadership. Democracy's greatest weakness was its tendency to give itself over to its lowest elements and bring the superior individual down to the level of the undistinguished mass. The problem of leadership, then, was one part of the Humanists' efforts to fit aristocratic

could only be a "humanitarian chimera" (More, *Aristocracy and Justice*, p. 144; see also Arthur Hazard Dakin, *Paul Elmer More* [Princeton, 1960], p. 167n; Babbitt, *Democracy and Leadership*), pp. 268, 288.

[12] Malcolm Cowley, "Humanizing Society," p. 84.

principles within the democratic framework and thereby provide the checks that alone could contain its inherently expansive tendencies. Socialism, to Babbitt and More, illustrated all the dangers of a democracy loosed from its moorings.

The aristocratic principle was first of all a matter of priorities. More and Babbitt despaired of regaining or preserving civilized society through democratic exhortation. No program of social improvement could rely on general uplift, for the hope of civilization would always rest, not with the democratic mass, but with a small and select group of individuals. With these the fate of others would be inextricably bound. More could thus ask the question, "Is the main purpose . . . of government to raise the material welfare of the masses, or to create advantages for the upward striving of the exceptional? . . . Shall our interest in mankind begin at the bottom and progress upward, or begin at the top and progress downward?" For More there could be only one answer. But that elitist preference unfortunately led Babbitt and More to a vehement defense of the rights of property that identified both in the eyes of their critics as relentless conservatives. Indeed, there was little of the Humanist moderation and restraint in that defense, and the force of their pronouncements turned many heads. More spoke most bluntly. "To the civilized man," he said, *"the rights of property are more important than the right to life."* No line from all the Humanist literature was more widely quoted, and always with the intention of casting the school into a reactionary mold. It is fair to question whether More himself intended a literal reading of that statement, even though he added no qualifying remarks to it. Property had for More a symbolic meaning more significant than the literal. Specifically, property represented a visible and positive element of distinction among men in a democratic age that had already gone too far in blurring distinctions. That was the malady the Humanists found prevalent in politics, art, and education. Their concern for the elite of ability, or the natural aristocracy, translated in social terms to the rights of that group in property. More in fact maintained that the growth of human society out of barbarism concurred with a change from concern over wrongs done to persons to the protection of material possessions. "The main care of advancing civilization," he said, "has been for property." All real progress has revolved around that defense, and the concern for this protection was identified in More's judgment with the protection of the better human elements against the rest. That protection alone made civilization possible. Any social scheme that ignored these distinctions would surely halt the wheels of progress or "throw the world back into temporary barbarism." He who is frank and clear in his judgment must admit that "the security of property is the first and all-essential duty of a civilized community."[13]

Their special concern for the protection of the advanced and better members of society was a critical part of the Humanists' views on leadership. Society, Babbitt said, will have leaders, whether they be good or bad, and the notion that mere numerical majorities reflecting the "general will" could be a substitute for a leadership class was only a "pernicious conceit." "In the long run democracy will be judged, no less than other forms of government, by the quality of its leaders." But here again a constant threat to democracy was the loss of its best people. Too often its citizens bestow the highest honors on the man of the hour to the neglect of the "true philosophers." The latter More described in Platonic terms as those "who have won the difficult citadel of their own souls." Their withdrawal from public affairs to an ivory tower is a serious loss, for the most able were likely then to devote their energies to isolated work and thus deprive society of the talent and wisdom it needed. The better citizen, then, must have surer access to positions of authority. "The state cannot progress," More said, ". . . unless a certain advantage of honour accrues to those individuals who are themselves governed by reason, with the privilege of imposing their will on those who, from the rational point of view, are inferior to them."[14]

The same sense of priorities governed Babbitt's and More's attitudes toward the working class. Babbitt objected that Marxist labor theories of value were strictly quantitative measures that fostered a misleading standard of measure. But there was also in the socialist's philosophy a distinctly romantic perspective that saw something inherently superior in manual labor, as opposed to intellectual productivity or managerial talent. Rousseau fitted that moral identification into his primitivistic creed, and, Babbitt said, reduced work "to its lowest terms." Babbitt rejoined that society had best reassess its priorities and do more to honor the "higher forms of working." For its own advantage it should encourage those who work with their minds over those who work with their hands. The quality of a man's work, Babbitt said, should determine his place in the social order. Civilization demands that certain persons be relieved from the necessity of working with their hands, and from this group should come its leadership class. This practice would not work solely for the benefit of the privileged few; rather, the encouragement of this class's talents was the surest prescription for the amelioration of the working class and society altogether. "As a result of the concentrated mental effort of the

[13] More, *Aristocracy and Justice,* pp. 31, 132–33, 135–36. The quotations are on p. 136.

[14] Babbitt, *Democracy and Leadership,* p. 16; More, *Aristocracy and Justice,* pp. 119–20.

gifted few," Babbitt remarked, "an effort displayed either in invention or else in organization and management, the common laborer may to-day enjoy comforts that were out of the reach even of the opulent only two or three generations ago." The laborer himself, if he wishes to preserve these advantages, would shun the agitator who tries to instill in him a sense of superiority. More agreed, and on the matter of priorities made the same emphasis as Babbitt. "Let us, in the name of a long-suffering God," he said, "put some bounds to the flood of talk about the wages of the bricklayer and the trainman, and talk a little more about the income of the artist and teacher and public censor." [15]

Not only were society's elite the major agents of progress, but at the top also lay the greatest danger of decay. The Humanists were not at all enamored with the leadership class in America and warned that any reform efforts that would confront the real crisis of the nation must consider that group first. Babbitt and More believed that history supported their contention. The decay of Rome, More argued, spread from the top down. Not the plebeians, but the corrupt factions of the Senate and the treachery of the patricians corroded the empire. And in France, Babbitt said, the dissipation of the aristocracy was the first seed of the revolution. [16] But if corruption and decay were rampant in high places, one had better deal with the problem there than seek a revolution by inflaming the passions of the masses below or by proclaiming some abstract ideal of social justice. Both Babbitt and More found American life pervaded by the financial greed and dishonesty of the wealthy classes. But they insisted that society would improve only with the reform of that group and not through an attack on property or wealth. This was a definite problem for the Humanists, for if property and power did not accrue to the disciplined and responsible, their defense of social distinctions on that basis was invalidated. "Our real hope of safety," Babbitt urged, "lies in our being able to induce our future Harrimans and Rockefellers to liberalize their own souls, in other words to get themselves rightly educated." The remedy for the evils of corruption was "in the moderation and magnanimity of the

[15] Babbitt, *Democracy and Leadership,* pp. 191–93; More, *Aristocracy and Justice,* p. 32. Babbitt was not wholly unsympathetic to the plight of the laborer. He was part of a system that reduced him to a mere cog in a giant machine and deprived his work of human qualities. The industrial revolution that had triumphed through the ruthless cult of efficiency resulted in an endless subdivision of labor, Babbitt explained, so much that the industrial workers contributed but an infinitesimal part of himself to his labor. Therein was the cruelest aspect of his situation (*Democracy and Leadership,* p. 212).

[16] More, *Aristocracy and Justice,* p. 33; Babbitt, *Democracy and Leadership,* p. 124.

strong," and not in any "sickly sentimentalizing over the lot of the under-dog." Society, Babbitt warned, could not raise itself by its bootstraps; though its men of power were capable of much harm, they held the only promise for useful leadership.[17]

Babbitt remarked once that whereas it had been the effect of Christianity to make the rich man humble, Rousseau had the effect of making the poor man proud. The external dualism of the romantic philosophy made the unsuccessful appear in his own eyes a victim of society. This shift in emphasis boded ill for genuine social improvement and even placed bombs in anarchists' hands. Here also Babbitt identified the attack on property with an attack on distinctions. Social reform that turned from the essential business of curbing the desires of the man at the top to inflame the desires of the man at the bottom was entirely misplaced. An attack on the institution of property, Babbitt said, will invariably be an attack on in-dustry and thrift in favor of laziness and incompetence. The humanitarian dreamer and the radical reformer alike deluded themselves in imagining that egalitarian schemes could assure any meaningful progress. Even though competition produced its evils, no real justice could be fulfilled without it. Competition and the promise of reward, Babbitt believed, could alone arouse man from his natural indolence. The material rewards that honored success were the just rewards of the virtuous and the marks of distinction that always divided the ranks of men.[18]

The critique of democracy in the early decades of the twentieth century was not the sole prerogative of the New Humanists. Indeed, from H. L. Mencken the attack came with even greater flair. In the pages of his *American Mercury* Mencken scored the democratic mediocrity of American life and rivaled the Humanists in disdaining the humanitarian meddler and the political leveler. Mencken and the Humanists recognized their affinity on the general issue. Babbitt's essay on Mencken noted their common distaste for the present state of American politics, while Men-cken in turn praised Babbitt's *Democracy and Leadership* for the "effective blow" it struck at the "stale sentimentalism" rank in the American mentality

[17] Irving Babbitt, *Literature and the American College* (Boston, 1908), p. 71; idem., *Democracy and Leadership*, p. 205. More wrote: "It is an ugly fact, as the world has always seen, that, under cover of the natural inequality of property, evil and greedy men will act in a way that can only be characterized as legal robbery. It is strictly within the province of the State to prevent such action as far as it safely can. Yet even here, in view of the magnitude of the interests involved [i.e., the rights of property] *it is better that legal robbery should exist along with the maintenance of law, than that legal robbery should be suppressed at the expense of law*" (*Aristocracy and Justice*, p. 141).

[18] Babbitt, *Democracy and Leadership*, pp. 77, 205.

and "the whole degraded buffoonery of Americanism."[19] Often Mencken's political language was identical with Babbitt's and More's. He thus summarized American democracy: "What baffles statesmen is to be solved by the people, instantly and by a seraphic intuition. . . . The cure for the evils of democracy is more democracy." Mencken was equally aristocratic in his notions and shared the Humanists' prescriptions for social progress. "All growth must occur at the top." "The strong must grow stronger, and that they may do so, they must waste no strength in the vain task of trying to lift up the weak."[20] But, the manifest similarities notwithstanding, the real thread of common opinion between Mencken and the Humanists was actually thin, scarcely enough to make them allies. In fact, a serious difference on fundamental questions divided them.

Mencken had emerged early in his career as a champion of the German philosopher Friedrich Nietzsche. He found in him the critical fuel for his own assault on democracy: Nietzsche's repugnance toward the "herd morality" and his endorsement of the superior individual, the "superman." Here, however, was the point of separation between the Humanists and Menckenites, even though there are shared views. Both insisted that the able and creative few, what Mencken always called the "civilized minority," were the victims of the inferior many in democratic society. Mencken too judged American democracy a conspiracy of the weak against the strong and saw in its Puritan morality and in the legislative mill the fetters forged by the herd to hold the intelligent and free soul in conformity. Nietzsche's hero became a rebel against society, posing against prevailing convention the force of his own "will to power."[21]

But on this note the Humanists and the Nietzsche-Mencken school severed ties. No less menacing to civilization than the self-righteous do-gooder, the Humanists believed, was the ruthless seeker after power. And this danger was most often a threat from above, the work of the un-scrupulous politician or businessman that constituted a serious betrayal of the leadership class. It stemmed from a dislocation of humanist values that Babbitt and More traced to the ascendancy of naturalistic and romantic principles, particularly visible in the Nietzschean influence.

More tied the deficiency of the Nietzschean ethics to its violation of human duality. For, like Rousseau, Nietzsche posited a dualism not of man

[19] Irving Babbitt, *On Being Creative and Other Essays* (Boston, 1932), p. 207; Seward Collins, "Criticism in America: The Origins of a Myth," *Bookman,* 71 (1929–1930), 362.

[20] H. L. Mencken, *Notes on Democracy* (New York, 1926), pp. 3–4; quoted in Richard Ruland, *The Rediscovery of American Literature* (Cambridge, Mass., 1967), pp. 100, 102.

[21] Quoted in Ruland, p. 102.

against himself but of man against society. The shift in emphasis, however, produced dangers of different extremes, even though they derived from the same original fallacy. That is, the external dualism yielded not only the anarchist and the humanitarian but also the superman. For the plight of the superman derived from without, from the restraints imposed by the mediocre many, the democratic masses. Rousseau and Nietzsche, recognizing the only reality as "the world of passions and desires," both looked for solutions through the liberation of the natural instincts. These might be universal sympathy deriving from the benevolent instinct, but this romantic expansion Nietzsche himself scorned. He substituted in its place the will to power. Babbitt could therefore charge that Nietzsche merely replaced one will with another, and so, like Rousseau, lacked the humanist inner check. In both cases there was the promise of progress through the expansion of individual temperament rather than restraint, a misconception that pointed more to social chaos than to social cohesion. [22]

In a larger context it is clear that the Humanists shared many social views with the earlier Victorian critics of democracy, especially Carlyle, Ruskin, and Arnold. It was a common ground, furthermore, that made the Humanists' position ultimately impotent and ineffective. Like these critics, the Humanists, as we shall see, upheld an organic view of society against an atomistic and individualistic one and were also severely averse to traditional laissez-faire economics. With Ruskin they condemned economic orthodoxy for its one-sided view of human nature and saw its endorsement of the acquisitive and competitive instincts playing directly into the hands of the Nietzschean individualists. The ethics of power built on this tradition had so brutalized American life that it elicited even from More a note of compassion: "History pronounces the philosophy of Manchester one of the most heartless creations of the human brain." [23] But, like their Victorian

---

[22] Paul Elmer More, *Studies of Religious Dualism* (1909; rpt. New York, 1967), p. 239; idem., *Drift of Romanticism*, pp. 179–80; Babbitt, *Democracy and Leadership*, p. 228. It should be noted too that although the Humanists shared with Mencken distinct elitist sympathies, they were never so excoriating as Mencken in their references to democracy. The Nietzschean breastbeating of Mencken discouraged that possibility. More and especially Babbitt did appreciate human freedom, and in a reference to the founding fathers, whose political realism he extolled, Babbitt confirmed that "the type of constitutional liberty that we owe to these men before all others is one of the greatest blessings that has ever been vouchsafed to any people" (*Democracy and Leadership*, p. 250; see also More, *Aristocracy and Justice*, p. 30).

[23] More, *Aristocracy and Justice*, p. 172. On this point too the Humanists, though holding much in common with the earlier Mugwump and Genteel critics, broke from their brand of nineteenth-century conservatism. See John J. Sproat, *"The Best Men": Liberal Reformers in the Gilded Age* (London, 1968), pp. 177–78.

counterparts, the Humanists had no faith in the masses, turned with distaste from the values and quality of mass society, and tolerated no leveling schemes of social reform. Their own program had to turn, then, as any truly conservative program must, on the successful location of an elite leadership, the aristocratic principle within the democratic structure.

In the end the Victorian answer was little help to the Humanists, and they were unable to find alternatives. Carlyle found an answer by borrowing from German romanticism, particularly from Fichte, the ideas for his Hero, who reveals the Divine Idea at the particular historical moment and emerges as the principle of order. Carlyle eventually bestowed this honor on the new captains of industry, proper successors to Cromwell and Frederick the Great. Carlyle's ideas, it has been observed, anticipated in precise outline the whole fascist movement of the twentieth century.[24] But not for this reason alone did Babbitt find them inadequate. Carlyle's hero was imperialistic, expansive rather than disciplined in temperament, and "a first cousin of the Nietzschean superman"; both have "an authentic descent" from the original genius of the romantic era.[25]

The Humanists were actually closer to Matthew Arnold's social program, to some extent because it derived largely from his dualistic philosophy. But Arnold had greater cause for despair than either Carlyle or Ruskin, because he saw no hope that an English aristocracy that worshipped Mammon would pursue a course of self-reform. Only a fractional minority of society's souls could ever follow their higher selves, but it was on this element alone that society depended for growth. Like the Humanists, Arnold looked to an effective educational system to supply the professions, the universities, the churches, and the civil service with a cultured elite. Arnold could trust to social salvation neither through a social class nor a charismatic leader but relied ultimately on the ideal of humane civilization and its beneficial influence.[26] But the Humanists, it is worth noting, never appealed directly to Arnold for social enlightenment as they did for aesthetic. Indeed, it is hard to avoid concluding that the Humanists simply despaired that an ideal such as Arnold's could ever realize itself in an American democratic milieu. The Humanists saw only two means of resolving the democratic dilemma, and both were terribly feeble. They themselves certainly had little confidence in either one.

Caught between their fears of radical democracy on the one hand and their disdain for the cult of individual and corporate power on the other,

[24] Benjamin Evans Lippincott, *Victorian Critics of Democracy* (Minneapolis, 1938), pp. 22, 47–49.

[25] Babbitt, *Democracy and Leadership,* p. 212.

[26] Lippincott, pp. 94–95, 109–110.

the Humanists were neutralized into a middle position that lacked the vitality, strength, substance, and popular appeal of the extremes. Their critics rightly pointed to one of the major deficiencies of the movement—its lack of program. The Humanists, insofar as they pointed to any solution at all, appealed to a standard of justice that barely transcended the individual person as the unit of action.

The best illustration of this characteristic is Babbitt and More's concept of justice. They found in both egalitarian schemes and doctrines of individual power a violation of true justice. But their own efforts to present a usable theory began, not with a large social principle, but with a theory of individual conduct. Specifically, both Babbitt and More appealed to the Platonic concept of justice. They summarized Plato's position by saying that justice is not concerned at first with the outer man, his behavior toward his fellows, but with the inner man. For the just man is he whose house is in the right order through the harmony of his faculties. It is he who has achieved a true humanist proportion of the will, the reason, and the sensibility. "Justice," as Babbitt presented the Platonic concept, "results when every part of a man is performing its proper function," and especially when the higher self is coordinating and controlling the inferior parts of his nature. The just thing, then, is what preserves this harmony in whatever activity of life, and the knowledge which promotes it is wisdom.[27]

The Humanists' view was simple in essence, but also fundamental. Babbitt and More pronounced it the basic categorical difference in the approach to social problems that distinguished the Humanists from the humanitarians. Between the man who puts the main emphasis on the inner life and the man who puts it on the "progress and service of humanity," there was, Babbitt insisted, an opposition "of first principles." The second course sprang directly from the dissolution of the inner dualism by the humanitarian. For the Platonic notion required that one put his own work before the world's work and argued that any ethical union, whether on the communal, national, or international level, emerges not from the emotional expansion of universal benevolence "but only by the pathway of the inner life."[28]

Their reflections on social life and the imagination demonstrate again the persistence of the dualistic philosophy as the governing framework of the New Humanists in all categories of thought. The application of the imagination to political life was a direct extension of its place in the

---

[27] More, *Studies of Religious Dualism*, pp. 336–37; Babbitt, *Democracy and Leadership*, pp. 197–98.

[28] Babbitt, *Democracy and Leadership*, pp. 26, 310.

human condition. In the contest between the lower and higher self for mastery of the individual, the imagination always held the critical balance; it would unite either with the reason to check the pull of the expansive impulses of the natural man, or it would join with those drives to enhance their power against an inner check. And the alliance that prevailed was as crucial in society as in the individual, because here too no amount of abstract reasoning would serve by itself to stay the passions of the multitude. Society's check on itself, like that of the individual against himself, required the pull of the imagination, not with the emotion of the moment, but against that tide. Babbitt even argued that the battle that had been waged in political affairs for over a century was really a battle between the conservative spirit of Burke and the liberal spirit of Rousseau, and that contest was above all an "opposition between two different types of imagination."[29]

The ascent into the higher life, the Humanists maintained, required the discovery by the individual of an imaginative, or illusionary, world that set itself against his natural state and its control by the instincts and passions. The problems for the state and for society were similar in nature and linked inseparably to that of the individual. "The idea that the State should have a permanent or higher self that is felt as a veto power upon its ordinary self," Babbitt said, "rests ultimately upon the assertion of a similar dualism in the individual." For Babbitt and More the higher self of society was the acquired wisdom of tradition and the past that should always claim priority over the prevailing sentiments of the hour. Here was the familiar battle of the permanent against the flux writ large in the affairs of society. For tradition was nothing less than the established experience of any community, its permanent self that unites the past with the present and is the rational restraint against the popular whim. "There is an opposition of first principles," Babbitt asserted, between those who contend for the prevalence of the popular will immediately and unrestrictedly through the registration of majority opinion and those who maintain that it should be purified first of what is merely ephemeral and impulsive in it.[30] Each view derived from radically different conceptions of the nature of man and the nature of the state.

Babbitt defined the imaginative appeal of Rousseau as the most powerful force in the modern world. Behind its many-sided assault on civilized society and its institutions was the "idyllic imagination" of Rousseau's romantic naturalism. Babbitt recognized that philosophies of nature and natural rights were in the air before Rousseau, but it was the effect of Rousseau to cloak abstract and inert ideas in the pastoral image, thereby

[29] Ibid., p. 69.
[30] Ibid., pp. 273, 99, 247.

giving them a motivating content. Babbitt explained that the forms in which Rousseau constructed his philosophy of nature replaced the earlier Christian pattern, in which saintliness derived from one's nearness to God, with a new emphasis that made virtue the product of one's nearness to nature. Within that scheme the plain man of the common people loomed most conspicuously. Romantic literature celebrated the uncorrupted state of the peasant and found a blissful innocence "in huts where poor men lie."[31] Babbitt was sensitive to the force of that motif in the American popular mind and regarded it as one of the real dangers of the Rousseauistic influence. The idyllic imagination unduly flattered the man at the bottom of the social ladder, he said, fostering in his mind the illusion that he was the moral and intellectual superior of the upper ranks. Rousseau further compounded that fallacy by picturing the state of nature as the natural and happy condition of things, so that when reality refused to fly in the face of that fancy it was all too easy to convince the simple-minded that failure is due neither to the ideal nor to himself; it was the working of some conspiracy of persons or things. So invariably society was the culprit, and the result of this felicitous rationale was usually a vicious contempt for the existing order and an inflamed passion to destroy it all. One need only do away with the artificial restraints of civilization to recover the pristine natural order that was the original gift to man in his natural state. This fallacy and the social consequences attending it led Babbitt to recall a comment by Anatole France: when one starts with the assumption that men are naturally good and virtuous, one ends by wishing to kill them all. The indiscriminate lover of men emerges finally in the clothes of the anarchist.[32]

The idyllic imagination left society with no restraints upon itself, no quality to temper the passions of the multitude by appeal to a higher reason. That deficiency was largely an extension of the fallacies that governed the romantic's view of human nature. For Rousseau knew only the individual and could get outside himself only through a natural benevolence based on emotional expansion. He could offer for the guidance of the state only the collective wisdom of its individual members drawn together in the general will. But the Humanists well knew that the general will was only the instant register of prevailing feelings and thus subjected the state to the immediate and the impulsive. The second danger was Rousseau's original assumption that men are in essence individual units. Celebrating the qualities that differentiated one man from the next, Rousseau in turn conceived society only in terms of its autonomous units

[31] Ibid., pp. 68–69. The quotation from Rousseau is on p. 75.
[32] Ibid., pp. 80–83.

and dismissed the force of its collective tradition and experience. Prescribing that the individual need only follow the emotional path of least resistance, he could urge only that the state yield to the voice of the people in the prevailing popular will. In Rousseau's thinking, Babbitt charged, the religious and political traditions of society were both arbitrary and artificial. The state, like the individual, therefore had not a dual self, but a single self; Rousseau deprived it of appeal to the permanent and unchanging in itself and acknowledged only the exclusive claim of the present.[33]

Against the idyllic imagination of Rousseau both Babbitt and More placed "the moral imagination" of Edmund Burke. Defender of tradition and outspoken critic of Rousseau and the French Revolution, Burke won the allegiance of the two Humanists both for the conservatism of his politics and his recognition of the imaginative force of the past. "In his imaginative grasp of all that is involved in the task of mediating the permanent and the fluctuating element in life," Babbitt said, ". . . he has had few equals in the field of political thinking." It was the merit of Burke to perceive how much the stability of society and the wisdom of the individual consist in the imaginative apprehension of the past and its infusion with the present.[34]

Burke's social ideas, like Rousseau's, derived from a particular view of the human condition. In opposition to the individualism of Rousseau, Burke maintained that along with his private self each person has a self that he shares in common with others. That commonness is the bond of social cohesion. Burke and the Humanists after him found in traditional institutions the higher social self that Rousseau neglected. The conventions of a particular time and place, Babbitt said, must serve as barriers to the "unchained appetites of the individual." They constitute the permanent self of society and, as Burke insisted, were as real in their imaginative content as the immediate and changing. Summarizing Burke's position, More elucidated the relationship between the individual and the social principles of the humanist: "The aim of Burke was to set the stability of aristocratic institutions against the innate restlessness of human nature and to use the imagination as a force for order and self-restraint and political health."[35]

Rousseau's individualism led him to describe the state as by nature atomistic, while Burke's dualism recognized it as organic. More, using

[33] Ibid., p. 100.

[34] Ibid., pp. 105–6.

[35] Babbitt, *Rousseau and Romanticism*, pp. 46–48; More, *Aristocracy and Justice*, p. 188.

that difference to explain the conservative viewpoint of the Humanists, said that the first conception holds as a single standard the prevailing opinion of the majority, while the other is a consecration of the past and looks for the permanent and unchanging to moderate the opinion of the moment. The one knows only mutability, while the other honors "a binding law of duty which cannot be abrogated by the interests of the living generation." The Rousseauistic theory confirms the individual in his inclination, while the conservative prescription seeks to transcend his personal whim and incorporate the "wider meanings of tradition." There is no surer test of the quality of a man's mind, More believed, than the degree to which he feels the "long-remembered past as one of the vital and immediate laws of his being." In their right sense and example, the traditions of society are not merely artificial and arbitrary; they are the selected wisdom of its collective and permanent experience. The imaginative power of the symbols of the past, Babbitt said, draws the individual back to an ethical center, a standard with reference to which he can set bounds to "the lawless expansion of his natural self." The support of society's institutions and the ultimate hope that they will serve as stabilizing forces depend, More added, on their "symbolic sway over the imaginations of men." Without that kind of support, they would "crumble away beneath the aggressive passions of the present."[36]

But in the battle for the imagination it was clear to Babbitt and More that their side was not winning. The whole direction of the modern world, they felt, conspired against the restoration of an imaginative conservatism, for that direction ran increasingly toward change, the new and the transient in human affairs. The imagination, Babbitt said, had been drawn away more and more from the elements of unity in things to the elements of diversity. The modern sense of reality had come to be associated with change and difference, a fact tied closely to the phenomena of expanding knowledge and the material improvement of the race through technological advances. Life in the modern era, Babbitt remarked, "no longer involves

[36] More, *Aristocracy and Justice*, pp. 178–79, 19–20; Babbitt, *Democracy and Leadership*, p. 109. Both Babbitt and More praised the political thought and practice of Benjamin Disraeli, and More illustrated through Disraeli the link between the imaginative concept of the state and its traditions and the conservative principles that he and Babbitt shared. For Disraeli the institutions of England were its higher self, the basis of unity among its citizens and the imaginative force that cemented them. More quoted from an early speech by the British statesman: "By the Conservative Cause I mean the splendor of the crown, . . . the privileges of the Commons, the rights of the poor. I mean that harmonious union, that magnificent concord of all interests, of all classes, on which our national greatness and prosperity depends" (*Aristocracy and Justice*, p. 180).

any reverence for some centre or oneness, but is conceived as an infinite and indefinite expansion of wonder and curiosity."[37]

Nowhere were these tendencies more pronounced than in democratic America. More emphasized that point by citing the superiority of the imaginative quality of British life over the less traditional United States. A nation born in revolt against the past and prospering richly if ingloriously from its material achievements was particularly susceptible to the appeal of the moment, a vulnerability enhanced all the more by its democratic expansiveness. The society that More observed thrived on that appeal and reveled in sensationalism and sentimentalism. It had developed elaborate media to provide the thrills. Its key, More said, was "always appeal to the emotion of the hour, and present it in terms which shall justify its excess." The central problem for modern American society was the vitalization of institutions that would hold a countersway over the imagination. But by its very nature democracy was the least equipped of all social forms to create and perpetuate such symbols.[38]

More and Babbitt tried diligently to tie their social views to a Humanist framework and place them within the larger context of a general conception of human nature. But was there a necessary link between Humanism itself and a conservative political creed? The democratic defense of Stuart Sherman, though largely unsystematic, uncritical, and heavily emotional, showed that Humanism did not necessarily lead to Burke. Even during the period when Sherman was most under the influence of Babbitt, his democratic enthusiasm was intense and rivaled his Humanism in dominating his literary criticism. Sherman's position troubled Babbitt and More from the beginning, and others within the camp regarded him as something of an alien. G. R. Elliott thought that Sherman's own term for his credo, democratic humanism, was really a contradiction, in fact if not in theory. Elliott insisted that Humanism could never give effective aid to democracy and even charged that democracy had already seriously undermined Humanist values.[39] But Sherman in turn urged that if humanism did not integrate itself with the democratic spirit and ideals of America, it would assign itself to futility, to the detriment of its advocates and the democratic system that stood to profit from it.

Sherman differed with Babbitt and More on fundamental attitudes, but his approach to social and political matters reflected characteristics similar to theirs. Like the two older Humanists, Sherman did not consider

[37] Babbitt, *Democracy and Leadership*, pp. 103, 114–15.

[38] More, *Aristocracy and Justice*, pp. 18–20, 27 (the quotation).

[39] G. R. Elliott, *Humanism and Imagination* (Chapel Hill, N.C., 1938), p. 84.

himself a political philosopher and took little interest in the political issues of the day. Both his published writings and his private correspondence rarely refer to the pages of the morning paper. Quite significant about Sherman's democratic defense is the fact that it emerges most strongly in his literary criticism. For democracy, to Sherman, was really an affair of the imagination, and he was no less aware than Babbitt or More that any successful political program must win on that level. Sherman expressed that awareness in the very designation he gave his ideals, the "religion of democracy." In that term Sherman included both principles of his creed and suggested the manner by which they merged into a moving imaginative unit. In a 1918 letter to More, Sherman offered his "definition" of democracy, one that manifests the emotional and religious character with which he endowed it: "Democracy is government by *divine revelation to the people of the 'right of man.'* We begin with a sacred book of abstract principles which we call our constitution or what not. These principles summarize our 'divine intuitions.' They oppose the natural tendency of things. They will never be realized on earth, for they constitute a divine plan, a picture of an ideal state—like the Beatitudes or the Decalogue." Sherman admitted that the definition was crude and needed polishing, but the sense that it conveyed was important. For a national religion, one that would spring from the common political heritage of all Americans, should expand to include not only the mere allegiance to principles but also an imaginative grasp of all things American. That was the enlivened consciousness that would create a truly national literature and lift America out of its spiritual slumber. Sherman had even his own Humanist colleagues in mind when he called on "superior men" to slough off their aristocratic notions and accept "the purified religion of democracy." To oppose it, he said, "is to oppose the formative spirit of our national life and to doom one's self to sterility." America must somehow effect a renewal of the national will "on the basis of a genuinely democratic humanism, recognizing as its central principle the duty of bringing the whole body of the people to the fullest and fairest human life of which they are capable."[40]

Sherman's appeal to democracy never left the plane of emotion, and this above all disturbed Babbitt and More. The latter thought Sherman uncritical if not naive. He and Babbitt were vexed particularly at their younger colleague's disinclination to deal with democracy on rational and intellectual grounds. So More told Sherman not to get "slushy." "The sure way to turn democracy from a blessing to a curse," he said, "is to puff

[40] Sherman to More, Mar. 12, 1918, Sherman Correspondence, University of Illinois Archives, Urbana-Champaign; Stuart P. Sherman, *The Genius of America* (New York, 1923), pp. 230–31.

it up with conceit and call it heroic and curse those who criticize it."[41]
Such easy enthusiasm too quickly passed over important human distinctions and flattered the lesser sorts along with the better. Sherman himself
was impatient with More's kind of criticism and argued back that democratic idealism was the strongest power against a crude naturalism.
Rightly exercised, it would furnish the spiritual content of the higher self
against the brutal qualities of the natural. Said Sherman: "If 'P. E. M.' had
a bit more of that natural sympathy, of which he is so distrustful, he
would have perceived that what more than anything else today keeps the
average man from lapsing into Yahooism is the *religion of democracy*."[42]

The political question, as the Humanists approached it, invariably involved the problem of control. Sherman knew that as much as Babbitt
and More, though they disagreed fundamentally on programs and technique. Sherman sought to supply the content for a higher national self
from America's democratic ideal, imbued with a pervasive religious quality.
That spirit, he thought, would redirect democracy's citizens away from
their brutish instincts and check the naturalistic forces rampant in modern
society. Babbitt and More's reply to Sherman merely discounted Sherman's
promised results; they believed his program simply would not work.
Democratic idealism might not lead to yahooism, but its uncritical flattery
and pomp were more likely to be expansive than constrictive in nature,
emotional rather than reflective. Babbitt perceived here only a false
idealism that he considered the mainspring of the most troublesome
quality in the American national psychology, the imperialist temper. And
he was quick to warn of the dangers. America's waxing imperialism, he
feared, posed one of the greatest threats to stability in the nation and the
world at large.

The imperialist temper joined with the nationalist, and in the latter

[41] Quoted [by Seward Collins] in "Chronicle and Comment," *Bookman*, 70
(1929–1930), 295.

[42] Dakin, *Paul Elmer More,* pp. 187–88. Sherman, however, did not consider himself a leveler. He likened himself to a Walt Whitman who could celebrate the
plain and common and find in the mass of men a resounding moral energy. But,
like Whitman, he too was "a democrat with an exorbitant thirst for distinction."
Sherman said that he always looked for the person with large interests, the
powerful, free individuals whom Whitman celebrated. In Whitman were the
"germs of a new aristocracy" that could revitalize America's spiritual life. Though
Sherman looked first to the imaginative writer for this inspiration, he believed he
could fill the ranks from the real world of politics and business also. He demonstrated that wide selectivity in essays on Andrew Carnegie and Theodore
Roosevelt. See *Americans,* pp. 246–87. But surely when we consider Sherman's
selections and recall More's remarks on property, we recognize not only how
desperate but also how unproductive were the Humanists' efforts to locate an
aristocratic element within the American democratic structure.

Babbitt perceived the infectious mentality of romanticism. Its self-flattery and emotional expansiveness were dangerous in themselves, to be sure, but became all the more menacing when linked with the dominant commercial ambitions of modern American life. The flag-waving superpatriot roused Babbitt's animosity, and he could little distinguish the indiscriminate lover of humanity from the blind worshipper of the state. His distaste for the nationalist further separated him from Sherman, both in literary and political views. Sherman's essay "American and Allied Ideals" was in many parts only heated passion. But his insistence that "the American who has not been thoroughly indoctrinated with American ideals is a menace to the Republic" reflected in Babbitt's judgment a spirit that was anti-Humanist and potentially destructive. National idolatry of any kind Babbitt renounced. "One is here at the root of the most dangerous of all the sham religions of the modern age," he said, "—the religion of country, the frenzied nationalism that is now threatening to make an end of civilization itself."[43]

The nationalist and imperialist mentality, Babbitt believed, was the product both of the prevailing modern culture and of conditions peculiar to the American experience. He saw the nationalist movement as the child of the romantic age. Rousseau had first identified the important elements of personal character with individual temperament, and Babbitt explained that it was easy for Fichte and others in the German romantic school to make the next step of identifying the nation with the national temperament. The romantic cult of emotional expansion burst the bonds of restraint and was ready to worship at any altar, whether that of the individual, humanity, or the nation. But it also made for a peculiar cult of tradition. For in its search for original genius, the romantic nationalist looked invariably for the source of the national spirit. Thus the same sentimentalism that led to the celebration of childhood as the ideal and uncorrupted condition of natural man led the nationalist back to the Middle Ages and the earliest expression there of a pure national, or folk, spirit. Herder thus called the Germans to a greater awareness of their national genius and to the golden beginnings of that spirit in early poetry, legends, and folk tales. But if the romantic could be a traditionalist in this manner, the Humanist could not. For the function of traditional symbols had conflicting effects in each case. The romantic turned to the past for emotional outlet and expansion, and in doing so exercised not a common humanity but a narrowly national or racial temper. The ultimate failure of the romantics, Babbitt said, was neglecting to refer the national genius back

[43] Sherman, "American and Allied Ideals," p. 104; Babbitt, *Rousseau and Romanticism*, pp. 344–45.

to some ethical center that would set limits to its expansion. The tendency, then, was for the members of a whole national group to flatter one another and inbreed their national experience without reference to a common and universal humanity. Without that center the nationalist is without a restraining ethical check. Babbitt, writing in 1919, charged that Germany had lived mostly in a state of moral isolation respecting its relations with other nations.[44] He and More defended the symbols of the past and tradition explicitly for their restraining effects on the national temper and on individual behavior.

For a principle of international peace and justice, Babbitt and More returned again to the Platonic theme. The just state sprang from the just man, and the just man was master of himself. A nation is most likely to act toward its neighbors, Babbitt pointed out, as its citizens act toward each other. "For behind all imperialism," he said, "is ultimately the imperialistic individual, just as behind all peace is ultimately the peaceful individual." The path to world peace depended neither on the democratic extension of the rights of self-determination nor on the machinery of the League of Nations. One must return at last and inevitably to the individual unit. Wrote Babbitt: "A State that is controlled by men who have become just as a result of minding their own business in the Platonic sense will be a just State that will also mind its own business." It will be a service to other states not by its commercial ambitions nor by its idealism but, in the manner of all true leadership, by its example.[45]

To some extent the democratic dilemma, one that the Humanists were by no means the first to recognize or in their own day the only persons to confront, was a dilemma of their own making. Their discussion of the social imagination and its role was valid, and modern sociology has sanctioned much of its outline. But as a Humanist alternative it raised a problem for which Humanism did not have any applicable answer. Let us grant that conservative and traditional symbols can and do provide a check to individual temperament and a measure of value against the individual will and imagination. What, however, is to prevent them from becoming forces that are anything but disciplinary, both to the individual and the society in its collective outlook and its sense of itself? Babbitt rightly feared nationalism, but he never made it clear how the Burkean imagination itself was not conducive to the nationalism that has plagued modern history. Babbitt was not wholly insensitive to this problem, to be sure, and certainly was more comfortable with an appeal to a classical humanism

[44] Babbitt, *Rousseau and Romanticism,* pp. 346–47; idem., *Literature and the American College,* pp. 185–87.

[45] Babbitt, *Democracy and Leadership,* pp. 136, 309.

in the widest sense, one that brought Greek civilization, Christianity, and Buddhism within its imagination. Nonetheless, it must be admitted that Reinhold Niebuhr, in his *Moral Man and Immoral Society*, demonstrated a more sensitive appreciation and better social grasp of this problem than the Humanists, showing how it is nearly impossible for individuals, living and working in groups and organizations, to divert their own disciplining moral idealism from the immoral activity of the larger society.

Certainly one factor that failed to sustain the Humanist movement beyond the sudden popularity it attained at the end of the 1920s was its failure to translate its values into a program of social action. On this point other cultural conservatives like the Southern Agrarians were more effective and preserved their audience in the depression years while the Humanists' declined. On the surface it is plausible that it was the Humanists', dualism that brought the movement short. Their nearly total obsession with the higher life of the individual virtually blinded them to important movements in sociology, many of which could have been effective against their liberal opponents. The Humanists made the higher self a mystery, empirically evident but not susceptible to empirical analysis. And although they allowed that science could study natural man behavioristically, precisely because that was only half (and the least important half) of the human totality, they forfeited all interest in the conclusions. Surely this is one reason also why John Dewey and his followers maintained their public interest amid the Humanist decline. For not only did Dewey dissolve completely the mind-body dualism, he dissolved the individual-society dualism as well. Human nature was the virtual sum total of its multifarious interactions with its social environment, so philosophy was invariably social and practical in all its considerations.[46] The perspective itself does not confirm the correctness of Dewey's views, though they had monumental implications that the Humanists too easily passed over; it does, however, demonstrate the advantages and appeal of a philosophical system that takes all of life as its grounds of investigation and includes in it a careful attention to the behavior of social classes, groups, and institutions, as well as individuals.

But this is not the entire answer. It would be wholly incorrect to maintain that a dualistic human philosophy must invariably be indifferent to a contextual social analysis or incapable of presenting one. The Humanist movement was beginning just when modern sociology was emerging and even operating within a closer philosophical framework than it does today. Like the Humanists, Emile Durkheim "stood solidly in the classical tradition of moral philosophy that stemmed from Plato and Aristotle,"

[46] James Gouinlock, *John Dewey's Philosophy of Value* (New York, 1972), p. 106.

and, although critical of much in the Western dualistic tradition, he vehemently opposed all forms of reductive naturalism. Durkheim's 1914 essay "Le Dualisme de la nature humaine et ses conditions sociales" is worth quoting at one key part because it is so similar to the Humanists' own language. Durkheim wrote:

These two aspects of our psychic life are, therefore, opposed to each other as are the personal and the impersonal. There is a being in us that represents everything in relation to itself and from its own point of view; in everything that it does, this being has no other object but itself. There is another being in us, however, which knows things *sub specie aeternitis* [*sic*], as if it were participating in some thought other than its own, and which, in its acts, tends to accomplish ends that surpass its own. The old formula *homo duplex* is therefore verified by the facts.[47]

Furthermore, Durkheim shared with the Humanists an impatience with any system that linked the moral and spiritual self with a supernatural or transcendent reality outside the natural order of things, and opposed Kant on these grounds. Durkheim was interested in the higher self, especially as a social reality, and his sociology was to a large measure an effort to analyze its behavior. It was Durkheim's dualism in fact that enabled him to posit within the realm of nature an entity, "society," that is responsible for engendering collectively shared beliefs and values. Properly, human dualism translates into an "individual" self and a "social" self. Nor is this social self a merely expansive humanitarian sentiment that simply supplements the individual ego. No one appreciated more than Durkheim how critical for the health of society and the individual was the appropriation of the larger values and norms of the social whole by the individual. "If [these] dissolve, if we no longer feel [them] in existence and action about us, whatever is social in us is deprived of all objective foundation. All that remains is an artificial combination of illusionary images . . . nothing which can be a goal for our action."[48]

These perspectives led Durkheim into detailed examinations of social institutions—the family, the school, the state—for he was concerned with how the higher moral self of the individual and society works and what conditions are most conducive to its healthy exercise. It is not necessary to review Durkheim's investigations (on education, to make just one reference, his ideas were quite similar to the Humanists'); the point is merely to show that the Humanists' dualism did not exclude the possibility of

[47] Ernest Wallwork, *Durkheim: Morality and Milieu* (Cambridge, Mass., 1972), pp. vii, 13–14. The quotations are on pp. vii, 61.

[48] Ibid., pp. 17, 38, 49 (the quotation).

important social implications. One must be disappointed that these possibilities were barely glimpsed by the Humanists, for, with the exception of
education, they never grappled with the concrete in a manner that would
have given flesh and blood to their critique of modern America. The
Humanists, however, did make an intelligent plea for the priorities of
the gifted few and the enlarged arena for the exercise of their talents. In
a nation much given to indiscriminate leveling in its official rhetoric,
that plea required courage and merited more consideration than it received.
But in the end, though the Humanists perceived and effectively outlined
much of the problem of democracy, they scarcely began to solve it.

CHAPTER SEVEN

The Religious Alternative

When studied with any degree of thoroughness, the economic problem will be found to run into the political problem, the political problem into the philosophical problem, and the philosophical problem to be almost indissolubly bound up at last with the religious problem.

—Irving Babbitt

RELIGION WAS HUMANISM'S alter ego. It was Humanism's ally and friend, eliciting from the Humanists the warmest affection though also an occasional rebuke. The Humanists did have a quarrel with religion, but it was really a lover's quarrel, one that allowed for a sharp exchange of criticism only because each partner knew that beneath the surface of disagreement was an enduring bond of mutual affection. The situation is illustrated in a story told by Paul Elmer More. After Babbitt's death, More recalled an earlier visit with his friend and a stroll together on North Avenue in Boston. When they passed a church, Babbitt turned to More and cried, "There is the enemy! there is the thing I hate!" But that surprising outburst came from one who honestly acknowledged a debt to religion and even conceded that the Catholic church might be the only institution left that could uphold "civilized standards" in the modern world.[1]

This ambivalence pervaded much of the New Humanist's discussion of religious ideas and the place of religion in contemporary society. For many of them religion, both as a discipline and as a unifying tradition, was an ideal they believed could no longer prevail, and this group frankly asserted that Humanism, "critical and positive," as Babbitt called it, could alone offer modern man the path to the higher life that he would not accept from dogmatic religion or supernatural faith. Others, particularly More, traveled the route through Humanism to religion, or at least maintained an allegiance to both. A third group, of which T. S. Eliot was most outspoken, insisted that Humanism could never succeed without the help of the dogma and faith of the

[1] Paul Elmer More, *On Being Human* (Princeton, 1936), p. 37; Irving Babbitt, *Democracry and Leadership* (Boston, 1924), p. 186. Or: "I hold that at the heart of genuine Christianity are certain truths which have already once saved Western civilization and, judiciously employed, may save it again" (ibid., p. 22).

religious life and should therefore join with organized religion to reinvigorate modern society. The strictly Humanist and the religious factions, then, never quarreled over ultimate objectives—the spiritual regeneration and discipline of the modern world. They did divide seriously on programs, and the central question emerged whether Humanism could provide the cohesive faith by which religion in an earlier period had given purpose and cultural unity to human society. And as with the discussion of literature, the different reflections and considerations on religion greatly amplified the New Humanism itself. They showed again that Humanism was capable of embracing several variations on a main theme, leaving its own exponents to take positions often strikingly at variance with each other. Indeed, the religious question was probably the knottiest problem the Humanists tackled. On other matters—art and literature, education, politics—they spoke, albeit with different voices, with confidence. The answers to the questions raised by religion never came so easily.

Babbitt had reacted in his youth against both the harsh Calvinism of his boyhood Midwest and the easy spiritualism of his father. The latter long left a bad taste in Irving Babbitt's mouth. The various cults in which his father indulged smacked of complacent romantic indulgence and betrayed the self-disciplining exercise that for Babbitt was the true religious motive. The father, author of such works as *Health and Power, a Handbook of Cure and Human Upbuilding by Aid of New Refined and Powerful Methods of Nature* (1893), *Religion as Revealed by the Natural and Spiritual Universe* (1881), and *The Health Guide: Aiming at a Higher Source of Life and the Life-Forces, Giving Nature's Simple and Beautiful Laws of Cure* (1874), was always a reminder to the son of the age's pseudospirituality. Babbitt in fact took little interest in theology or religious history, and apparently the only books he read on these subjects were those of his friend More. But Babbitt did separate the spiritual core from the ecclesiastical shell of religion and, while always averse to the institutional church, personally respected religious faith as a force that lifted man above the natural plane of existence through its imaginative and spiritual qualities. With the consistency that typified all his endeavors, Babbitt looked throughout his life for a system that would preserve what he considered the useful, enduring elements of religion, but could dispense with the creed, dogma, and institutional paraphernalia that he always rejected because he believed they could no longer hold men's minds in a positivistic age. Babbitt believed that the modern world had suffered in its transition from an age of faith to an age of science and that the loss of the element of supernatural grace had given reign to the romantic and naturalist era that followed. "What I have been looking for," he wrote to a friend, "is the equivalent of this element [of grace], the possible recognition of such an element without the Christian outlook, since so many moderns cannot be Christian believers." Here was one indication of the pragmatic test that occurs throughout the Humanists' discussion of religion, and another illustration of Babbitt's interest in "results." For unless the modern age recovered the sense of need for discipline, he felt, "we shall but continue our naturalistic decadence." So Babbitt chose to "meet the positivists on their own grounds." He would not go beyond "the immediate data of consciousness" and would suspend all appeal to the transcendental and supernatural. And he furthermore insisted that observation and experience did themselves point to the reality of an inner check, the indispensable fact of the duality of the human condition, which was the equivalent in function to the Christian notion of grace.[2]

Though Babbitt was willing to offer Humanism to the modern world by making it critical and empirical, he could not himself abandon the elements of religion, the spiritual and traditional, that always brought from him a sympathetic response. Babbitt even admitted that although religion could get along without Humanism, the latter could not get along without religion; nor could it wholly take its place as an alternative. Christianity had supplied what was lacking in humanist Greece, Babbitt said, by setting up doctrines that humbled reason and by creating symbols that controlled men's imaginations and, through their imaginations, their wills.[3] Humanism would have to accomplish the same task, but without the religious base that disposed the mind to receive an imaginative insight built upon a supernatural framework. Babbitt illustrated that point in two comparisons of the religious and romantic personalities. The religious life, he said, led easily if not necessarily to humility, and humility, Babbitt thought, was essential to a moral life. And as humility diminishes, vain egoistic conceit rushes in to take its place. Babbitt seemed to doubt the ability of the Humanist life itself to provide the former quality. He thought that "humanism should have in it an element of

[2] Quoted by Louis J. A. Mercier, in Frederick Manchester and Odell Shepard, eds., *Irving Babbitt: Man and Teacher* (New York, 1941), p. 200.

[3] Irving Babbitt, "Humanism: An Essay at Definition," in Norman Foerster, ed., *Humanism and America* (New York, 1930), pp. 43–44; Babbitt, *Rousseau and Romanticism* (Boston, 1919), p. 380; idem., *Democracy and Leadership,* p. 175.

religious insight" and suggested that even in this sense Humanism and religion were only different stages along the same path.[4]

Babbitt saw that religion and Humanism were common allies against romanticism. The true Christian, Babbitt pointed out, always saw the world, not as an Arcadian dream in the fashion of the romantic, but as a place of trial and probation. Followers of Christ were not permitted the free indulgence of the instincts. Nature and God were so far from being one that natural man was judged to be so corrupt and sinful that he might bridge the vast gulf that separated him from God only by the miracle of grace. True religion, Babbitt said, is a process of concentration, "the result of the imposition of the veto power upon the expansive desires of the ordinary self." Here, clearly, religion was a Humanist ally. Both were the complete antitheses of the essentially expansive nature of the romanticist and his renunciation of the inner check. "Genuine religion," Babbitt summarized, "must always have in some form the sense of a deep inner cleft between man's ordinary self and the divine."[5]

This concern, as we saw earlier, was the basis of Babbitt's attraction to Buddhism, an attraction that highlights the Humanists' great interest in religion and their total disinterest in theology. For Buddhism was "the least mythological of religions" and dispensed entirely with any recourse to the supernatural or to divine revelation. It could get along without these supports and still uphold a dualistic account of human nature and the virtues of moral discipline. Foerster too made this appeal to an empirical age and even cast a wider net than Babbitt for the distilled essence of religiosity. Humanism, he wrote, "believes that there is need as well as room for a working philosophy mediating between dogmatism and scepticism and void of revelation and ecclesiastical organization." Humanism could supply all that was "essential" in religion and could borrow from a variety of religious traditions—Greek, Hebraic, Buddhist, Confucian, and Christian—to do so. "So long as the modern or critical spirit continues to dominate men's thinking, so long will a critical humanism be justified in seeking to reveal what is really central and normal and permanent in human experience."[6]

None of the Humanists, however, approached the religious question with more dedication than Paul Elmer More. The evolution in his thinking on this subject marks one of the most interesting

[4] Babbitt, *Rousseau and Romanticism*, pp. 380–81.

[5] Ibid., pp. 183, 115.

[6] Norman Foerster, "Humanism and Religion," *Criterion*, 9 (1929), 24, 26.

themes in the New Humanism, and one of the most challenging. For More went full cycle, from an early rejection of Christianity to a nearly complete endorsement at the end of his life. Yet More always stayed somehow within the Humanist framework that Babbitt had impressed so indelibly upon him in graduate school. The final position at which he arrived culminated a lifelong and difficult effort to find some reconciliation between his Humanism and the attraction to religion that never abandoned him.

Even more than Babbitt, More experienced in childhood the stern, moral Protestantism of the Midwest. He recalled later that in this period "I lived securely in the old inherited faith of Calvinism." But he grew impatient with the rigid logic of that system. "Doubts gathered with the years," and finally he cast off "once and for all, the faith that had nurtured the better life of my childhood and youth." But the break with Calvin did not produce in More, as it often has in others, a total alienation from religion. He had lost the attraction for dogmatic faith, but there persisted within him "that obsession of a mystery beyond the senses . . . those intimations of a whole ghostly world corresponding to something latent in the soul itself." More, then, was ready to accept a religion of "pure spirituality," one, like Babbitt's Buddhism, that did not even require the belief in a God. For this reason Babbitt's Humanism made a ready appeal to More, as did ancient Hinduism. More's views on this subject in fact so paralleled Babbitt's on Buddhism that they need not be reviewed. In the period of the *Shelburne Essays* More insisted that the extent of its recognition of the dual nature of man marked the depth of any religion. Religion in essence merely imposed on the war in the cave a superstructure of myth and dogma.[7]

One senses, in reading More during this period, a genuine attraction to the mysteries of religion to which his empirical Humanism prevented his fully surrendering himself. For example, More evidenced a strong admiration for Saint Augustine and his complete commitment to the Christian faith. There is a wistful note in More's reflection on Saint Augustine's experience of the beauties and mysteries of religion. He remarked in an essay on the early Christian thinker that through

[7] Paul Elmer More, "Marginalia," *American Review*, 8 (1936), 23–26. More wrote to his sister in 1888: "I do not believe as a Christian should and so far as I can judge myself never shall. I have found God and have learned some peace from this knowledge—but this is not to be a Christian" (Arthur Hazard Dakin, *Paul Elmer More* [Princeton, 1960], p. 29). Specific glimpses of More's religious attitudes in the early period may be found in his *Studies of Religious Dualism* (1909; rpt. New York, 1967).

the church sacraments there was permitted Augustine "that saving grace of the imagination, whereby the believer . . . might escape the hard element of rationalism that tends to petrify the definitions of dogma, and might live the pure life of the spirit within the fold of the Church."[8]

When Stuart Sherman spoke of the "Religion of Democracy" he meant just that. Sherman's statements on religion bear all the imprints of his nationalism and democracy and give to his account a quality that separates it clearly from Babbitt's and More's. Sherman was struck at an early age by the sterility of institutional religion and never maintained active ties with a church. Sherman the Humanist turned instead to literature for the spiritual fuel that he craved. He was convinced that great literature alone could "light a fire in the belly of the world."[9] He combined this faith with his commitment to democracy, and one can learn as much about Sherman's conception of religion through his critical writings on literature as in his separate statements on religion, which are scarce. Sherman was looking for the awakening of a religious sense that would unite the American people, an objective that required an appeal to American traditions and habits. He thus gave to religion a national and social dimension that was absent from Babbitt, Foerster, and More.[10]

One sees immediately the foundation on which Sherman constructed his conception of religion in his account of Matthew Arnold's writing on the question. Arnold's religion was both national and social, and neither rational nor supernatural. Arnold regarded the Church of England as essentially "a great national society for the promotion of what is commonly called *goodness*, and for promoting it through the most effectual means possible." Arnold specifically tied religion to conduct: "Religion means simply either a binding to righteousness, or else a serious attending to righteousness and dwelling upon it." Conduct of course implied an ethical code, but one enhanced by an emotional quality. For Arnold religion was "ethics heightened, enkindled, lit up by feeling," so that the passage to religion occurs

[8] More, *Studies of Religious Dualism,* p. 92.

[9] Henry Seidel Canby, "Stuart P. Sherman: 'The American Scholar,' " *Saturday Review of Literature,* 6 (1929), 202; Jacob Zeitlin and Homer Woodbridge, eds., *Life and Letters of Stuart P. Sherman* (New York, 1929), II, 627; Sherman to More, May 3, 1923, More Papers, Department of Rare Books and Special Collections, Princeton University Library, Princeton, N.J.

[10] Stuart P. Sherman, *Points of View* (New York, 1924), pp. 14–15.

when emotion is applied to morality. The true meaning of religion, Arnold stated, is *"morality touched by emotion."*[11]

Sherman built on this nontheistic framework. For the emotional content he looked to the literature of democratic America, which, as a whole, would constitute a national faith and a spiritual union for Americans. Here was the American counterpart to the Church of England. Sherman was willing, however, to look beyond this to the wisdom of the past for the ethical or the emotional source of religion, and appealed to Emerson as a model. The religious liberation that Emerson offered, Sherman said, suspended dry sectarian creeds and drew from history's greatest spiritual leaders—Confucius, Christ, Buddha, and Mahomet. These sources yielded the elevated thought and noble sentiments that Emerson, and Sherman, saw as the common endowments of all the best in the great religious traditions. That tradition, as it was for Babbitt and More, was also Humanist.[12]

Nonetheless, Sherman would have nothing to do with the fear of God that More wanted to reinstill in modern man. Sherman again appealed to Emerson and John Stuart Mill, who incorporated in their religion a motivating humanitarian concern. For the old tyrannies, Sherman said, they have substituted child welfare and a living wage, what Sherman called in general "the humanization of all the people." Here, said Sherman, "are tangible objects for the religious sense to work upon or to pray for." Sherman, like Babbitt and More, thought that he was stripping religion down to its bare essentials, shorn of the theological and dogmatic superstructure. But what emerged bore little resemblance to the religious core that Babbitt and More found. "When you 'scrap' your theology," Sherman asked, ". . . what is there left, for the modern skeptical mind . . . of positive content in the 'idea of God' but some more or less impassioned sense of what ought to be done on earth by men?"[13]

Because the Humanists considered religion, its spirituality, its tradition, and its moral content, as a supplement to their own program, or as a partner or ally, they reflected with concern on the prevalent religious trends in America. And this condition too helps explain the sudden attraction of the New Humanism at the end of

[11] Quoted in Stuart P. Sherman, *Matthew Arnold: How to Know Him* (Indianapolis, 1917), pp. 279, 292–93.

[12] Stuart P. Sherman, *Americans* (New York, 1922), p. 79.

[13] Stuart P. Sherman, *The Emotional Discovery of America and Other Essays* (New York, 1932), pp. 53–56.

the decade of the 1920s, a period that Sydney Ahlstrom has described as one of declining religious vitality in America. Much of the nation's religious energy had dissipated into a crude fundamentalism, symbolized by the famous "monkey trial" at Dayton, or a muscular moralism such as the Prohibition crusade that seemed to carry all Protestantism with it. On the other hand, to many the freshness of the earlier "Social Gospel" had become stale and empty, and some accused the churches of excessive cultural accommodation with the world. Particularly noteworthy in this period was the churches' loss of prestige among the intellectual and literary leadership of the country.[14] The attraction of Humanism among this group showed the need for a spirituality and moral discipline that the churches did not adequately supply. To the Humanists the fundamentalists were so beneath contempt that they scarcely troubled to present a critical case against them. More and Babbitt had early renounced a sharp dogmatism in religion and defended a place in it for intelligence and reason. In considering the contemporary status of religion, More simply said that the fundamentalists have "lost their case so utterly and finally that nothing can add to their discomfiture." Sherman labeled William Jennings Bryan "a prehistoric clergyman" who sought hopelessly to restore religion to American life by calling for the legislative suppression of the "most fruitful scientific theory of modern times," the Darwinian account of evolution. "The Fundamentalist," Sherman wrote to a friend, "is pitiful—merely pitiful. It would be as brutal to strike him as to use a horsewhip on a two-year old child."[15]

But though the fundamentalist erred in the direction of morbid emotional excess and anti-intellectualism, the other extreme, the Humanists found, equally distorted the true religious life. They found that tendency both in modern philosophical trends that offered a merely intellectual or metaphysical rendering of God and in a neoromantic reduction of religious spirituality to vague emotionalism. The Humanists treated neither form at length, but More did offer as illustration of the first the difficult process theology of Alfred North Whitehead, under which God emerges as the "principle of concretion."

[14] Sydney E. Ahlstrom, *A Religious History of the American People* (New Haven, 1972), pp. 899–915.

[15] Paul Elmer More, "An Absolute and an Authoritative Church," *Criterion*, 8 (1929), 621; Sherman, *Points of View*, pp. 12–13; Sherman to "McNitt," July 12, 1925, Sherman Correspondence, University of Illinois Archives, Urbana-Champaign.

More cared little for the logical consistency or lack of it in Whitehead's system, showing the general Humanist disdain for metaphysics. The greater objection stemmed from More's insistence that both Humanism and religion were as much affairs of the heart as of the head and that the excessive intellectualism of Whitehead deprived them of an imaginative quality that could stir the soul and invigorate human lives. More revealed that point in considering Whitehead's God and asking the question, How could anybody really pray to that? More thought that "between religion and metaphysics there is a deep gulf fixed and an irreconcilable feud."[16]

But though religion must touch the heart, it needed also to be more than a warm, comforting feeling to meet the Humanist standards of a regenerating spiritual force. More and Babbitt argued that genuine religion must retain the sense of the higher and lower selves within the individual, a sense they were both convinced was yielding in their day to mere aestheticism, optimism, and humanitarian sympathy. More referred to the exponents of the "inner light," who, he felt, reduced religion and spirituality to vacuous thoughts on the wonders of the cosmos. Their God, he said, "fades off into the vaguest sort of pantheism or the flimsiest aura of transcendentalism." Theirs was a religion that required virtually nothing of them and wholly ignored the critical war in the cave. On that basis, too, More criticized Sherman's Emerson. Emerson, he said, was insufficiently aware of the internal conflict within man and sought to pass over it by merging the divine and the human soul in a transcendental unity. But More distrusted the facileness with which Emerson pictured a happy state resulting for man from this realization. Specifically, More charged that Emerson too easily passed over the problem of evil, and for this, one of the difficult and real problems of life, More argued that genuine religion was better equipped. The power of religion, More said, derived from "its feeling for evil as a tremendous reality." And for it there was no easy emotional substitute. "To be reconciled so cheerfully to this dark dilemma," More added, "is not a reconciliation of the dilemma itself, but argues rather some deep-lying limitation of spiritual experience."[17]

[16] Paul Elmer More, *The Demon of the Absolute* (Princeton, 1928), pp. 44, 49; idem., *The Sceptical Approach to Religion* (Princeton, 1934), p. 116.

[17] More, "An Absolute Church," pp. 631–32; idem., *A New England Group and Others* (1921; rpt. New York, 1967), p. 89. Babbitt treated the problem similarly. See *The Masters of Modern French Criticism* (1912; rpt. New York, 1963), pp. 70–71. There is likely to be a confusion of terms here, especially when one picks up this subject in the early 1930s. A group of "religious humanists" also assumed the name "New Humanism" and used as its vehicle of expression a journal entitled the *New Humanist*. It published the famous "Humanist Manifesto"

At Harvard one time, when Babbitt had invited some of his students over to his home to meet More, the latter teased Babbitt about his unwillingness to attend church. Babbitt replied that the churches had ceased to be genuine religious institutions. "What you get in the churches nowadays," he explained, "is religiosity, the religion of feeling, aestheticism, the cult of nature, official optimism, talk about progress, humanitarian sympathy for the poor." More could only concur in Babbitt's complaint, for both saw in the merging of social welfare and humanitarianism with religion the sorest blight on the modern church. For every sermon one heard on the obligation of man to God, or on the need for personal regeneration, or on the beauty of holiness, More said, one heard a score on the virtue of social sympathy. The social content of religion was one subject in which More engaged in intense conversation with his students. Against their Christian socialism, which he defined as a "vaunting materialism," More called for a return to service for God above service for man as the truly religious life.[18]

Babbitt, and especially More, who gave greater attention to the problem, insisted that Christianity departed from its true spirit when it turned to offer the world material salvation. Humanitarianism, Babbitt argued, cannot be a substitute for religion, though the humanitarian may say that the Christian spirit is the same as his own when stripped to its essentials. But to substitute human altruism for a supernatural God was to deprive religion of its antiexpansionist influence. Babbitt in this case sided wholly with revealed and dogmatic religion as a source of personal discipline and spirituality, in opposition to the materialistic secularism of the humanitarian. Christ, More argued, never contemplated the introduction of a religion that would rebuild society. "What a mockery is made of the gospel if it cannot be preached to a man until the iniquities of society

---

signed by John Dewey and others, which outlined a bland and rather trite set of "religious" ideas that tried to give an ethical and spiritual dimension to their governing naturalistic philosophy. It insisted on rejecting "the traditional dualism of mind and body" as the basis for any conception of human nature *(New Humanist,* 6 [1933], 1–5). For a fuller account of this liberal religious movement see Arthur Hazard Dakin, *Man the Measure: An Essay on Humanism and Religion* (Princeton, 1939). Recently a sequel to the manifesto appeared, the equally uninspiring "Humanist Manifesto II," in *Humanist,* 33 (1973), 4–9.

[18] Quoted by William F. Maag, Jr., in Manchester and Shepard, p. 75; Paul Elmer More, *Aristocracy and Justice* (1915; rpt. New York, 1967), pp. 207–8; Dakin, *Paul Elmer More,* p. 67.

have been set right. . . . The call of religion," he added, ". . . is
first of all and last of all to offer to a soul despairing of this
world's peace the promise of eternal life." Here was the sole proper
concern of Christianity, "the one valid consolation of mankind" that
it could offer, and that, More thought, the church was bartering
away for "an impossible hope," the improvement of the human
lot through its material amelioration.[19]

In this sense particularly, religion was the ally of Humanism. It
promised with Humanism a form of spiritual consolation amid the
material pressures of life, a feeding of the soul. True religion, More
said, directed man inward, offering peace of mind and the beauty
of solitude. Babbitt once remarked in observing a statue of Buddha that
the eyes appeared to be closed, but were not entirely. His was the
pose not of sleep but of concentration and contemplation. More called
it the "joy of spiritual insight," which he found in Buddha and Christ
and which appealed to him as the "pure religious spirit." Both
leaders, More claimed, taught that human society could not supply the
needed nurture of the soul. The sorrow of Christ, More wrote,
was not the cry of one despairing at the wrong and injustice
of the world; rather it was the "brooding pity of one who sees
that the fashion of this world passeth away, and that rich and poor
alike are in the bondage of sin. . . . The world is dark to
him because it lies outside the great and wonderful radiance of
the kingdom of heaven."[20]

Paul More's intense involvement with Platonism formed a transitional
stage between his Humanism and his acceptance of Christianity.
The studies that engaged him in this period, roughly 1915 to
1925, showed More using Plato to give a stronger philosophical
basis to Humanism, but also finding through Plato an appeal to a
kind of transcendentalism that prepared his endorsement of a Christian
theism. Three of the five volumes that formed *The Greek Tradition*
dealt with the Hellenistic philosophies and Plato, and three with
Christianity. Indeed, the major theme of the entire series is the
underlying unity between the Greek and Christian traditions. More
at first regarded Christianity as a religious adjunct to Platonism, one
that drew upon the philosophical truths of Platonism and rendered them

[19] Babbitt, "Humanism: An Essay at Definition," p. 36; Paul Elmer More,
Shelburne Essays: First Series (1904; rpt. New York, 1967), pp. 230–31, 234; idem.,
On Being Human, pp. 152–53; Dakin, *Paul Elmer More*, pp. 67–68.

[20] Frederick Manchester, in Manchester and Shepard, pp. 134–35; More,
Shelburne Essays: First Series, pp. 230–31, 218.

symbolically in the myths of the faith. Christianity for More was a culmination of a great tradition in the cultural history of the Western world. Without that tradition, he said, "we should have remained barbarians; and, losing it . . . , we are in peril of sinking back into barbarism." The modern world, More believed, needed urgently to return to Greek idealism, this "purer source of our spiritual life."[21]

More's recovery of the Greek tradition continued the search that he had made in the first part of his Humanist phase for the basic truth of the human condition, though he turned now to Greek philosophy to buttress the structure. Religion still interested More as a force that was in essence Humanistic, and at the beginning of the series he announced his intention to look beyond the Christian myth and dogma to the "Hellenistic fathers of the Church," its humanist foundation, to seek what "is universally valid in religious experience." Here was the real truth, for example, of Platonism: "the truth that is in religion but is not bounded by religious dogma, and which needs no confirmation by miracle or inspired tradition."[22]

More's gradual and difficult passage from the philosophical framework of Plato to the religious framework of Christianity belongs to a later consideration of the final stage of his intellectual life. It remains to note here only how the idealism of Plato was the catalyst that sped the transition from Humanism to Christianity. More found in Plato's concept of the ideas a symbolical rendering of the dualism that lay at the basis of his own Humanism. Plato posited these both as rational and moral entities that existed above the phenomenal world, as independent entities. More as Humanist accepted the truth of the moral absolutes as elements of unity in the experience of men that function as restraints on the natural self. But More at first acknowledged these as facts of human experience only and accepted them without their transcendental and nonempirical character in the Platonic philosophy. The important change came with More's increasing receptivity to the actual and the independent, rather than the merely symbolic reality of the Platonic ideas. More remarked, in a statement clearly indicative of his changing perspective, that Plato had touched on one of the true elements in religion in his visualization of the world of ideas as "very real entities, existing . . . out of space and above the sphere of phenomena visible to the eye of flesh." In addition, More, in the fashion of the Humanists,

---

[21] Paul Elmer More, *The Religion of Plato* (Princeton, 1921), pp. vii–viii.

[22] Ibid., pp. 4, vii–viii.

endorsed Plato's contention that the ideas themselves, beginning as intuitions of the mind, are perceptible only to the ethical imagination, that although they are the "most intimate realities of experience," things of which we are certain, they are incapable of rational or logical explication.[23] What is most important here, however, is More's new dualism, that of a phenomenal world and a transcendent spiritual world. For More was defending with Plato the independent reality of the moral truths, not as "mere conceptions in the mind," but as "powers, principles, laws of the spirit, things actually existing."[24] More had begun here the first shift in his thinking that soon took him through Plato to Christianity.

The religious question pitted members of the Humanist camp against one another and Humanists against those who defended religion alone. But the debates dealt little with the validity and truths of religion, and there was disappointingly little earnest searching into the crucial questions about the existence of God or the meaning of Scripture. More alone of the Humanists studied these questions at length. Rather, the participants in the discussion reflected their concern that either Humanism or religion serve as a spiritual and disciplinary force in the modern age, and were often led to side with one or the other as the movement that could do more service in directing the energies of men to worthwhile human ends. Babbitt of course showed his concern with this question in insisting that Humanism must replace religion in an age that could no longer accept dogma and superstition, but might turn to Humanism as a realistic description of the facts of human experience with an imaginative content that would offer an appeal beyond mere rational consent. But others were not so convinced that religion had lost forever its power to inspire.

T. S. Eliot shared Babbitt's concern that modern man had lost all meaningful direction and was wandering in a secular wilderness. But Eliot was also convinced that Babbitt's Humanism was incapable, by itself, of supplying the necessary guidance. Babbitt wanted to make an appeal to the individual himself, who, by a conscientious effort, might gain an awareness of his higher self and find the means to its realization. Specifically, Babbitt was willing to rely upon the vital check against the natural instincts, an effort that required only the imposition of one part of the personality against the other. Eliot had no quarrel with this appeal to the inner check and acknowledged

[23] Paul Elmer More, *The Christ of the New Testament* (Princeton, 1924), pp. 16–18.

[24] Robert M. Davies, *The Humanism of Paul Elmer More* (New York, 1958), pp. 114–15.

its value in a democratic and romantic age that increasingly was sloughing off all restraints. But Eliot did question the wisdom of relying on the individual to find the necessary frein vital by himself. Eliot therefore argued that more effective than the inner restraints of Babbitt's Humanism were the "external restraints" supplied by orthodox religion. It alone could provide the unity and discipline as a spiritual force that the relativism of Humanism could not. To hope that regeneration in the modern age might spring from each individual checking himself through his private notions and judgments, Eliot thought, was "pretty precarious." Babbitt, in short, was trying "to build a Catholic platform out of Protestant planks," and the structure suffered in strength because it lacked the hard cement of a single spiritual core and a dogmatic creed. [25]

Without these elements, Eliot felt, Humanism lacked a central purpose. He agreed with Babbitt in asserting that rationalism ultimately left men unsatisfied and that some imaginative appeal was necessary to pull against the natural self. Here again, though, Humanism failed to provide what was needed. Babbitt, in insisting that Humanism be modern, that it be experimental and critical, appealed to the higher self as an empirical reality. But in positing a higher will, Eliot charged, Humanism had still to ask what exactly was the object of the will. Where, in other words, Eliot asked, were all the scientific and empirical qualities of Humanism going to lead? "What is the higher will to *will*, if there is nothing either 'anterior, exterior, or superior' to the individual?" Eliot pointed here to what he considered the essential inadequacy of a nontheistic Humanism in opposition to orthodox religion, and the primary difference between the two. [26]

But Eliot was careful to point out that he was not concerned with the question whether Babbitt's civilization was desirable, only whether it was possible. He believed it was not. Nonetheless, Eliot was clearly sympathetic to Humanism and did not wish to set up religion and Humanism as alternatives to each other. "The need of the modern world," Eliot wrote, "is the discipline and training of the emotion," and that was the objective both of Humanism and religion. Like the Humanists, Eliot was critical of modern tendencies in religion and saw the excesses of humanitarianism, emotionalism, and intellectualism all depriving religion of its discipline and inspiration. Too often the churches offered only watery sentiment or "emotional debauch" on the one hand and the "fleshless dogma" of theology or the "monstrous Life Force"

[25] *For Lancelot Andrewes* (New York, 1928), pp. 150-51.
[26] Ibid., pp. 152-54.

of Whitehead's God on the other. Eliot thought Humanism a genuine
mediator between harsh dogma and vague sentiment in the church
and believed that without Humanism religion was sterile. That was
its true role—not an independent agency but the spiritual ally of
religion and the church.[27]

Another English writer, G. K. Chesterton, brought the same charges
against Humanism and against Foerster in particular. Eliot was an
Anglican and Chesterton a convert to Catholicism. Both saw in
the bonds of the church, its tradition and dogma, the unifying spiritual
power that Humanism and its individualism could not provide.
"Where," Chesterton asked, "is the *cement* which made religion corporate
and popular, which can prevent it falling to pieces in a debris
of individualistic tastes and degrees?" Humanism could not, Chesterton
said, become a substitute for religion in the manner suggested by
Babbitt and Foerster.[28]

Foerster replied directly to the contentions of Eliot and Chesterton
in the pages of Eliot's journal, the *Criterion.* He challenged
Eliot on Humanism's ability to outpoll religion in the modern age
and insisted that the advantages were clearly with Humanism. In it
the role of the imagination was equally as great and effective as
in religion, and the materials of the New Humanism might offer
as much inspiration as the traditional and orthodox church.
The real issue for Foerster was not the need for a uniform discipline,
but for any civilizing discipline. To an age that had already rejected
dogmatism, Foerster reemphasized, there was little left for religion
anyway, and those who were genuinely interested in finding spiritual
redirection for modern man must rely on a critical and individualistic
Humanism. Foerster, incidentally, felt that for this reason Humanism
should ally itself with some form of Protestantism, an opinion at
variance with most of the other Humanists—Babbitt, Shafer, and Elliott,
for example—who, were the choice necessary, would have preferred
the tradition and unity of Roman Catholicism.[29] But Foerster
challenged this alliance and Chesterton's specific defense of Rome. "The
final effort of the modern or critical spirit," he said, "must be
to render clear and commanding an inner authority competent to

[27] Ibid., p. 158; "Religion without Humanism," in Foerster, *Humanism and
America,* pp. 107–11.

[28] "Is Humanism a Religion?" *Criterion,* 8 (1929), 393.

[29] Foerster, "Humanism and Religion," "Correspondence" in *Forum,* 8 (1928),
470–71. G. R. Elliott wrote to More in 1928 that after being raised an Anglican
he had wandered from the church but was now returning and joining the Roman
Catholic fold (June 23, 1928, More Papers).

take the place of outer authority." It might do that, not by appealing to the narrow tradition of a single institution, but through Humanism's effort to clarify and restore "all that is sound in the old institutions."[30]

At a second level the debate over Humanism and religion was far more technical, but raised important questions that demanded resolution. Here again the case against the Humanists was brought by individuals somewhat, if not greatly, sympathetic with Humanism, but ultimately convinced of its inability to replace religion. Allen Tate, the American poet, critic, and defender of the Southern Agrarian position in the late 1920s and '30s, defined himself, like the Humanists, as a believer in "tradition, reason, and authority." His essay in *The Critique of Humanism*, however, offered the same challenge as Eliot, that Humanism supplied no valuable medium for acquiring values and reduced itself ultimately to a vague program of restraint and proportion for their own sakes.[31]

Tate's essay, the most complex in the anti-Humanist collection, struck first at the Humanists' dualism. Tate charged that their rejection of reason as a guide to truth sprang from their need to go beyond the naturalistic plane of existence. But the Humanists, Tate pointed out, were also insisting that the "supernatural intuition," or the foundation of religious faith, must be tested by the intellect. It was therefore distinct from the intellect. Tate felt that the Humanists were reverting to the naturalistic eighteenth century's desire to break down all irrational, and therefore particularly religious, constructions of the universe. The Humanists themselves, Tate charged, were thrown back upon naturalism. "For naturalism," he said, "contains the only idea of reason that is available to the Humanist." Were this not true, the Humanists would not feel the necessity of superseding reason. The Humanists' own appeal to the ethical imagination as an adjunct to reason and as the escape beyond the rational level of existence failed to convince Tate of its effectiveness. The Humanists failed to give any explanation why the ethical imagination is "above" the reason. Humanism failed because it was expecting naturalism to unnaturalize itself; so long as it insisted on using the intellect, it was using the natural to check the natural, a hopeless effort that made the dualism of the Humanists merely verbal.[32]

---

[30] Foerster, "Humanism and Religion" (the *Criterion* article), p. 31.

[31] Allen Tate, "The Fallacy of Humanism," in C. Hartley Grattan, ed., *The Critique of Humanism* (New York, 1930), pp. 131–32.

[32] Ibid., pp. 138–39.

Tate, however, defended religion for its ability to do what he thought Humanism could not, that is, lift man wholly above naturalism. Religion alone could answer the question, How shall we know when we have values? "The religious unity of intellect and emotion, of reason and instinct, is the sole technique for the realization of values," he argued. But Tate did not here illustrate the interplay of these elements or distinguish their use in religion as opposed to Humanism.[33]

Eliot also added to his case for religion in a manner similar to Tate's. The Humanists, he said, believed that a recognition of the dualism of the human and natural levels of existence was an exercise sufficient to pose to the natural self the needed restraints. But Eliot replied that the supernatural level, for which the Humanists had no definite need, was necessary for the maintenance, indeed was an integral part of, the human plane of existence. And if this third stage is suppressed, the dualism of man and nature collapses "at once." "Man is man," Eliot wrote, "because he can recognize spiritual realities, not because he can invent them. Either everything in man can be traced as a development from below or something must come from above." Religion alone could preserve the human capacities that were necessary to resist the pull of the natural. There is no escaping that dilemma, Eliot warned; "you must either be a naturalist or a supernaturalist."[34]

Eliot related this argument to the one he presented earlier. He recalled a charge made by Babbitt that the spokesmen for naturalism hoped naively to enjoy the benefits of the past achieved through a humanistic or religious discipline.[35] Eliot, however, thought that Babbitt was trying to cash the checks of Humanism on the credit of religion. He would ask in return whether the Humanists hoped to live on their own and enjoy the benefits of the past achieved through the discipline and spiritual strength of religion. For the Humanists, he said, in repressing the religious qualities of faith and dogma, are left only with the human qualities of reason and imagination, and *these* are likely to descend again to the animal or natural level.[36]

[33] Ibid., pp. 160–61.

[34] T. S. Eliot, "Second Thoughts about Humanism," *Hound and Horn,* 2 (1929), 343. Eliot wrote to More respecting Christian dogma: "I consider that one must be a whole-hogger or nothing." He confided to More that Christianity was to him the one source of meaning in the otherwise all-pervasive void of life. "Only Christianity helps to reconcile me to life, which is otherwise disgusting" (Aug. 10, 1930, and "Tuesday 1928," in the More Papers).

[35] Babbitt, *Democracy and Leadership,* p. 47.

[36] Eliot, *For Lancelot Andrewes,* pp. 143–44.

In the last period of his life, the years after 1925, More's consuming interest was Christianity. His extensive study of the religion and his long examinations of its validity were the most exhaustive efforts of any of the Humanists to deal with the entangled question of Humanism and religion. Even though More moved to a position friendly to Christianity, the particular endorsement he gave bore strongly the still viable perspective of his Humanism. Indeed, More's final thesis was a unique and delicate merging of Humanism with Christianity that distinguished his variety from orthodoxy.

If one picks up the thread of More's thinking on religion with his *The Christ of the New Testament* (1924), one senses throughout that More felt a strong attraction to the faith but was constrained by the positivism in his thinking that remained from the Humanist and even the Platonic periods. More stated that he was not interested in debating the truth of the Christian religion itself but sought only to establish what constituted true Christianity. That was the opening through which More could pass to set up a Christian model to which he ultimately gave his own endorsement. More, at this point, was finding what was true Christianity without conceding that it was true in itself; but the qualities that he gave to it were the forms for which he worked thereafter to justify rationally and intellectually. And of those qualities the most important, and subsequently the most challenging to More's thinking, was the unquestionable supernatural basis of Christianity.[37] His final endorsement would thus take him far from the earlier perspective.

More's *The Sceptical Approach to Religion* (1934) was in essence the final reconciliation between More the Christian and More the Humanist. It is the clearest statement of the terms on which he accepted Christianity, a remarkable synthesis of all the elements of his belief that greatly clarifies the doubts and ambivalence that

---

[37] The year of this publication (1924), which documents an intellectual shift in emphasis, may have coincided with an emotional or spiritual shift in More also. One derives this impression from his correspondence with Babbitt. More was in England in 1924 and from there detailed his travels to Babbitt. Writing from Oxford, More commented on his visits to the English cathedrals and attendance at worship services. "I was overcome by a rush of emotion," he wrote unabashedly. Standing at the church, he felt as though he "stood at the heart of England." More too, it seemed, was finding, like Eliot, the filling of a spiritual void in his discovery of the historical church. He further bared his soul to Babbitt: "And the conclusion? It is simply the query whether in these days of mental confusion and insolvent materialism the first and most effective protest may not be simply to go to church. A lame and impotent conclusion, I fear you will say; but there is something in it, believe me" (Sept. 5, 1924, More Papers).

pervaded his earlier thoughts on religion. More here was seeking to show how a skeptic, or even a positive and critical Humanist, might accept theism, and particularly Christianity. He thus announced at the outset that he addressed the ideas offered to those who, like himself, "find intellectual difficulties in the way of accepting the traditional dogmas of faith." He would not, he said, go beyond "the immediate data of experience."[38]

More appealed first to intuition and maintained that our consciousness itself gives us the intuition of right and wrong. We know, More wrote, that some acts are right and some are wrong, and we perceive their character from the sense of self-approval or disapproval that accompanies them. From this fact More inferred that "inherent in my very nature as a man" is a purpose, however faint it may appear, which is a call to "shape my life and character after a pattern which is associated with a *telos* or 'end' of self-approval." More pointed to this condition as a given fact of experience in the internal life of each individual; it was not a rational concept but "a direct perception." Every human being has an end, visualized or grasped through the conscience or moral sense, that he has the capacity of freedom and the responsibility, also intuited, to fulfill.[39]

More then shifted ground and asked his readers to consider the conditions of the external world. Here what we observe of life, he said, contrasts sharply with our internal teleological intuition. For whatever that intuition may tell us of purpose, will, and end for ourselves, the facts of observation indicate that the experiences of the world do not fit this pattern. We see, that is, no ultimate purpose governing life and directing it to an apprehended end. Hence the contradiction between intuition and observation, and the dilemma it poses. For both impressions come to us as immediate knowledge, leaving us the problem: "Is the human world, then, at once both teleological and non-teleological?"[40]

The skeptic, More said, will likely take one of two routes out of this dilemma. He may accept the data of observation and regard the world as a mechanism, and then infer that the empirical data that it yields are the only valid kind, thereby rejecting the data of the intuition. More labeled this option rationalism. But in contrast to rationalism is faith. It is the element that fixes our attention on the content of intuition as more significant and real than the data of observation. And

[38] More, *Sceptical Approach to Religion,* pp. 1–2.

[39] Ibid., pp. 4–5.

[40] Ibid., pp. 6–7.

the life directed and controlled by faith, More said, is religion. Moreover, although faith does not transfer our consciousness of freedom, responsibility, and purpose to the observed phenomena of the world itself, it does infer "the existence of a free and responsible agent, whose purpose is operative in the world while He Himself is transcendent to [it]." Faith, that is, is the transference to the world at large of a truth of the inner life. Here was More's first step to theism. He defended the choice, however, as entirely reasonable, as the more probable of the two choices that any thinking individual is forced to confront in a serious consideration of life and its meaning. "To faith," More wrote, "the whole world thus becomes teleological just as the individual is conscious of being teleological."[41] And here also was the first statement of the new dualism that More drew from Plato, the world of matter and the world of spirit that he now accepted as real and made the basis of religion.

More's case here was something like Pascal's wager. "I must either believe or disbelieve," he explained, "that there is within the world, or, rather, beyond the world, that which corresponds to my intuition of freedom and responsibility." More specifically: "I must either regard the universe as teleological . . . or I must regard it as without purpose. There is for the honest and serious mind . . . no middle ground." As Pascal observed, the question involved no inconsequential choice. More insisted that the acceptance of the intuitional inference as opposed to the rational observation constitutes a wholly new life for him who makes it. For the theist will accept a responsibility to conform his actions to the will of God and take on an obligation to a supreme Ruler and Judge. The object of faith, that is, assumes a reality to its holder; the probability of belief becomes a truth of experience. Here one sees that More has imposed a religious principle upon a Humanist framework. For the religious life is akin to the Humanist's higher life. The life of faith, More said, implies a power within the individual to move toward the fulfillment of his purpose and a commitment to it. The life of infidelity, on the other hand, recognizes no such discipline; it yields to the flux. It is, More said, "a facile surrender to the streaming impressions that crowd upon us from the outer world and to the tides of sensation that ebb and flow within us."[42] Religion now was doing for More what he had earlier called upon Humanism to do.

More now had the skeleton of religious faith that needed only the flesh of Christianity. Here again the vital factor in More's thinking was a teleology, one that he found in the record of history. What struck More above

[41] Ibid., pp. 11–14.
[42] Ibid., pp. 24, 14–15.

all was the teleological nature of the Christian religion itself, "the only completely teleological religion of the world." More marveled at the record that traced from the early prophets and Moses to the Incarnation and the coming of the Messiah in the Christian doctrine. He followed this evolution of consciousness through that first source to the Greek philosophers, of which Platonism offered a "high form of teleology," to its fulfillment in Christ's appearance. Then More asked the crucial question: Was the evolution of the Judeo-Christian tradition a simple form of cultural evolution, a mere process of change through some inner human force, or was it something more profound? Was it, More wondered, at least in part controlled "by a conscious superhuman agent who from the beginning was directing it towards a proposed end?" Did this evolution come from an actual God who was purposely making himself known through the limiting conditions of time? "Were the prophets of Israel," More asked, "uttering merely what they believed, with no warrant in fact, or was Jehovah revealing Himself through their halting words?"[43]

For More, the outstanding fact about Christianity, then, was the remarkable correspondence of its record to the facts of human experience. More linked this discovery to his earlier points. Faith is the transference of the moral sense, the teleological experience of the individual, to the belief in something similar at work in the world itself. But nowhere, More asserted, except in the Christian religion, do the inner and outer facts of teleology correspond. Here was its uniqueness. "Alone in the Judaeo-Christian tradition the ideas of God and morality and redemption . . . move straight on through the line of prophets to a convergence and a culmination in the Messianic fulfillment of prophecy." We have in the objective facts of history, More said, what might be described as the psychological experience of the individual writ large, the growth from a sense of longing to a reality of experience in faith. "What the individual tells of himself, that the persistence of voluntary faith brings an ever-growing assurance of the living reality of the object of his belief, we seem to see here actually occurring in the line of prophets among a peculiar people." The coincidence astounded More. "There is no other religious phenomenon so challenging to thought," he said. "To brush this distinction aside as a mere accident, won't do; to pass it by as insignificant won't do; it calls for a cause commensurate with its magnitude."[44]

The outline of More's thought here only suggests the means by which he passed from Humanism to religion and Christianity. He elaborated at length on the general thesis by showing further the correspondence of the

[43] Ibid., pp. 145–46.
[44] Ibid., pp. 158, 156.

important elements in the Scriptures with the facts of human experience. But although More had made the passage from Humanism to theism, the route was governed throughout by his early thinking, and even the final form of his religion reflected important elements of Humanism. More's case for religion began with an appeal to universal human experience, and More never asked the skeptic to suspend his reason and intellect for dogma or revelation without an empirical basis. More even argued that the inference from personal intuition to a theistic teleology was a representatively human act. Prayer, worship, ritual, and sacrifice have always been in human societies the articles of faith that spring from the first perceptions of a moral purpose in life. And finally, even in his Christian defense, the factor of illusion remained as critical as it had been for More and Babbitt in Humanism. Christianity, he said, ultimately rests on a myth whose truth we can grasp only in symbols and signs. "We cannot totally rise out of the realm of illusion." [45]

More had become deeply interested in the life of faith peculiar to the truly religious person, and it now outweighed Humanism in its appeal to him. But, like the Humanists as a group, More was still concerned with the pragmatic test, the question as to which spiritual force might more effectively stir the soul of modern man. Babbitt and Foerster continued to hold resolutely for Humanism, but More now turned to religion. That shift was apparent as early as 1924 when More observed the emerging new perspective that now divided him from Babbitt. "I cannot see things as he does," More commented. "To me the only possible release from the present trend towards materialism and dissipation seems to lie through the awakening of the sense of what I call otherworldliness. I do not believe the mass of people ever was or ever can be rational or positive; I do not believe the positive scientific view of life will ever have the power to restrain the passions." That conviction grew with More to the end of his life. In his last work he wrote that "without the restraining content born of superstition [religion] the turbulent desires of the masses would throw the world into anarchy and barbarism and universal misery." But besides this social concern, More was defending religion from a personal perspective as well, and he now proclaimed that the life of faith can offer the only genuine happiness to the soul. Humanism might afford a kind of resignation to the world, but true joy in life was the gift of religion, a gift that, more than Humanism, could "move the world." [46]

[45] Ibid., p. 156. The quotation is in Dakin, *Paul Elmer More*, p. 256. See also More, *Sceptical Approach to Religion*, pp. 164–69.

[46] Dakin, *Paul Elmer More*, pp. 221–22; More, *On Being Human*, p. 124. More wrote to Babbitt: "It is just impossible to get the psychological benefits of Christianity

But even more telling was More's own intellectual turnabout. For he now virtually conceded the points made by Eliot, Chesterton, and Tate, the Christian critics of Humanism. The supernatural, but not superhuman, element that was Babbitt's surrogate for divine grace, More now labeled a principle of naturalism. In refusing to recognize a power and authority entirely transcending the human realm, More said, Humanism was hopelessly entrusting the natural to check the natural. It could not work. "Will not the Humanist," he asked, "unless he adds to his creed the faith and hope of religion, find himself at the last, despite his protests, drawn back into the camp of the naturalists?" The Humanists' "higher reality" is either a supernatural reality or it is "suspended in a vacuum," a mere chimera. And without the religious elements, Humanism was inert; it could not pass from the critical to the productive state. In fact, for More, Christianity even outplayed Humanism at its own game. Nothing was more decisive in the contest for the imagination than the whole Christian mythology, far more likely than an imaginative Humanism to restrain the expansive instincts of the individual and to rejuvenate the spiritual life of the modern world. The debate then ended where it began. "The question is primarily pragmatic," More said, "but at the last it involves a whole philosophy of faith." [47]

Finally, one of the curious facts about the religious phase of More's intellectual career was his marked ambivalence toward institutional religion. He regularly attended church but was never a member of any church. Regarding religion in general, More's interest was mostly intellectual and emotional, never corporate. He was friendly to Anglicanism and a serious student of its history. [48] On the other hand he strongly opposed Roman Catholicism and spelled out his case in an essay in the *Criterion*.

More began his presentation by questioning the validity of revelation and the strict authority either of the Scriptures or the Pope for the Christian faith. In the face of the higher criticism, the general uncertainties, obscurities, and even contradictions of the Bible, More charged, he

---

while rejecting the Christian (and Platonic) conceptions of the super-natural as a reality" (May 17, 1932, More Papers). Babbitt in turn was noticeably distressed by his friend's lapse into Christianity. "I don't know what has happened to Paul Elmer More!" he said. "He seems to think that all truth was arranged at the Council of Nicea!" (quoted by Warner Rice, in Manchester and Shepard, p. 261).

[47] More, *On Being Human*, pp. 38–39, 15; Dakin, *Paul Elmer More*, pp. 256, 221–22, 276, 285.

[48] With Leslie Cross he edited *Anglicanism: The Thought and Practice of the Church of England, Illustrated from the Religious Literature of the Seventeenth Century* (Milwaukee, 1935).

who would preserve both his faith as a Christian and his integrity of mind must insist that we have "no infallible revelation vouchsafed us either in the Bible or in the Church." When the Vatican Council passed the burden of infallibility to the shoulders of one man, More said, it "set up for our credence the sharpest and most brittle Absolute the world has ever known." With other articles of Catholicism More was equally impatient. The doctrine of transubstantiation he labeled "a metaphysical absurdity." The doctrine of original sin was "a pure fabrication of occidental theology, as baseless in fact as it is in logic." The sacraments he called a confusion of religion with magic.[49]

More's harshness to the Catholic church is unaccountable, especially in view of the fact that he balanced his severity with a special plea for organized religion. For More was not prepared to throw the religious life back entirely upon the individual anymore than the Humanists would trust education to the college sophomore. More allowed that although the "absolute church" was unacceptable, an "authoritative church" was not. Let us admit, More said, the possibility, even the probability of a revelation in the church or in the Bible, which, while not wholly authoritative, does possess "sufficient authority." More was anxious now to preserve in religion the sense of tradition and common spirituality that he defended as prerequisites for the Humanist life and as the disciplinary and restraining forces for the modern world. "For our growth and sanity in religion," he wrote, "we must have something to supply what the inner light will not afford to the isolated souls of men, something to make us conscious of our citizenship in the communion of the saints, to supplement our limited intuition with the accumulated wisdom of the race, and to fortify our moral sense with the authority of ancient command." So far as the church responded to these needs, he added, we will hold it to be an inspired institution. "This," he said, "is what I mean by an authoritative as contrasted with an absolute Church."[50]

The final position at which More arrived was the result of long reflection and study of religion and the church. And More never really resolved his ambivalence toward the latter. A bishop of the Episcopal church visited him several times when More was near death in 1937 and, seeing that he would not ask of his own accord, offered

[49] More, "An Absolute Church," pp. 616–18, 628–30. The quotations are on pp. 628 and 633.

[50] Ibid., p. 633.

him confirmation. More said that he would think it over, but in the end declined. He had made his bed, he said, and "ought to lie on it."[51]

This final and intriguing development in More's thinking left the New Humanism in a curious position in the 1930s. More was now laboring to show the integral relationship between Humanism and Christianity, contending that Christianity necessarily completes a Humanist view of life and lifts it into the realm of absolute truth. This perspective itself affords a vantage point from which to make a concluding reflection about the place and context of the New Humanism within the Western cultural tradition.

When the Humanist movement began as an effort to rescue critical elements of the inherited culture that it saw under attack by romanticism and naturalism, it looked first to the classical past as its immediate concern. But as Humanism phased out some three decades later, religion, and especially the Christian tradition, had become the critical consideration. That denouement was not at all improbable, for though the Humanists themselves were scarcely cognizant of the fact, their movement was to a great extent an effort to save the Judeo-Christian tradition from its appropriation by its own enemies. Had the Humanists more completely understood the romantic movement they would have recognized what M. H. Abrams, with brilliant insight, has shown to be a secularization and internalization of the Judeo-Christian view of life—a model that romanticism inherited, partly refashioned, but could not discard. The romantics too lived out the drama of grace and redemption, recovery and renewal, the quest for a new heaven and a new earth; they undertook to give new and personal meaning to these Christian categories. "What is exceptional in the period beginning in the 1790s," Abrams writes, "is the scope of this undertaking. . . . A conspicuous romantic tendency, after the rationalism and the decorum of the Enlightenment, was a reversion to the stark drama and superrational mysteries of the Christian story and doctrines and to the violent conflicts and abrupt reversals of the Christian inner life, turning on the themes of destruction and creation, hell and heaven, exile and return, death and rebirth, dejection and joy, paradise lost and paradise regained." In essence, the Christian apocalyptic vision, traditionally an eschatology, now centered in the individual, who was free to pursue his own quest for the Kingdom of God within.[52] The Humanists' effort to make their inner check, or frein

[51] Dakin, *Paul Elmer More*, p. 348.

[52] Abrams, *Natural Supernaturalism* (New York, 1971), pp. 13, 46–51, 66. The quotation is on p. 66.

vital, do the work of grace was their own claim to be within the essential heritage of the Christian tradition. But actually it made them rivals with the romantics for that tradition. Babbitt, who believed he could best appropriate the Christian outline by demonstrating that Christianity simply gave a supernatural statement to the empirical truth of a positivistic Humanism, was working along the same lines as the romantics, who, dispensing with an overruling God, left only the soul and nature by which to work out the terms of the older Christian program for salvation. For this reason too, as Abrams observes, romanticism took over the Christian symbols and tried to make them "intellectually respectable" and "emotionally pertinent, for the time being."[53] To the extent that this concern governed the romantics' interests, their movement actually shared with Humanism the effort to sustain the inherited cultural order. The Humanist-romantic quarrel, then, was the contesting of a legacy that involved the real and larger meaning of the spiritual heritage of Western civilization.

In the last years of his life Paul More believed he was reverting to that tradition in its purer form; he admitted that he had changed his thinking completely. He defended Christianity and defended it against his own earlier Humanism. He became skeptical that Humanism could do for the modern world what Babbitt continued to insist it alone could do. Intellectually, More's dissent was the death knell of the movement, and when he made his own contribution to *Humanism and America* in 1930, his heart was no longer in it. Discounting the personal considerations in More's conversion, one may nevertheless judge his break with Humanism unfortunate. The Christian critics of Humanism had a clear advantage in contesting for the right to reply to the naturalistic philosophies, for the appeal to the supernatural was, intellectually, the easiest, if not the most logical, course to pursue. But it did not in the least invalidate the Humanists' effort to overturn the common enemy without this recourse. The Christian apologists were undoubtedly correct in pointing to the precariousness of Babbitt's and Foerster's reliance on an inner discipline and a personal authority that sought no support from external creeds or supernatural authority. Just this factor, indeed, may account for the inability of Humanism to move from a fleeting popularity to an enduring appeal. But again this does not warrant the pessimistic conclusion that a satisfactory answer to naturalism and skepticism can come only from theology. The challenge to both naturalism and skepticism will suffer if that conclusion gains consent. Babbitt outlined what

[53] Ibid., p. 68.

experience proves to be an obviously more difficult philosophy to accept and a less popular way of life than the religious. But the Humanistic reliance on the empirical validity of the higher will and its dogmatic quest for a moral certitude in human experience was not discredited by the more despairing turn to religion as an answer to the spiritual confusion of the modern world.

Epilogue

THE NEW HUMANISM protested against what its adherents took to be romanticism and naturalism and their attendant effects in American life and culture. It grew to intellectual maturity amid the revolutionary impact of science and relativism on American thinking and the new conceptions about the nature of man and the universe. These ideas have had significant and permanent effects. Nonetheless, the twentieth century has already witnessed a sustained effort, emanating from different intellectual quarters, to undo the philosophical premises of the previous century. The New Humanism is significant as the first part of a comprehensive counterattack that began with the writings of Babbitt and More in the first decade of the century and has persisted well into the post–World War II era. Each of the different aspects of this reconstruction has to a large degree located the roots of contemporary disorders in the cultural relativism and naturalism inherited from the late nineteenth century. To this extent they usually shared with the Humanists a conviction that the problems of modern man would find no easy answer in technological, scientific, or economic adjustment, or in any grand schemes for human perfection. The roots of the human dilemma in the modern period were judged by these persons to be cultural and intellectual. For the Humanists and others the most critical problem was the imperative need to recover permanent and universal values. A concluding statement will illustrate how different aspects of the New Humanist critique were shared by other individuals and groups.

The Southern Agrarian movement arose just when the New Humanism was gaining its greatest influence at the end of the 1920s. Beginning in the middle of the decade with the "Nashville Fugitives" at Vanderbilt University, the Agrarians issued their collective manifesto, *I'll Take My Stand: The South and the Agrarian Tradition,* in 1930, the year of *Humanism and America.* The Southern movement, with John Crowe Ransom, Allen Tate, Donald Davidson, and Robert Penn Warren as major spokesmen, saw a cultural war developing in the United States. The cultural divisions paralleled regional ones and set the spirit of materialism and relativism in the North against the spirit of religion and tradition in the South. Although the critical threat to America lay in the evils of industrial living, the roots of these ills derived from the empirical, scientific, and materialistic temper in which they flourished. The product, the Agrarians argued, was the rootless and fragmented man of modern society, dissevered from the loyalties to family, church, and community and adrift amid the pervasive moral relativism of the present.[1]

The major effort of the Southern movement was its defense of an agrarian tradition in the South and the superiority of the agrarian life over the urban and industrial. But there was a marked metaphysical and religious dimension to the ideas of the Agrarians. Allen Tate, as already seen, argued that even Humanism was insufficiently antinaturalistic and appealed to an absolute realm of being and an absolute moral authority wholly outside the human realm. John Crowe Ransom also exposed the iniquities of naturalism, not only in modern philosophies but in Christian thinking itself. Modern man, he contended, must return not simply to Christianity, but to the postulates of the old-time faith, the myths and fundamental truths of Scripture.

Ransom's book *God without Thunder* attempted, like the Humanists' writings, to assess the impact of naturalism. He found that this view of reality, exercised through the modern world's faith in science, had fostered the pervasive belief that "the universe is largely known . . . and that there exists no God or other entity beyond or above this demonstrable nature." With the rise of this conviction there had occurred a dramatic and significant change in the Christian view of the world. The "Old God," the deity that Ransom defended, was mysterious and unknown. He was a personality, one that willed, ordered, and judged, in his divine arbitrary way. He worked by fiat, not by natural law. Above all, he inspired awe, fear, and humility on the part of his subjects. The "New God," the god of the modern age, was by contrast shaped by the exigencies of a scientific faith and a priority placed on the material improvement of the human lot. The New God was rational and benevolent and worked within the limitations of his own mechanical universe. Science thus constructed a world that yielded all its mysteries to man's understanding and control. It was a world that was usable and hence profitable, and it made man the master of all things. The New God, then, embodied the principle of universal benevolence and physical well-being. The essence of Christianity became "concern for the common good." "Today," Ransom wrote, "in the degree that scientific naturalism has dispossessed [true] religion, the service of God has become merely the service of man." Ransom shared with the Humanists a disdain for humanitarianism and materialism, which they both linked together. Ransom's solution, however, was not Humanism but Fundamentalist Christianity. Although he shared with the Humanists a con-

[1] Ronald Lora, *Conservative Minds in America* (Chicago, 1971), pp. 107–23.

viction that the modern faiths, and above all liberal Protestantism, failed to deal adequately with the problem of evil and the need for humility, he departed from Humanism in returning to the Bible as the single valid source of truth and the certain means of recovery from modern decadence.[2]

The greatest merit of the Agrarian movement was its perceptive critique of industrialism, which was far more penetrating than the Humanists'. The Agrarians, like the Humanists, were searching for a usable past but believed that Babbitt and More were too abstract. They consequently drew the lines of their own defense narrowly and upheld the regional tradition of the rural South, a retreat that made the movement ultimately impractical and unpopular. But, more than this, the Agrarians illustrated the 'major weaknesses of a recoil from modernism through the efforts to recover a specific culture. The movement often had the air of a search for a lost golden past. Their turn to Christianity not only found Donald Davidson defending William Jennings Bryan at the Scopes trial, it also found the Agrarians adhering closely to T. E. Hulme's *Speculations* (1924) and its long lament over the breakdown of the Middle Ages and to T. S. Eliot's *The Idea of a Christian Society* (1939), with its notion of a society that could only effectively preserve its homogeneity without a large number of free-thinking Jews. The same perspective governed the Agrarians' views toward American Negroes. In the 1930s the Agrarians contributed heavily to Seward Collins's fascist-minded *American Review* and their movement came to parallel in ideology and sentiment the reactionary developments in Europe.[3] The Humanists had better reasons than the Agrarians to distrust the fascist temper, for their traditionalism drew from many sources and was more vigilant toward expansive tendencies on the Right as well as the Left.

Another sustained effort to reconstruct the bases of modern culture was the "Neo-orthodoxy" movement in Protestant theology led by Reinhold Niebuhr. Niebuhr's extensive writings, from the late 1920s to his death in 1971, sought, like the Humanists', not merely to expose the spiritual crisis of modern man but to trace the intellectual roots of modern liberalism in the intellectual past. It is fascinating to read Niebuhr against the perspective of the Humanists. There is a remarkable correspondence both in their identification and diagnosis of the spiritual ills of the modern age, even though the usual empirical basis of the Humanists radically separates them from the solutions to the dilemma that Niebuhr pursued through biblical faith.

[2] John Crowe Ransom, *God without Thunder* (1930; rpt. Hamden, Conn., 1965), pp. 3–51, 61–67, 95–109. The quotations are on pp. 27, 35.

[3] Alexander Karanikas, *Tillers of a Myth* (Madison, Wis., 1969), pp. 8, 14, 26, 30–31, 39, 88–93.

Modern man, Niebuhr believed, rejected the historical faiths, not from a formulated opposition to their tenets and creeds, but from his sense that they were irrelevant to him. In a secular age dominated by science and technology men found the historical religions devoid of meaningful content. The tragic view of life, the problem of redemption, the sense of sin, all dissipated before science's promise to open new avenues of human power and control. Religious faith in a redemptive God thus yielded before the fact of human pride; the need for repentence lost its force in a secular age that shifted attention away from the original sin in the souls of all men to an external process that prescribed material and technological adjustment.[4] But Niebuhr shared with the Humanists a conviction that this problem was not one of science and technology alone; it derived, rather, from modern fallacies of human nature. Niebuhr and the Humanists thus tried to analyze the currents of thought and the tendencies of their effects over some three or four centuries of time. He agreed with the Humanists to the extent that "modern culture, that is, our culture since the Renaissance, is to be credited with the greatest advances in the understanding of nature and with the greatest confusion in the understanding of man." Niebuhr traced the intellectual misconceptions of the past through a two-fold influence somewhat similar to the Humanists' own war with romanticism and naturalism. Niebuhr differed to the extent that he attacked the idealist (or rational) philosophies on the one hand and the naturalistic on the other. Niebuhr believed that the combined force of these, opposed though they were to each other, had the effect of denying the reality of a transcendent human self. That is, the naturalistic conceptions placed man irretrievably within nature and the flux of experience. The idealists either lost the self in some undifferentiated ground of being or tried to define man or human nature too much from the point of view of his rational faculties, thereby failing to recognize a spirit, the ultimate human self, that exists above this part of his finite nature. This is not the place to examine all the aspects of Niebuhr's criticism, but it will be helpful to indicate the extent to which he shared in the efforts of the Humanists and other twentieth-century thinkers to reorder the assumptions of the nineteenth century.[5]

To Niebuhr's Christian perspective man was a creature with an essentially dual nature. Man obviously is a child of nature, subject to its vicissitudes and compelled by its necessities. But he is also "a spirit who stands outside

[4] Reinhold Niebuhr, *The Nature and Destiny of Man: A Christian Interpretation, Vol. I, Human Nature* (New York, 1941), p. 94; idem., "The Dilemma of Modern Man," *Nation,* 164 (1947), 206.

[5] Niebuhr, *Nature and Destiny of Man,* I, pp. vii, 69–70. The quotation is on pp. 4–5.

of nature, life, himself, his reason and the world." This by analogy was proximate to the Humanists' notion of a higher and lower self and established the means by which each judged inadequate both the naturalistic and romantic conceptions of man, even though the two dualisms were by no means identical. Niebuhr intended by the higher self "a capacity for self-transcendence, the ability to make oneself his own object." Any monistic conception of man was incomplete and dangerous in its exercise. Romanticism, Niebuhr thus argued, saw all of human nature in terms of a self-justifying vitality that reduced everything to flux, breaking down form and order. Even more serious was the happy optimism of this view of man. Failing to measure man against any higher dimension of his personality, the romantic, Niebuhr said, defined all goodness in terms of this vitalism. Evil was thus extraneous to human nature and romanticism became "a primitivistic effort to recover the innocence of nature." The notion, furthermore, had pernicious effects. Translated onto the political arena, this conception of man left a thinker like Rousseau, as Niebuhr and the Humanists both argued, with no criteria but the unrestrained will of the majority as the measure of social right. The effect, Niebuhr believed, was to put the instruments of tyranny "in the hands of a given and momentary majority."[6]

Niebuhr saw the naturalistic philosophies growing out of Hobbes, Locke, and Hume through William James and John Dewey. Naturalism too was a one-dimensional conception of man that disintegrated the soul or merged it entirely with nature. Niebuhr believed modern behaviorist psychology advanced little beyond the sensationalist psychology and materialistic metaphysics of Hobbes. The effect was a complete dissolution of individuality. The effort to hold man within the confines of physical and organic nature, Niebuhr said, reduced psychology to physiology, and physiology to biochemics. In defining individual reality by an exclusive reference to the external sensuous world, the naturalistic philosophies had the same effect as the romantic; both were easy reconciliations of the problem of evil that removed sin from its inherent ground of existence in the human constitution.[7]

Here is the most important similarity between Niebuhr and the Humanists. The latter described the twin influences of romanticism and naturalism merging to despoil their own conception of humanity as defined by a higher and a lower self. With the eradication of the inner check the human problem no longer centered on the evil in the self; it yielded in both romanticism and naturalism to the new duality of man and society. Niebuhr too saw the result of modern fallacies in the same misplaced

[6] Ibid., pp. 3, 105–6.

[7] Ibid., pp. 72–73.

emphasis, a phenomenon he elaborated in describing the "easy conscience" of modern man. There is little, he said, that today disturbs man's good opinion of himself. "He considers himself the victim of corrupting institutions which he is about to destroy or reconstruct. . . . He continues to regard himself as essentially harmless and virtuous."[8]

Although Niebuhr and the Humanists were in essential agreement here, a critical difference set them apart. The Humanists had faith in the efficacy of the reason, when supported by the ethical imagination, to control and discipline the natural man. But Niebuhr maintained that those who trust the rational faculty tend to set up a false duality between the reason, which is good, and that part of our being that is in nature, which is evil. They err, he believed, in failing to see that man's reason is also part of his natural state. The Christian view of man, on the contrary, describes a creature whose duality places him in nature, but which also posits a self that transcends nature. This duality was critical and defined for Niebuhr the whole human problem. We can never find full meaning or value in life from a reason that is part of a natural and finite being. That is, human spirit cannot identify the principle of meaning with rationality, since that spirit transcends its own rational processes. The human spirit is essentially "homeless" in this world and can define itself only against some higher absolute and unconditioned ground of existence, God. This, Niebuhr said, is the basis of all religion. "For the self which stands outside itself and the world cannot find the meaning of life in itself or the world." All the modern philosophies thus commit the fundamental error of attempting to find the whole of meaning within the finite historical conditions of human life. The totality of meaning, however, can be grasped and judged only in terms of a religious faith that has discovered the source and center of life to be at least partially beyond finite existence. This center is the God who is both the creator and judge revealed in Scripture.[9]

Niebuhr's views are a useful footnote to the discussion of Humanism and Christianity, for they continue and state most emphatically the theistic critique of an empirical dualism and suggest also how that view passes easily over into religion. Both Niebuhr and the Humanists warned against the reality of evil in the human condition, but it is clear that Niebuhr much more effectively translated his account of human nature into a social program. His experience in the industrial community of Detroit surely gave Niebuhr a better perspective on social realities than Cambridge and Princeton gave Babbitt and More. But what is more informative, as Niebuhr's *Moral Man and Immoral Society* shows, is that the reaction

[8] Ibid., p. 94.

[9] Ibid., p. 103.

to Deweyan naturalism and the recourse to a dualistic philosophy do not necessarily lead to social and political conservatism. Niebuhr was probably the most important twentieth-century critic of Dewey, but their politics differed little in substance. Niebuhr utilized a dualistic Christian account of human nature in a career-long effort to construct a democratic society that could defend itself against the concentration of wealth and power in massive social and economic organizations; in the hands of the Humanists, especially Babbitt and More, the effort became a quest for the aristocratic and elitist few that could save American democracy from its self-destructive tendencies.

The intellectual movement that shows most clearly the extension or continuation of the Humanist critique is the New Conservatism that emerged after the Second World War. It too was a sustained effort to undo the effects of philosophical relativism and thus joined with other schools of thought in a wider pattern of criticism first articulated by the Humanists. The New Conservatives had the additional perspective of a second world conflict in the twentieth century. They protested against the irrational secular ideologies, fascism and communism particularly, which they believed had caused a cultural hemorrhage in the Western world, shattering the ethical basis of the Judeo-Christian and Greco-Roman traditions.

The New Humanists and the New Conservatives best document the emergence for the first time in American thought of a well-articulated philosophical or cultural conservatism in the tradition of Edmund Burke, Thomas Carlyle, and others. Both movements to this extent mark a new direction in American conservatism. They are distinct from another line of conservatism that links nineteenth-century liberalism, with its commitment to laissez-faire, and nineteenth-century Social Darwinism, with its celebration of the rude competitive order, to twentieth-century right-wing apologists such as Barry Goldwater and William F. Buckley, Jr. What is remarkable is the very existence of a movement in America philosophically biased toward tradition, custom, and the past. This conservatism was not strictly a question of self-interest or the allegiance to the status quo as a preserver of any special property or economic "rights." It was in fact a "cultural" conservatism that sought to reawaken a society immersed in the drift of technological change to the enduring values of the whole Western heritage.[10]

[10] Lora, pp. 5, 176–77. The difference between Buckley's conservatism and Babbitt's and More's is indicated by the fact that when anthologizing twentieth-century American conservative thought, Buckley ignored the New Humanists. See William F. Buckley, Jr., ed., *Did You Ever See a Dream Walking?* (Indianapolis, 1970).

The poet and historian Peter Viereck was the first to indicate the intellectual dimensions of the New Conservatism. His views closely correspond to the general propositions of the New Humanists, and Viereck himself acknowledged Babbitt as one of the best modern spokesmen against materialism. Viereck's diagnosis of contemporary ills was similar to the Humanists'. Modern society, he wrote, was witnessing the triumph of an ethical relativism that had created a moral vacuum and deprived society of a meaningful and unifying cultural center. At the root of the moral chaos of the modern world was a two-hundred-year-old romantic rebellion against discipline, measure, and sanity that had unleashed in the twentieth century its most vile product, the barbarism of the unchecked ego. The modern "isms," Viereck believed, had built on the Rousseauistic notion of the natural goodness of man to promise new secular utopias around a collective faith in the masses of mankind.[11]

Viereck constructed his own conservatism around the necessary means of finding limitations to the unchecked egotistical expansiveness of the age. Man would need to come first to a proper notion of himself and of his capacity for evil. Conservatism, then, was for Viereck the "political secularization of original sin." Man had ignored the problem of evil, he warned, by flaunting his pride and celebrating his ill-conceived "natural goodness." The result was the self-defining morality of the Nietzschean superman, a threat to the whole civilized order. Viereck insisted that the world must recover from its insanity by rediscovering universal moral truths that would restrain individual power and provide some direction for the drift of mass man. It could best achieve this by recapturing its own tradition. "Conservatism," Viereck wrote, "is a treasure house . . . of generations of accumulated experience, which any ephemeral rebellious generation has a right to disregard—at its peril." Conservatism was not a political dogma but an "emotional elan" holding together the centrifugal forces of society and cementing together what Western society has built.[12]

In three specific ways that were similar to the Humanists, Viereck suggested means of recovering from the modern chaos. Education was critical. The universities, he believed, must return to literature and the classics as their major focuses and renounce "the shortsighted cult of utilitarian studies." Only by such a return can we educate the whole man rather than the fragmentary man. Education must also be concerned with man and society, with the wider experience of the race. "Its purpose must be to create a community of persons, not a mere aggregation of people." And finally, the school must overcome its fixation with individual

[11] Peter Viereck, *Conservatism Revisited* (New York, 1962), pp. 142, 47–48.
[12] Ibid., pp. 47–50, 32.

whim. Its function was not to deify the child in his " 'glorious self-expression,' " but to limit his natural instincts and behavior by "unbreakable ethical habits." [13]

The church, like the university, Viereck believed, must also become an agent for moral recovery. Like most of the Humanists, Viereck dispensed with the theological problems about God and the afterlife to give attention to religion as a spiritual and moral counterthrust against the disrupting forces of the present. The church must lead in instituting inward spiritual reform as a substitute for the one-sided preoccupation with material progress. Marx was right, Viereck said, in condemning religion as the "opiate of the people"; it was the tamer, pacifer, and civilizer of the masses. The modern barbarians, then, are only logical in persecuting the church. [14]

Finally, Viereck also shared with the Humanists a concern for creating an organic society, one united by its own sustaining and cohesive institutions and traditions. He similarly shared a prejudice for the social distinctions within it. He apologized for his elitism no more than did Babbitt and More. The leveling and homogenizing tendencies of the modern age and the democratic and socialist ideologies had succeeded only too well in producing the age of the common man. And they had raised in the process a bland mass society of uprooted souls. Viereck defended social distinctions and contended that the only meaningful reform of society must begin at the top and work down, and it must not come through radical change or mob action. Viereck's overall views were parallel to the Humanists'. They were a call for aristocratic principles within a democratic system. Conservatism, and democracy properly exercised, must exhort all its citizens to be more than undistinguished elements in the mass whole. "Democracy," Viereck wrote, ". . . is the best government on earth when it tries to make all its citizens aristocrats." [15]

Despite his affinity with the New Humanism, Viereck probably improved on Babbitt and More in at least one way. In his break with the Goldwater conservatives in 1964, Viereck demonstrated that in the United States a true conservatism is one that is necessarily at home with the democratic traditions of the country, traditions that Viereck saw running from Jefferson through the New Deal. A genuine American conservatism, in short, must help preserve the liberal tradition of American politics. [16] Here Viereck more exactly echoed Stuart Sherman than Babbitt and More, who

[13] Ibid., pp. 33–34.
[14] Ibid., pp. 46–48.
[15] Ibid., pp. 134, 34–35, 38.
[16] Ibid., p. 142.

never successfully showed how their appeal to the stabilizing presence of tradition in America could support the ideal of social aristocracy that they elaborated. The danger was precisely that the American tradition led to a political course which Babbitt and More feared but which Viereck felt the need to appropriate.

It would be easy to extend the references and comparison of the New Humanists with other thinkers, Russell Kirk or Richard M. Weaver for example. Kirk has referred to Babbitt as "my mentor" and believes him "perhaps the strongest conservative author in the whole range of modern American letters."[17] But the effort here is mainly to show that the New Humanism was one part of a twentieth-century intellectual counterrevolution in America, one that made a significant collective critique of the intellectual changes coming mostly out of Darwinism in the late nineteenth and early twentieth centuries. This redirection of American thought was only one aspect of the total picture. Indeed, neither the cultural conservatism first articulated by the Humanists nor the Neo-orthodoxy of Niebuhr has by any means become the mainstream of American thought. Most intellectuals in fact continue to endorse an intellectual liberalism that is relativistic and pragmatic, at least regarding ethical, moral, and aesthetic questions. This pattern is part of a curious transformation of the intellectual in American society. For it was the conservative thinkers, such as Babbitt, Foerster, More, Viereck, and Kirk, who became and remain the alienated intellectuals. It is they, appealing to tradition, the past, and the recovery of religious and spiritual values, who seem most to be standing on the outside of mainstream America. The liberal thinkers, on the contrary, acquired in the postwar period a sense of rapprochement with American life and culture. They were mostly comfortable with the pluralistic character of American life, and the pragmatic political style that became increasingly prevalent with the New Deal and with progressive education. Writers and artists continually innovated in their work and found a sizable public willing to take notice. In 1952 a survey of twenty-five American artists and intellectuals found an overwhelming consensus that alienation was no longer appropriate or necessary for the liberal intellectual.[18]

[17] Russell Kirk, *A Program for Conservatives* (Chicago, 1954), p. 18.

[18] See Richard Hofstadter, *Anti-Intellectualism in American Life* (New York, 1962), pp. 394–95. This review has not taken account of parallel movements in Europe that were akin in spirit to the New Humanism. And although there were similarities to Humanism in several European intellectual currents, these ought not to be exaggerated. None corresponded precisely with the empirical dualism that was the distinguishing feature of the American Humanists. Nor did Babbitt and More and their followers identify with, or for that matter even take

Against this change the articulation of a cultural conservatism by the New Humanists and others in the twentieth century is particularly significant. All of these thinkers felt the loss of something sacred and meaningful in the industrial and urban mass society of the modern age. They have felt little identity or integration with the mainstream of American living and have been uncomfortable with the cultural, political, and educational directions of the United States in their times. Their critique of American life suffered from their failure to appreciate or even to confront the challenge of technology. To the extent that they recoiled from the horrors of mass society they were unable to analyze critically the intricate workings of an advanced industrial system. The Humanists made the universal and permanent their frame of reference, but in so doing they overlooked the shifting and circumstantial, the obstinate and omnipresent problems of everyday life. But apart from this weakness their selected framework did afford the Humanists perceptive insights on modern life and culture. Theirs was a serious and sophisticated effort to judge America by the best traditions of the human past, and this endeavor did not fail to point to some of the deficiencies of the age. In a nation committed to change and celebrating material progress in all phases of its existence, an eloquent defense of tradition and the priorities of the past deserved a hearing.

---

cognizance of, the Europeans. But in the year of the Humanist furor, 1930, Gorham Munson did point to a "classical revival abroad" that he thought might be the basis of a transcontinental alliance with the Americans. In addition to T. S. Eliot he included in the English group Philip S. Richards, Herbert Read, Wyndham Lewis, Hilaire Belloc, and G. K. Chesterton. In France he looked to Julien Benda, Charles Maurras, and Jacques Maritain. Munson took only a superficial look at these thinkers and clearly hoped too much from persons who were often tied to Roman Catholicism, Anglicanism, or French royalism to a degree that the Humanists would find uncomfortable. See Gorham Munson, *The Dilemma of the Liberated* (New York, 1930), pp. 79–106. The most deliberate effort to bridge the Atlantic and propagate a New Humanism abroad was Louis J. A. Mercier's *Le Mouvement Humaniste aux Étas-Unis: W. C. Brownell, Irving Babbitt, Paul Elmer More* (Paris, 1928).

Select Bibliography

Index

Select Bibliography

PRIMARY SOURCES

Manuscripts

Correspondence of Stuart Pratt Sherman. University of Illinois Archives, Urbana-Champaign.
Irving Babbitt Correspondence. Harvard University Archives, Cambridge, Mass.
Norman Foerster Papers. University of Iowa Archives, Iowa City.
Paul Elmer More Papers. Department of Rare Books and Special Collections, Princeton University Library, Princeton, N.J.

Books

Arnold, Matthew. *Culture and Anarchy.* New York, 1883.
_____. *Essays in Criticism.* Boston, 1865.
Babbitt, Irving. *Democracy and Leadership.* Boston, 1924.
_____, trans. *The Dhammapada: Translated from the Pāli with an Essay on Buddha and the Occident.* New York, 1936.
_____. *Literature and the American College: Essays in Defense of the Humanities.* Boston, 1908.
_____. *The Masters of Modern French Criticism.* 1912; rpt. New York, 1963.
_____. *The New Laokoön: An Essay on the Confusion of the Arts.* Boston, 1910.
_____. *On Being Creative and Other Essays.* Boston, 1932.
_____. *Rousseau and Romanticism.* Boston, 1919.
_____. *Spanish Character and Other Essays.* Boston, 1940.
Brooks, Van Wyck. *America's Coming-of-Age.* New York, 1915.
_____. *The Ordeal of Mark Twain.* New York, 1920.
Canby, Henry Seidel. *Definitions: Essays in Contemporary Criticism, First Series.* 1922; rpt. Port Washington, N.Y., 1967.
_____. *Definitions: Essays in Contemporary Criticism, Second Series.* 1924; rpt. Port Washington, N.Y., 1967.
Croce, Benedetto. *Guide to Aesthetics.* 1913. Translated by Patrick Romanell. Indianapolis, 1965.
Dewey, John. *Experience and Nature.* 1929; rpt. New York, 1958.
_____. *Philosophy and Civilization.* New York, 1931.

Eliot, T. S. *For Lancelot Andrewes: Essays on Style and Order.* New York, 1928.
————. *The Sacred Wood: Essays on Poetry and Criticism.* London,1920.
————. *Selected Essays: 1917–1932.* New York, 1932.
Elliott, George Roy. *The Cycle of Modern Poetry: A Series of Essays toward Clearing Our Present Poetic Dilemma.* 1929; rpt. New York, 1965.
————. *Humanism and Imagination.* Chapel Hill, N.C., 1938.
Flexner, Abraham. *Universities: American, English, German.* New York, 1930.
Foerster, Norman. *American Criticism: A Study in Literary Theory from Poe to the Present.* Boston, 1928.
————. *The American Scholar: A Study in Literrae Inhumaniores.* Chapel Hill, N.C., 1929.
————. *The American State University: Its Relation to Democracy.* Chapel Hill, N.C., 1937.
————. *The Future of the Liberal College.* New York, 1938.
————, ed. *Humanism and America: Essays on the Outlook of Modern Civilisation.* New York, 1930.
————. *Towards Standards: A Study of the Present Critical Movement in American Letters.* New York, 1930.
General Education in a Free Society: Report of the Harvard Committee. Cambridge, Mass., 1945.
Grattan, C. Hartley, ed. *The Critique of Humanism: A Symposium.* New York, 1930.
Hofstadter, Richard, and Wilson Smith, eds. *American Higher Education: A Documentary History.* 2 vols. Chicago, 1961.
Hutchins, Robert Maynard. *The Higher Learning in America.* New Haven, 1936.
Kirk, Russell. *A Program for Conservatives.* Chicago, 1954.
Lewisohn, Ludwig, *Expression in America.* London [1932].
Manchester, Frederick, and Odell Shepard, eds. *Irving Babbitt: Man and Teacher.* New York, 1941.
Meiklejohn, Alexander. *The Liberal College.* Boston, 1920.
Mencken, H. L. *A Book of Prefaces.* Garden City, N.Y., 1917.
————. *Notes on Democracy.* New York, 1926.
————. *Prejudices: Second Series.* New York, 1920.
————. *Prejudices: Third Series.* New York, 1922.
Mercier, Louis J. A. *American Humanism and the New Age.* Milwaukee, 1948.
More, Paul Elmer. *Aristocracy and Justice.* Shelburne Essays, Ninth Series. 1915; rpt. New York, 1967.
————. *The Christ of the New Testament.* The Greek Tradition, Vol. III. Princeton, 1924.
————. *Christ the Word.* The Greek Tradition, Vol. IV. Princeton, 1927.
————. *The Demon of the Absolute.* New Shelburne Essays, Vol I. Princeton, 1928.
————. *The Drift of Romanticism.* Shelburne Essays, Eighth Series. 1913; rpt. New York, 1967.
————. *A New England Group and Others.* Shelburne Essays, Eleventh Series. 1921; rpt. New York, 1967.

_____ . *On Being Human.* New Shelburne Essays, Vol. III. Princeton, 1936.

_____ . *Platonism.* Princeton, 1917.

_____ . *The Religion of Plato.* The Greek Tradition, Vol. I. Princeton, 1921.

_____ . *The Sceptical Approach to Religion.* New Shelburne Essays, Vol. II. Princeton, 1934.

_____ . *Shelburne Essays: First Series.* 1904; rpt. New York, 1967.

_____ . *Shelburne Essays: Second Series.* 1905; rpt. New York, 1967.

_____ . *Shelburne Essays: Fourth Series.* 1906; rpt. New York, 1967.

_____ . *Shelburne Essays: Fifth Series.* 1908; rpt. New York, 1967.

_____ . *Shelburne Essays: Seventh Series.* 1910; rpt. New York, 1967.

_____ . *Studies of Religious Dualism.* Shelburne Essays, Sixth Series. 1909; rpt. New York, 1967.

Munson, Gorham B. *Destinations: A Canvass of American Literature since 1900.* New York, 1928.

_____ . *The Dilemma of the Liberated: An Interpretation of Twentieth Century Humanism.* New York, 1930.

Niebuhr, Reinhold. *The Nature and Destiny of Man: A Christian Interpretation.* Vol. I, *Human Nature.* New York, 1941.

Pater, Walter H. *Studies in the History of the Renaissance.* London, 1873.

Ransom, John Crowe. *God without Thunder: An Unorthodox Defense of Orthodoxy.* 1930; rpt. Hamden, Conn., 1965.

Shafer, Robert. *Paul Elmer More and American Criticism.* New Haven, 1935.

Sherman, Stuart P. *Americans.* New York, 1922.

_____ . *Critical Woodcuts: Essays on Writers and Writing.* 1926; rpt. Port Washington, N.Y., 1967.

_____ . *The Emotional Discovery of America and Other Essays.* New York, 1932.

_____ . *The Genius of America: Studies in Behalf of the Younger Generation.* New York, 1923.

_____ . *The Main Stream.* New York, 1927.

_____ . *Matthew Arnold: How to Know Him.* Indianapolis, 1917.

_____ . *On Contemporary Literature.* 6th ed. New York, 1931.

_____ . *Points of View.* New York, 1924.

Spingarn, Joel E. *Creative Criticism and Other Essays.* New York, 1931.

_____ , ed. *Criticism in America: Its Function and Status.* New York, 1924.

Stearns, Harold. *America and the Young Intellectual.* New York, 1921.

[_____] , ed. *Civilization in the United States: An Inquiry by Thirty Americans.* New York, 1922.

Taine, H. A. *History of English Literature.* New York, 1879.

Viereck, Peter. *Conservatism Revisited.* New York, 1962.

Wilson, Edmund. *The Triple Thinkers.* New York, 1938.

Articles

Babbitt, Irving. "Croce and the Philosophy of the Flux." *Yale Review,* NS 14 (1925), 377–81.

_____. "The Modern Spirit and Dr. Spingarn." *Journal of Philosophy, Psychology, and Scientific Methods,* 11 (1914), 215–18.

_____. "President Eliot and American Education." *Forum,* 81 (1921), 1–10.

_____. "Reply to Dr. Spingarn." *Journal of Philosophy, Psychology, and Scientific Methods,* 11 (1914), 328.

Bandler, Bernard. "The Individualism of Irving Babbitt." *Hound and Horn,* 3 (1929), 57–70.

Bart, Peter J. "The Christianity of Paul Elmer More." *Catholic World,* 135 (1932), 542–47.

Blackmur, R. P. "Humanism and Symbolic Imagination: Notes on Re-Reading Irving Babbitt." *Southern Review,* 7 (1941), 309–25.

Bourne, Randolph S. "Paul Elmer More." *New Republic,* 6 (1916), 245–47.

_____. "The Puritan's Will to Power." *Seven Arts,* 1 (1916–17), 631–37.

Brody, Alter. "Humanism and Intolerance." *New Republic,* 61 (1930), 278.

Canby, Henry Seidel. "The New Humanists." *Saturday Review of Literature,* 6 (1929–30), 749–51.

_____. "Stuart P. Sherman: 'The American Scholar.' " *Saturday Review of Literature,* 6 (1929–30), 201–2.

Chesterton, G. K. "Is Humanism a Religion?" *Criterion,* 8 (1929), 382–93.

[Collins, Seward]. "Chronicle and Comment." *Bookman,* 70 (1929–30), 289–305.

_____. "Criticism in America: The Origins of a Myth." *Bookman,* 71 (1929–30), 241–56.

_____. "Criticism in America: The Revival of the Anti-Humanist Myth." *Bookman,* 71 (1929–30), 400–415.

_____. "Criticism in America: The End of the Anti-Humanist Myth." *Bookman,* 72 (1930–31), 145–64.

Dreiser, Theodore. "Life, Art, and America." *Seven Arts,* 1 (1916–17), 363–89.

Eliot, T. S. "Experiment in Criticism." *Bookman,* 70 (1929–30), 225–33.

_____. "Second Thoughts about Humanism." *Hound and Horn,* 2 (1929), 339–50.

Elliott, George Roy. "Irving Babbitt as I Knew Him." *American Review,* 8 (1936), 36–60.

_____. "Mr. More and the Gentle Reader." *Bookman,* 69 (1929), 143–47.

_____. "The Religious Dissension of Babbitt and More." *American Review,* 9 (1937), 252–65.

Farrar, John. "The Fiction of the Uncontrollable." *New York Herald,* Apr. 29, 1923.

Foerster, Norman. A letter. *Forum,* 80 (1928), 470–71.

_____. "Humanism and Religion." *Criterion,* 9 (1929), 23–32.

_____. "The Impressionists." *Bookman,* 70 (1929–30), 337–47.

Lippmann, Walter. "Humanism as Dogma." *Saturday Review of Literature,* 6 (1930), 817–19.

Lovett, Robert Morss. "Criticism Past and Present." *New Republic,* 28 (1921), 247–49.

[Mather, Frank Jewett, Jr.]. "Academic Studies and Degrees." *Nation,* 74 (1902), 284–85.

[_____] . "For an Improved M.A." *Nation,* 92 (1911), 186–87.

[_____] . "Higher Education Made in Germany." *Nation,* 72 (1901), 332–34.

[_____] . "Scholarship and Research." *Nation,* 85 (1907), 276–77.

[_____] . "The Small College." *Nation,* 75 (1902), 6–7.

[_____] . "University Teaching of English." *Nation,* 83 (1906), 387–88.

Mencken, H. L. "The Motive of the Critic." *New Republic,* 28 (1921), 249–51.

More, Paul Elmer. "An Absolute and an Authoritative Church." *Criterion,* 8 (1929), 616–34.

_____ . "Marginalia." *American Review,* 8 (1936), 1–30.

_____ . "The Problem of Poverty." *Unpopular Review,* 6 (1916), 231–45.

_____ . "Taste and Tradition." *Unpopular Review,* 8 (1917), 112–32.

Mumford, Lewis. "The New Tractarians." *New Republic,* 62 (1930), 163.

Nickerson, Hoffman. "Irving Babbitt." *Criterion,* 13 (1934), 179–95.

Niebuhr, Reinhold. "A Faith to Live By: The Dilemma of Modern Man." *Nation,* 164 (1947), 204–9.

Read, Herbert. Review of Irving Babbitt's *Democracy and Leadership. Criterion,* 3 (1924), 129–33.

Richards, Philip S. "An American Platonist." *Nineteenth Century and After,* 105 (1929), 479–89.

_____ . "Irving Babbitt: A New Humanism." *Nineteenth Century and After,* 104 (1928), 433–44.

Salpeter, Harry. "Irving Babbitt, Calvinist." *Outlook and Independent,* 155 (1930), 421–23.

Shafer, Robert. "The Definition of Humanism." *Hound and Horn,* 3 (1930), 533–56.

_____ . "University and College: Dr. Flexner and the Modern University." *Bookman,* 73 (1931), 225–40.

_____ . "University and College: Is Liberal Education Wanted?" *Bookman,* 73 (1931), 387–400.

_____ . "University and College: A New College in the Modern University." *Bookman,* 73 (1931), 503–21.

_____ . "What Is Humanism?" *Virginia Quarterly Review,* 6 (1930), 199–209.

Sherman, Stuart P. "American and Allied Ideals: An Appeal to Those Who Are neither Hot nor Cold." U.S. Government *War Information Series,* No. 12 (Feb. 1918).

_____ . "The Liberal Arts Course at the University of Illinois." *New Republic,* 32 (1922), 12.

Spingarn, Joel E. "The Ancient Spirit and Professor Babbitt." *Journal of Philosophy, Psychology, and Scientific Methods,* 11 (1914), 326–28.

_____ . Review of Irving Babbitt's *The Masters of Modern French Criticism. Journal of Philosophy, Psychology, and Scientific Methods,* 10 (1913), 693–96.

Sypher, Wylie. "Irving Babbitt: A Reappraisal." *New England Quarterly,* 14 (1941), 64–96.
Warren, Austin. "A Portrait of Irving Babbitt." *Commonweal,* 24 (1936), 234–36.

SECONDARY SOURCES

Books

Abrams, M. H. *The Mirror and the Lamp: Romantic Theory and the Critical Tradition.* London, 1953.
_____. *Natural Supernaturalism: Tradition and Revolution in Romantic Literature.* New York, 1971.
Berthoff, Warner. *The Ferment of Realism: American Literature, 1884–1919.* New York, 1965.
Bloom, Harold, ed. *Romanticism and Consciousness: Essays in Criticism.* New York, 1970.
Boller, Paul F., Jr. *American Thought in Transition: The Impact of Evolutionary Naturalism, 1865–1900.* Chicago, 1969.
Child, Ruth C. *The Aesthetics of Walter Pater.* New York, 1940.
Dakin, Arthur Hazard. *Paul Elmer More.* Princeton, 1960.
Davies, Robert M. *The Humanism of Paul Elmer More.* New York, 1958.
Duggan, Francis X. *Paul Elmer More.* New York, 1966.
Fisch, Max H., ed. *Classic American Philosophers.* New York, 1951.
Gouinlock, James. *John Dewey's Philosophy of Value.* New York, 1972.
Hoffman, Frederick J. *The Twenties: American Writers in the Postwar Decade.* New York, 1949.
Hofstadter, Richard. *Anti-Intellectualism in American Life.* New York, 1962.
Karanikas, Alexander. *Tillers of a Myth: Southern Agrarians as Social and Literary Critics.* Madison, Wis., 1969.
Lippincott, Benjamin Evans. *Victorian Critics of Democracy: Carlyle, Ruskin, Arnold, Stephen, Maine, Lecky.* Minneapolis, 1938.
Lora, Ronald. *Conservative Minds in America.* Chicago, 1971.
Lovejoy, Arthur O. *Essays in the History of Ideas.* Baltimore, 1948.
Lucy, Sean. *T. S. Eliot and the Idea of Tradition.* London, 1960.
McCormick, John. *The Middle Distance: A Comparative History of American Imaginative Literature, 1919–1932.* New York, 1971.
May, Henry F. *The End of American Innocence: A Study of the First Years of our Time, 1912–1917.* London, 1959.
O'Connor, William Van. *An Age of Criticism: 1900–1950.* Chicago, 1952.
Randall, John Herman, Jr. *Aristotle.* New York, 1960.
Rudolph, Frederick. *The American College and University: A History.* New York, 1962.

Ruland, Richard. *The Rediscovery of American Literature: Premises of Critical Taste, 1900–1940.* Cambridge, Mass., 1967.

Smith, Huston. *The Religions of Man.* New York, 1958.

Sproat, John C. *"The Best Men": Liberal Reformers in the Gilded Age.* London, 1968.

Stovall, Floyd, ed. *The Development of American Literary Criticism.* Chapel Hill, N.C., 1955.

Sutton, Walter. *Modern American Criticism.* Englewood Cliffs, N.J., 1963.

Tomsich, John. *A Genteel Endeavor: American Culture and Politics in the Gilded Age.* Stanford, Cal., 1971.

Veysey, Laurence R. *The Emergence of the American University.* Chicago, 1965.

Wallwork, Ernest. *Durkheim: Morality and Milieu.* Cambridge, Mass., 1972.

Wellek, René. *A History of Modern Criticism.* 4 vols. Vol. I, *The Later Eighteenth Century* (New Haven, 1955). Vol. IV, *The Later Nineteenth Century* (New Haven, 1965).

White, Morton. *Social Thought in America: The Revolt against Formalism.* New York, 1949.

Wimsatt, William K., Jr. and Cleanth Brooks. *Literary Criticism: A Short History.* New York, 1957.

Zeitlin, Jacob, and Homer Woodbridge, eds. *Life and Letters of Stuart P. Sherman.* 2 vols. New York, 1929.

Articles

Hoffman, Frederick J. "Philistine and Puritan in the 1920s: An Example of the Misuse of the American Past." *American Quarterly,* 1 (1949), 247–63.

Unpublished

Flanagan, Mary Frances. "The Educational Role of Norman Foerster." Diss. University of Iowa 1971.

Index

Abrams, M. H., 51, 176-77
American Criticism (Foerster), 19
American Review, 24, 181
Americans (Sherman), 16
American Scholar, The (Foerster), 22
American State University, The (Foerster), 22
Anderson, Sherwood, 82, 85, 86, 103-4
Anglicanism. *See* Church of England
Aristocracy, 132-33, 136; defended by Mencken, 89; Humanists' plea for in higher education, 118; defended by Viereck, 187
Aristophanes, 31
Aristotle, 35, 37, 51
Arnold, Matthew: as model for Humanists, 25; and Humanists' program, 40; and moral element in art, 64; on Emerson, 90; social views of, 138; religous views of, 157-58
Augustine, Saint, 156

Babbitt (Lewis), 105
Babbitt, Edwin Dwight, 5, 153
Babbitt, Irving: biography, 5-10; character and personality, 8; on Sherman, 16, 18; and the Midwest, 24; disdain for poetry writing, 24; on the modern age, 31; on popular faith in progress, 32; on modern spirituality, 32; on dualism, 36-38; on the One and the Many, 37, 40-41; and empirical Humanism, 37, 42; and Platonism, 37; on Buddhism, 42-43, 155, 162; on characteristics of romanticism, 45-46; on originality in art, 52, 77; on excesses in neoclassicism, 54; on German style of romanticism, 55-57; on romanticism in aesthetics, 57; on the use of the past, 57; on Pater, 59; ctitique of Croce, 60-61; on impressionist criticism, 62; on judgment in criticism, 62-63; on the moral imagination in art, 64-65;

on moral element in romantic aesthetic, 65; and Matthew Arnold, 67-68; on historical criticism, 69-70; on Tolstoy, 72-73; criticized by T. S. Eliot, 74-75, 164-65; on Emerson, 91; on Edwards, 91; on Whitman, 95; aloofness from modern literature, 100-101, 105; on altruism in education, 107; on education and tradition, 109; defense of classical languages, 110; on individualism in education, 111; on the elective system, 112; on materialism in higher education, 115; on the research emphasis in higher education, 116-17; relation of his political views to philosophical, 125-27; on aristocratic principles, 127-28; on Progressive movement, 128; on humanitarianism, 128-31; on socialism, 131-32; on the decay of the leadership class, 134-35; on economic competition, 135; and Mencken, 135-37; on Nietzsche, 137; his concept of justice, 139; on tradition in political life, 142; on Burke, 142; on the imagination in politics, 142-44; criticizes Sherman's democratic ideals, 146; on imperialism, 146-47; on nationalism, 147; on international politics, 148; on the Catholic church, 152; on Humanism as surrogate for religion, 153-55; on religion as support for Humanism, 154-55; on dualism in religion, 160; on modern churches, 161; on self-discipline through religion, 161; acknowledged by Kirk, 188
Bacon, Francis, 12, 47
Barren Ground (Glasgow), 103
Baudelaire, Charles, 58, 83
Beattie, James, 64
Behaviorism, 32, 47
Belinski, Vissarion Grigorievich, 68